European Political Thought, 1815–1989

EUROPEAN POLITICAL THOUGHT, 1815–1989

Spencer M. Di Scala

University of Massachusetts

Salvo Mastellone

University of Florence

WestviewPress

A Division of HarperCollinsPublishers

Copyright © 1998 by Westview Press, A Division of HarperCollins Publishers, Inc.

Published in 1998 in the United States of America by Westview Press, 5500 Central Avenue, Boulder, Colorado 80301-2877, and in the United Kingdom by Westview Press, 12 Hid's Copse Road, Cumnor Hill, Oxford OX2 9JJ

A CIP catalog record for this book is available from the Library of Congress.
ISBN 0-8133-1738-X (hc.)—ISBN 0-8133-1739-8 (pbk.)

The paper used in this publication meets the requirements of the American National Standard for Permanence of Paper for Printed Library Materials Z39.48-1984.

10   9   8   7   6   5   4   3   2   1

FOR LAURA AND BARBARA

CONTENTS

PREFACE AND ACKNOWLEDGMENTS

Because of the authors' background, this book represents a blending of perspectives, European and American, regarding the seminal political ideas of the last two centuries. We believe that approaching a subject from different angles and from distinct cultural viewpoints promotes a broader outlook, and we hope that we have accomplished this objective. In addition, we aimed particularly at synthesizing complex ideas and conveying their import and impact to readers in a clear and understandable manner. Frequently political science, and intellectual history in general, becomes very abstract because of the manner of presentation. For this reason, we concentrated on providing an overview of the historical contexts in which the ideas we discuss appeared and developed so that readers may comprehend the concrete issues that different political theorists confronted as well as why they made certain choices. Too much information would have weighed down the text, and too little would have meant failure in achieving this goal. Consequently, we have striven to achieve a balance that will not bore readers but will allow them to understand the complex problems involved. In this way, the reader may discover that the doubts and dilemmas of earlier ages on how to organize life in common have not disappeared and, perhaps, will gain greater insight into our own pressing questions.

One of the pleasant aspects of writing this book was the level of cooperation between the authors. If this collaboration is any indication of the capacity of people to get along, the human species is in good shape. This teamwork extended to our wives, Laura Di Scala and Barbara Mastellone, supreme pragmatists, whose suggestions and support made the work of composition speedier and more efficient than it otherwise would have been. Ashley Di Scala gave at least one of the authors a greater sensibility for the conduct of everyday politics.

Besides personal debts, we would like to acknowledge professional ones. Charles L. Killinger and Armand Patrucco read the entire manuscript and made detailed and important comments that improved the book. With the rapid changes in technology it would be unwise to undertake any large writing project without an adviser in the library. We thank Stephen Haas, business and documents librarian at the Healey Library, University of Massachusetts, Boston, for counseling us in the use of the powerful tools available to researchers. Peter Kracht, our editor at Westview Press, and his assistant, Rob Williams, not only encouraged the writing of this book but also, despite an overwhelmingly busy agenda, did more than their share to see it into print. For all of this help, we are very grateful.

Spencer M. Di Scala
Boston, Massachusetts

Salvo Mastellone
Florence, Italy

A NOTE ON TITLES

The dates of titles cited in the text are those of publication. In order to keep the sense of chronology clear for the reader, when an English translation is readily available, the title of the translation is cited with the year of publication of the *original* work, not the translation. If an English-language translation is unavailable or not easily accessible, the title has been cited in the original language with the author's translation of the title in brackets.

INTRODUCTION:
THE SCOPE OF MODERN
EUROPEAN POLITICS

The history of European political thought from the fall of Napoleon Bonaparte in 1815 to the fall of the Berlin Wall in 1989 presents historians with a daunting task, given the intersecting political events, ideological motivations, and national differences that must be considered. Despite these difficulties, however, we have attempted throughout this work to follow clear thematic lines regarding ideas on forms of government and the problems presented by new economic, social, and political developments. We have aimed especially at achieving clarity in presenting the solutions that political thinkers elaborated in order to resolve and conciliate issues that appeared at times mutually contradictory. Given the great scope and complexity of the topic, we make no pretense of having provided anything more than a clear introduction that will serve to familiarize students with the basic European political ideas that circulated in Europe during the past two centuries and with the theoretical problems that a rapidly modernizing society presented to political observers. We believe that, with the passage of time, it becomes increasingly imperative for students of the modern world to understand how and why certain tendencies in politics emerged if they are to understand the present. Unfortunately, with the passage of time, the tendency is to emphasize historical periods that are ever closer to the present, a trend in which ideas are abstracted from their context, leaving people less equipped to comprehend rapidly unfolding developments. This book, we hope, will provide a solid foundation for anyone wishing to gain a more complete understanding of particular thinkers or movements and to build on that knowledge.

In political thought, as in so many other fields, the period known as the Enlightenment (roughly, the eighteenth century) set the tone for the modern world. The French Baron de Montesquieu, for example, in his most famous and influential work, *The Spirit of the Laws* (1748), altered the categories that had served previous thinkers in their study of different forms of government. It was not important to know whether power was theoretically in the hands of the many (democracies), of the few (aristocracies), or of one person (monarchies), Montesquieu thought, but rather to understand how governments actually wielded power. According to Montesquieu, three forms of government existed—republics, monarchies, and despotisms. In republics, the people ruled through their representatives; in monarchies, one person governed, but only according to the rule of law; in despotisms (a corrupt form of government) one person ruled, but without law, without any control, and according to individual will and to whim.

Montesquieu himself preferred constitutional monarchies of the English type, founded on the principles of political liberty and the separation of powers. This kind of government had already been examined by seventeenth-century English thinker John Locke in the second of his *Two Treatises of Government*, which Montesquieu had read in translation. But in *The Spirit of the Laws*, Montesquieu also analyzed the nature of republics and pointed to ancient Athens and Rome as models of republican government. In these ancient republics, Montesquieu wrote, the people selected, in a wise manner, representatives in whom they invested part of the authority they alone possessed.

This consideration led Montesquieu to state that the laws governing the right to vote were fundamental to the proper functioning of a democratic republican government. For Montesquieu, constitutional monarchies and republics concerned themselves primarily with different issues. Basic to constitutional monarchies was the issue of civil liberty; republics developed the overriding theme of equality.

According to Montesquieu, democratic republics based upon "virtue," a quality highly emphasized by Renaissance thinkers, had only existed in the ancient world. In the modern world, democratic republics did not exist. In the most famous and influential collaborative work of the Enlightenment, the *Encyclopédie* (1751), Jean Le Rond d'Alembert foresaw a period of uprisings, and his friend Denis Diderot confirmed that these would be necessary revolutions in order to modify existing forms of government. In his *Social Contract* (1762), Jean-Jacques Rousseau, the most influential political thinker of the age, proposed a state founded on an association of citizens who governed themselves through the "general will." In fact, wrote Rousseau, only the general will could guide the state according to its overriding goal—the common good. Montesquieu and Rousseau set the tone for the second half of the eighteenth century; the European political debate sought ideological justification in the doctrinal context of Montesquieu's *Spirit of the Laws* and in a popular assembly capable of elaborating a "social contract" that would confer political power on ordinary citizens—as elaborated by Rousseau.

By the latter part of the century, Europeans looked not only to Montesquieu and Rousseau but also, in practical terms, to the American and French Revolutions, in order to develop future governmental forms. From these revolutions emerged two new and different republican models of government. Among the fundamental principles of the American republic enunciated in the Declaration of Independence (1776) were that all men had certain inalienable rights and that governments are created by the governed to guarantee these rights. The fundamental principles of the French republic were attached to the preamble of the Jacobin Constitution of 1793, which stated that the right to equality is antecedent to the rights to liberty, property, and security.

Although the Jacobin Constitution never went into effect and the Jacobins themselves were overthrown in 1794—to be replaced by the more conservative Directory in 1795—the egalitarian principles embodied in the French Revolution's most radical phase received widespread acceptance in Europe. The Committee of Public Safety, which had embodied Jacobin rule, succeeded in turning back the conservative European forces that had seemed on the verge of restoring the French monarchy and set up—with the aid of enthusiastic local supporters—sister republics based on the French revolutionary model. In these republics the French imposed the reforms that revolutionaries had already implemented in France. The result, at least initially, was great support for the French. Although continuing war and the need to raise money and troops aroused the ire of the populations of these republics against French dominance, French revolutionary methods and principles took root in other parts of western Europe. The Directory, unable to give France stable government or to maintain the revolution's conquests, gave way to Napoleon's coup d'état in 1799. Napoleon preserved the revolution's basic gains even though he did away with its most radical innovations. He then turned to foreign affairs, and his military conquests allowed him to reorganize Europe.

In order to gain support, Napoleon continued exporting the most basic social changes of the French Revolution to areas outside of France. Since a nation that is repressed by foreigners or native princes cannot achieve liberty without revolution, Napoleon promised national liberty to the different European peoples who came under the influence of French revolutionary principles. Although he had no intention of fulfilling his promises, his rhetoric aroused hopes of national independence, liberty, and equality. Instead, he parceled out kingdoms to his family and supporters. Since Napoleon's despotic methods belied his words, a powerful ideological opposition developed against the Napoleonic regime. In 1790

Edmund Burke (1729–1797), polemicizing against the French developments of 1789, had published *Reflections on the Revolution in France* (1790).
Translated and widely diffused, the *Reflections* had been utilized against
revolutionary ideals by European conservatives during the last decade of
the eighteenth century. But when moderates and defenders of constitutional liberties accused Napoleon of having organized a despotism, and
of having exploited the army to impose his personal power, these moderates made use of Burke's writings, which viewed constitutional monarchies as the antidote to despotisms. Burke had argued that in England,
the country's problems were debated in the British Parliament, where
both government and opposition had the right to speak. He had also
explained how the separation of powers praised by Montesquieu worked
in practice. In this context, it is understandable why the restored king of
France, Louis XVIII, believed it opportune on his return from exile in 1814
to concede a constitution—the "Charter"—modeled on the British legislature with its two houses. Other European sovereigns, however, failed to
follow Louis XVIII's example.

After Napoleon's defeat in 1815 the statesmen of the Congress of
Vienna imposed a return to the pre-1789 political situation as much as
possible. If it satisfied princes and sovereigns, however, the Congress of
Vienna failed to reassure people who had hoped to see the beginning of
an era of liberty and justice. In fact, it seemed that with restoration of the
kind of governments that had existed before the French Revolution (the
"old regime"), absolutism would prevail. As a result, writers and political
progressives studied with attention those forms of government that they
believed were most apt for their own countries and viewed them as political models to be imitated.

Political models are studied in particular historical circumstances in
order to propose alternatives to existing governmental institutions. A
model can be derived from a "functioning" political system when the
regime of a particular country becomes an example that another country
wishes to follow. It can be a "historical" model when it comes from the
image of a political system that has existed in the past. It can also be
"utopian" in the sense that it is created with the aid of the imagination
and the reason of a political theorist. Recently the theme of political models has been examined by political scientists in order to understand in
what way state structures have been inspired by ideological considerations (V. I. Comparato, *I modelli politici* [Political Models], 1987–1989).

After 1815 European jurists and political thinkers counterposed free
governments to the absolutist governments in power. By "free governments," they meant both constitutional monarchies and republics.
Supporters of the British constitutional monarchy continued reading
Burke as well as the work of the Swiss jurist Jean Louis De Lolme, *The*

Constitution of England (1771), which had been translated into English, German, Spanish, and Italian and reprinted in a fifth edition in 1819.

While sympathizers of monarchical systems showed most interest for the British constitutional model of government, supporters of republican systems were divided into two camps: those who preferred the American republic and those who preferred the French.

The United States attracted the more moderate republicans. The Americans had achieved their own independence, had created a democratic political order, and had developed an advanced system of civil liberties; in short, they had established themselves as an admirable example worthy of being imitated. During the early decades of the nineteenth century, many progressive thinkers kept the ideal of American popular government alive in Europe. In Italy, Carlo Botta wrote the *History of the War of Independence of the United States of America* (1820–1824), and Giuseppe Compagnoni published *Storia dell'America* [History of America] (1820–1821). In France, Armand Carrel and a group of republican colleagues founded the *Revue Américaine* [American Review], in which George Washington and Benjamin Franklin received praise, and American federalism was cited as an ideal means of conciliating local tradition and national interests. The American political system found its main European theoretician in Alexis de Tocqueville, who in 1835 published *Democracy in America.*

Tocqueville presented the United States as the country that had developed the concept of democratic liberties to the fullest; in fact, liberty and democracy coexisted in the reality of American politics. In the United States, Tocqueville wrote, "the people" was composed of all the citizens; the people named those who made the laws, those who executed them, and those who punished their infraction; the people directly nominated the representatives; and, though the form of government was representative, it was the majority that governed in the name of the people. Tocqueville's views were an implicit but powerful criticism of those French republicans who favored the French revolutionary tradition and demanded a national program of political and social equality.

Thus in the first half of the nineteenth century the French revolutionary theme of the free nation fed the hopes of the people who refused to accept the authority of the restored governments. This was true above all in Germany and Italy, where the "patriots" looked forward to national independence and unity. The French constitutions of 1791, 1793, and 1795 were read and commented upon. The champion of French egalitarian democracy was Filippo Buonarroti. His fundamental work, published in Brussels in 1828, was *Babeuf's Conspiracy for Equality*, translated into English in 1836 by famed Chartist leader Bronterre O'Brien, the story of the failed 1796 attempt of François-Noël Babeuf (known as Gracchus Babeuf) and his followers to overthrow the Directory and install a communist regime in France; Babeuf was executed and Buonarroti jailed in the aftermath. Rather than a history, however, the book is a fundamental ideological statement that greatly influenced European radical thought. For Buonarroti, popular democrats were those people who struggled on behalf of the working class and for the "complete reform of society." Political struggles were nothing other than class struggles, and Buonarroti taught that no compromise was possible. In 1847, in the *People's Journal* (London), Italian patriot in exile Giuseppe Mazzini designated Filippo Buonarroti as the theoretician of communism. Invited by the Communist League of London to draft a manifesto of the Communist party, Karl Marx confirmed Mazzini's judgment, but modified Buonarroti's interpretative line by counterposing the working class and the bourgeoisie.

At midcentury, the year of revolutions began. In February 1848, disorders exploded in Paris, and the Second Republic was proclaimed. Revolutions followed in Austria, Hungary, Italy, Germany, Switzerland, and Poland. Agitation was greatest in cities that had populations over a hundred thousand and had either social or nationalistic aims. The 1848 revolutions profoundly influenced the political debate, which concentrated on two themes during the period following the disorders: association and representation.

Historians have generally failed to emphasize that in the second half of the nineteenth century, the English term "union," the German "*Verein*," and the French "*association*" expressed a common yearning for political and social renovation. Associations—national or international, based on either category or class—came to be understood as an essential form of national organization for free citizens. After 1848, liberals, democrats, economists, and moralists theorized associations as instruments that were essential to confronting the disruption of traditional social associations such as the family as a result of the galloping industrialization of the era. In France, Britain, Germany, Belgium, and Italy observers viewed associations as capable of ending social and political injustice.

A glance at the history of associations in Europe confirms this statement. At the origin of the German Workers' party, founded by Ferdinand Lassalle in 1863, was the *Verein* concept, as its German name makes clear ("Allgemeiner Deutscher Arbeiterverein"); in France, workers' organizations emerged from various *associations* demanding improved working conditions and better salaries; from the idea of a "labour union" in England was born the International Workingmen's Association (November 1, 1864), in which Marx had such a prominent role. In short, in the second half of the nineteenth century, the pre-1848 concept of humanitarian solidarity transformed itself into a sociopolitical type of associationism whose goal was to transform existing society.

The question of representation had a similar evolution. The issue became whether the suffrage should be extended and whether individuals, groups, or classes, as such, should be represented. Representation, however, could not be separated from the issue of participation in politics. The suffrage could remain restricted to citizens who were rich or cultured, but with increasing wealth the number of people possessing the right to vote would increase. Thus modification of the voting system in a progressive direction automatically meant modifying the concept of the state.

The English thinker John Stuart Mill analyzed the implications of association and political representation in a subtle manner. In 1848 his *Principles of Political Economy* underlined the political importance of associationism and the economics of social reform. Here Mill not only discussed social philosophy but also pronounced labor to be the basis of production. He advocated an understanding between private and public utility as a progressive model of economic development that would benefit all society. Political thinkers of all stripes owe much to Mill's *Principles*—socialists like Marx, anarchists such as Pierre-Joseph Proudhon, French liberals like Dupont White, British democrats like Thomas H. Green, and even jurists like the Swiss-German Johann Kaspar Bluntschli.

The different editions of the *Principles of Political Economy* should be read in sequence to comprehend their true importance and to appreciate Mill's observations on workers' associations, electoral systems, political representation, and the state's role. Although the book was first published in 1848, the definitive edition appeared in 1871, after the foundation of the International Workingmen's Association (1864), the extension of suffrage in Britain (1867), German Unification (January 1871), and the events connected with the French Commune (April 1871). For Mill, representative parliamentary governments in national states signified the ideal political system.

After 1880, however, powerful groups on both left and right unfriendly to parliamentary systems emerged. On the left, socialists, anarchists, syndicalists, economists, and sociologists conducted the war on bourgeois parliamentary governments; and the antiparliamentary polemics of the right, from Heinrich von Treitschke to Vilfredo Pareto, were no less fierce. Before World War I, both sides accused parliamentary regimes of the inability to make decisions, of administrative inefficiency, and of political instability; they condemned deputies for their dirty business affairs, politicians for looking after their own interests, and parties for their ambiguous policies. It was not people noted for the high level of their culture, morality, or competence who governed—representatives of both extremes argued—but mediocre exemplars capable only of manipulating rules and exploiting power for their own personal ends.

In order to end this chaotic, unstable, and deplorable situation supposedly characteristic of parliamentary regimes, political observers at the beginning of the twentieth century theorized the triumph of a "dominant party." This dominant party could be the workers' party, composed of salaried people; the moral crisis of capitalist states convinced members of these parties that they could dominate the political life of their countries. However, "nationalist" parties could also become dominant. These were the parties that considered themselves to be associations linking state and nation; their members believed that they represented and defended the country's general interests.

Though the dominant-party concept lacked an organic theory during its early stages, it clearly claimed the political leadership. All executive decisions would be taken by the party leadership, which would then delegate policy implementation to its deputies in parliament and to its ministers in the government. Other parties could continue to exist, but the dominant party would run the country.

The concept of a dominant party had its origins not in the British or French political system but in the German term "*Herrschaft*," that is, dominance or supremacy. Already in the *Manifesto of the Communist Party* (1848), Marx had written that the proletariat must replace the bourgeoisie as the "dominant class." The idea of *Herrschaft* as a dominating function *(herrschende)* had subsequently been transferred to the party of the working class. The author of the German Socialist party's Erfurt program (1891), Karl Kautsky, had predicted that the party would have become the dominant party in the state *("die herrschende Partei im Staat")*, and he repeated this aim in his diatribe against Eduard Bernstein when the latter attempted to "revise" Marxism at the turn of the century.

The turning point in European political thought occurred as a result of World War I (1914–1918), when different political forces hoped to implement the dominant-party concept. In order to confront the first "total" war, the European countries employed not only military force but all their economic and moral resources as well. All the belligerent states conferred special powers on their executives to fight the war. Even before the conflict ended, observers of both the left and the right believed that authoritarian forms of government were necessary for the transition to a real peace. Socialists maintained that they would be able to take power with the support of the working masses and impose a dictatorship of the proletariat because the widespread class consciousness created by the conflict favored their coming to power. Nationalists, however, presented themselves as defenders of the fatherland and believed that with the determined support of the great number of war veterans returning from the front, they could implement a patriotic revolution in politics. Both sides abandoned parliamentary democracy, which seemed quaintly old-fashioned in its emphasis on issues such as civil liberties and the separation of powers; socialists and nationalists viewed parliamentary democracy as "bourgeois," and therefore hypocritical and egotistical.

Thus European history between 1918 and 1989 was conditioned by the formation in Russia, Italy, and Germany of a dominant party, transformed subsequently into a "single party." The single-party concept gave rise to a new form of government, and to a new literature that either exalted or condemned this new political reality. The transition from the dominant to the single party in the first part of the twentieth century characterized both fascism and communism. Though the historical literature has not paid much attention to this phenomenon, it is from this change that both World War II and the Cold War issued.

In Italy, with the entry en masse of nationalist organizations into the Fascist party (1923) after the Fascists had secured a favorable vote in Parliament, Mussolini informed the state administration that the Fascist party was now the dominant party because it represented the "totality" of the country. The sociologist Robert Michels, in the second edition of his study *Il partito politico nella democrazia moderna* [Political Parties in Modern Democracies] (1924), confirmed that "Benito Mussolini guides a dominant party composed of millions of people." After the murder of Giacomo Matteotti (a parliamentary Socialist opponent of Mussolini), the Liberal opposition accused "the Fascist dominant party of violating the traditional principle of separation between executive and bureaucratic spheres and of failing to respect the functioning of parliamentary institutions." In 1925 the historian Guglielmo Ferrero launched a sharp attack on Fascism in a work entitled *La democrazia in Italia* [Democracy in Italy]. According to Ferrero, the Fascists intended to become the "sole leader [of the country] as dominant party." Between the end of 1925 and November 1926, the Fascist regime imposed itself on Italy as a ruling single party without transforming the country's formal structure as a constitutional monarchy. In fact, the regime expelled the opposition deputies from the Chamber of Deputies and dissolved democratic political groups and associations.

The Italian Fascist party was not the first European example of a dominant party that had transformed itself into a ruling single party. From 1918 to 1921 in Russia, the Bolshevik (Communist) party declared its "hegemony"—that is, its dominant position—once it had obtained an absolute majority in elections. It then eliminated the opposition democratic parties so as to become the single party. At the end of 1922 Lenin outlawed all forms of pluralism and declared the Communist party the Soviet Union's only party.

After the Communist and Fascist examples, a similar phenomenon occurred in Germany, where the Weimar Republic had been hit hard by the Great Depression. With the elections of June 1932 the National

Socialist (Nazi) party became the dominant party in that country. The following year, having been named Reich Chancellor in January, Adolf Hitler had a law passed that declared that in Germany there existed a "single political party," the *National socialist* (July 14, 1933).

With one-party states flourishing in Russia, Italy, and Germany, after 1933 a debate ensued on the legal relationship between state and party. According to Soviet jurists, the Communist party was identified with the working class; consequently the party was engaged in the transformation of society in the name of the state. Fascist jurists argued that the party did not nullify the state but assumed the task of interpreting its political and social policies. National Socialist jurists—including Carl Schmitt—maintained that the party mediated between state and people; the party assumed a guiding role in the sense that the state was the legal instrument through which the party realized its goals in favor of the people.

The end of World War II witnessed the end of both the Fascist and the Nazi one-party states, but after 1948 the Cold War between the United States and the Soviet Union erupted. In Europe the conflict presented itself as an ideological struggle between two contrasting political orders—democratic pluralism versus a "monocratic" one-party system. It is true that the regimes of Eastern Europe called themselves "popular democracies," but after the signing of the Warsaw Pact (1955) and the uprisings of Berlin, Warsaw, and Budapest, it was abundantly clear that in these "popular democracies" the Communist party prevailed and that each of these organizations was in turn subordinated politically to the Communist Party of the Soviet Union.

During the Cold War, until 1989, several European political thinkers aligned themselves with the political regimes prevailing either in the United States or the Soviet Union. Nonetheless, Western Europeans attentively studied political developments in Britain, such as Clement Attlee's Labourism, and in France, such as Charles de Gaulle's presidentialism. Some authors, including Isaiah Berlin, Karl Popper, and Ralf Dahrendorf, indicated the British parliamentary system as a possible political model for European states. Berlin emphasized the "continuity of the European intellectual tradition" and studied British political theory from Hobbes to Locke, from Adam Smith to John Stuart Mill. Popper counterposed the "open society" to the "closed society" and criticized the German political philosophers Marx and Hegel, but he did not praise American industrial society; instead he underlined the British Parliament's role in the democratic development of that country. Dahrendorf, a scholar of Marx, described his "love" of Britain and his confidence in British institutions in his work *On Britain* (1982).

Other writers have pointed to France as a possible model because of the political standing of the president—not as powerful or isolated politically from the legislature, as the U.S. president—and because of the stability the Fifth Republic's constitutional structure has conferred on a national government previously noted for its instability. According to Maurice Duverger, an important proponent of the French model, this system is different because three governmental institutions operate within a multiparty context—the president of the republic, the government, and Parliament.

In Eastern Europe developments in the Italian Communist Party (PCI) were followed with attention, especially after the Twentieth Congress of the Communist Party of the Soviet Union in 1956, during which Soviet leader Nikita Khrushchev denounced Stalin's crimes. With the constitution of the Italian republic after World War II, the PCI skillfully and successfully operated as a powerful opposition organization within a Western parliamentary representative system. Following the thought of Antonio Gramsci, the Italian Communists fought fascism and criticized the Soviet leadership.

The fall of the Berlin Wall in 1989 and the end of the Soviet Union in 1991 marked the close of a tormented period for European political theorists and opened a new cultural era. We believe that a new democratic future has begun for Europe. The Italian political scientist Norberto Bobbio has exhorted Europeans to avoid the mythology of historical subjects such as "the proletariat," "the nation," and "the people" and to pursue the goal of solidifying individual liberty and civil rights. According to Bobbio, Europeans should concentrate on achieving reforms and respect for constitutional rules.

Certainly it is still too early to analyze completely and calmly the political questions and social problems that racked Europe between 1948 and 1989. For this task a certain distance is necessary, but we have attempted to provide an outline of the most crucial issues and the responses to them. In addition, a work such as this is necessarily selective, and we are aware of not having considered all political thinkers who had interesting perspectives on the crucial questions of their day. Throughout this book, however, we have aimed to present an overview of European political thought during the past two centuries by placing the major ideas within their historical context. We hope that this method will stimulate further interest in the subject and a desire on the part of readers to examine in greater detail the questions raised.

PART ONE

From Elites to Masses

1

RESTORATION MODELS AND UTOPIAN CONSTRUCTIONS, 1815–1830

On June 22, 1815, four days after the Battle of Waterloo, Napoleon Bonaparte abdicated for a second time and was conveyed by the British to St. Helena, in the middle of the Atlantic Ocean. This event—along with the Act of the Congress of Vienna published on June 9, 1815—marked the French revolutionary period's definitive end. The conservative powers, especially Austria, created a new European order that set its face against the French Revolution's ideals.

THE POLITICAL CONTEXT

In France itself, the Bourbon dynasty was restored in the person of Louis XVIII, brother of the executed king Louis XVI. Although Louis XVIII did not recognize the right of the French people to draft a constitution, political realities had spurred him to issue a Charter that created a two-house legislature with a Chamber of Deputies based on very limited suffrage and an appointed House of Peers. Instability marked Louis XVIII's reign, characterized by the struggle between a reactionary noble "Ultra" party led by the future Charles X and a tenacious liberal opposition animated by the "Doctrinaires" and supported by an economically dynamic bourgeoisie. The accession of Louis XVIII's brother in 1824 as Charles X and his attempt to return power once more to the "Legitimist" aristocrats who had been in exile (the émigrés) produced the July Revolution in 1830 that brought to power the "bourgeois king," Louis Philippe.

More serious discontent reigned in the other parts of Europe. In Spain the Bourbon dynasty was also restored in 1815 under Ferdinand VII, in whose name the Spanish people had risen against France in a bloody guerrilla war. Ferdinand, however, squandered that goodwill, provoking a serious revolution in 1820. The revolutionaries reinstated the Spanish Constitution of 1812—proposed by the parliament, the Cortes, at Cádiz according to the unicameral model of the French Constitution of 1791. With the blessing of the other major European powers, the French put down the Spanish revolution in 1823.

In Italy the old restored states and dynasties came under even greater Austrian domination than in the eighteenth century. The Italian monarchs had no wish to grant constitutions, and the Austrian emperor Francis II and his chancellor Metternich opposed such action because they feared the example such constitutions would set for their empire. Both liberalism and nationalism threatened the existence of Austria, because it was made up of disparate peoples held together by allegiance to the emperor, symbol of the empire. The restored Italian regimes and Austrian rule were so harsh that in 1820 and 1821 the discontent flared into revolutions in both south (1820) and north (1821), with the proclamation in both regions of the Spanish Constitution of 1812. The Austrians intervened to suffocate these uprisings, but they were followed by greater discontent with Austrian political hegemony in Italy.

In other European areas conservatism also set the tone. In Germany the Congress of Vienna established the German Confederation, a primarily defensive alliance consisting of thirty states and four free cities, which exploded the early hopes of German patriots for a unified country. Here also, Austria dominated, with Prussia incapable of challenging Austrian power. Austria had been unable to force those German states that had constitutions to revoke them, but the unrest following the Vienna settlement convinced the German Confederation to take drastic steps in July 1819 (the Carlsbad Decrees) that "fettered opinion and postponed constitutional liberty in Germany for a generation." In northern Europe, Belgium was forcibly attached to the Kingdom of Holland, an act that produced a revolution in 1830. In eastern Europe, Russia under the eccentric Alexander I and his reactionary successor Nicholas I subdued the subject nationalities along with Austria. Russian Poland rebelled in 1830 and 1831, but the revolt was suffocated in blood.

Within this troubled context theorists searched for new forms of political organization that would reform civil society.

WORKING MODELS

Political scientists have long employed the concept of a "model" as a useful tool with which to examine ideologies, to suggest forms of government, and to analyze economic and social programs. A more recent practice has been to analyze past political structures in order to determine whether and to what extent they served as guides in the construction of new institutions.

With the collapse of French revolutionary governmental forms at the end of the Napoleonic Wars (1815), three functioning forms of government existed that served as political models during debates among political thinkers of the period: the Prussian model, influenced by the concept of enlightened monarchy; the British model, based on limited monarchy and the parliamentary system; and the American model, which rested on a democratic republican form of rule that prevailed in the United States.

The Prussian Form of Government

In 1813 Madame de Stäel's *Considerations on the Principal Events of the French Revolution* was published in London. During the next few years, the discussion of German philosophy in this work resulted in the cultural discovery of Germany by Europe. Europeans came to view Prussia not as a "barracks state," as the French *philosophes* (eighteenth-century philosophers) had done, but as a country where the Enlightenment, a spirit of justice, and a sentiment favoring independence prevailed among all classes.

At the Peace of Tilsit (1807) Napoleon had deprived Prussia of half its territory, and it had seemed that Prussia had reached the end of its trajectory as a great power. It revived, however, by initiating a reform movement headed by people such as Heinrich Friedrich Karl von Stein, Wilhelm von Humboldt, and Karl von Hardenberg who were convinced that the nation could resurrect itself. Counting on the country's bourgeoisie, the reformers set out to alter the bureaucratic structure as a means of creating a modern state. The reformers astutely launched an agrarian reform in order to reconstruct the villages destroyed during the war with Napoleon. The feudal regime was abolished, and the bourgeoisie and the peasants were allowed to buy land. The old castes were replaced by social ranks (*Stände*) based on wealth and profession. The king gave up his domain lands and many who formerly rented their lands became landowners. At the same time, Stein's administrative reform retained traditional absolutist aspects of the Prussian bureaucracy but established consultative bodies with which government functionaries were bound to collaborate.

Stein and his supporters aimed at attaching the people to their sovereign—a lack held responsible for the disastrous defeat of the Prussians by the French—by forging links between the population and state institutions under the pressure of reform. Spurring this internal transformation would be national sentiment based on opposition to French domination in the name of liberty. The liberation struggle unified the country while thinkers such as Johann Gottlieb Fichte and Friedrich Schleiermacher spoke to the nation. In this context, Humboldt, then education minister, founded the University of Berlin in 1810.

After the victorious war against Napoleon, which owed much to Gebhard Leberecht von Blücher's military leadership and to Hardenberg's diplomatic ability, Prussia regained its status as a great power at the Congress of Vienna (1815). It grew beyond its 1792 boundaries with the addition of part of Saxony, the Grand Duchy of Posen, Swedish Pomerania, Westphalia, and other possessions on the left bank of the Rhine—over 2 million additional inhabitants in all.

In this situation, the reformers' ability manifested itself in all its clarity. They had to meld together Prussia's possessions in the east and the west. The formerly French-occupied territories had a different organization from that of the eastern lands, and it was necessary to create a single civil and judicial administration without alienating either the different populations or the old Prussian privileged classes. Even though they committed errors, the reformers did very well, so that Prussia achieved its own identity among the European nations. It had reconquered its liberty and had saved the German nation, but it also represented a specfic kind of reforming absolutism. Its counterbalancing of France on the Rhine had psychological repercussions in Europe and gave it a political function—Enlightened Prussia against Revolutionary France.

Thus the Prussian state drew widespread attention for its organization and efficiency, and it became a model for Europeans favoring a strong state. Many contemporary observers admired not only the Prussian state's legislative activity but also—and especially—its juridical and moral principles. Romantic Prussia built upon its own tradition and recognized the impossibility of having a general legislation that met the needs of different peoples. But this respect for tradition did not preclude the slow evolution of existing institutions. The Prussian ruling class recognized this, and was concerned primarily with the impact of changing economic conditions on those institutions. As a result of this consideration and of Prussia's changed geographical configuration after the Congress of Vienna, the government instituted a new tariff policy. It rejected the protectionist policies of France and England and decided that duties should not exceed 10 percent. This economic policy stimulated competition and encouraged cooperation among the commercial, agricultural, and industrial sectors. Prussia's attractive tariff policy produced understandings with neighboring states and led to a commercial union among the German states, known as the *Zollverein*.

Crowned with the halo of romantic cultural approval, the Prussian model also stood in contrast to the Austrian system. The latter lacked economic dynamism and, on the political plane, opposed the concept of nationhood. The Prussian model encompassed both "liberty" and "nation" because true liberty was embodied in the nation and, as the romantic philosopher Johann Gottlieb Fichte stated in his *Addresses to the German Nation* during the winter of 1807–1808, because the nation included all classes. These concepts were embodied in Humboldt's reform of the educational system, which affected all citizens by opening the elementary schools to everyone. The university system, which was selective, nonetheless had the duty of propagating national culture. Thus Prussian education became a model for other countries.

The political model of a romantic and reformist Prussia, with its economic implications, appealed not only to bourgeois groups with administrative functions but also to landowners anxious to profit from their recently acquired feudal lands and to young industrialists who feared British competition. There were also religious reasons, that is, a preference for Lutheran Prussia over Catholic Austria.

The opponents of representative democracy and constitutionalism had a reference point in the Prussia of enlightened reform, a well-organized state capable of educating its citizenry to make sacrifices for the collective good. In 1818 the philosopher G.W.F. Hegel even attributed a spiritual supremacy to Prussia. For him the Prussian state was the most typical manifestation of the German principle that, in his conception of the philosophy of history, came after the Eastern principle of Asia and the Western principle of Greece and Rome. Almost contemporaneously, Humboldt wrote that the Prussian state filled a role that was the result not of its material strength but of the spiritual energy of its rulers and the patriotic commitment of the nation.

British Parliamentarism

Madame de Staël dedicated the last part of her *Considerations* to England, the land of individual liberty and economic prosperity, where constitutional monarchy prevented both democratic excesses and authoritarian despotism. Britain had not only fought Napoleon and extended its commercial domination, but it also remained the model of governmental moderation that Montesquieu had praised.

The English political system was based on the separation of powers between the executive and legislative branches and the limits that the British constitution imposed on the monarch. In the English system, the people possessed the power to initiate legislation but chose representatives to whom they entrusted legislative authority. Representatives had no role in the executive branch, in the administration of government, or in the execution of the laws. The difference between a "representative" and a "popular" government lay precisely in this functional separation. The supporters of English constitutional government discussed the disadvantages of republican governmental forms and condemned the "communicability of power" because it jeopardized liberty, especially freedom of the press. They idealized political realities, but in the age following the Napoleonic period the British model provided a solid reference point for the postrevolutionary generation.

Europeans admired the English ruling class. Freedom of speech, of the press, and of association, which the British enjoyed, were political ideals to which the cultured classes of the Continent aspired. This view helps to explain the popularity of works on British history and literature on the Continent, but Europeans who opposed the French Revolution also admired the pragmatism of the British political system. They contrasted this pragmatism with the French Revolution and its penchant for abstract ideological slogans, which had blocked a true constitutional process. Real constitutions are not hasty emanations of a political group of a dominant power; they are an organic whole consisting of the laws, which represent the political tradition of a people, to be respected even by the sovereign. In 1688 the English had rebelled against a monarch who had not respected the country's political liberty. Since then Britain had evolved politically in such a manner as to avoid revolutionary outbursts and to achieve an extraordinarily high level of production and commerce. Above all, European landowners believed the British parliament to be a bulwark of property rights against sovereigns who had arbitrarily violated them.

After all, they believed, Britain was ruled by a parliament sensitive to national needs. In that body were representatives of different political groups, which retained their political independence but nevertheless resolved their special problems while working for society's benefit. Britain improved existing institutions while creating new ones, if necessary, without explosive upheavals. It was in the mentality of the British to adapt a practical approach toward problems, naturally avoiding general principles and theoretical constructions. The historian Guido De Ruggiero, in his classic *History of European Liberalism*, distinguished between English and French liberalism—the first, practical and reformist, the second, conceptual and theoretical.

American Democracy

Because they had rebelled against the motherland's despotism, the former American colonies were viewed with sympathy and interest in Europe. Not only had they chosen the republican form of government, but because the economics, local administration, and culture of the individual states varied widely, they had also established a federation.

Between 1789 and 1815, they thus became an object of attention for political writers who favored federalism or who criticized the authoritarian bent of European governments during this period.

After 1815 there was widespread discussion of the American political model as an alternative to the restored governments, which were absolutist, and to limited monarchies. The United States had succeeded in combining an antimonarchical system with governmental stability and economic development while avoiding a military dictatorship. These elements explain the attraction of American representative democracy for republicans whose ideas would otherwise have exposed them to the charge of advocating Jacobinism and terrorism.

The U.S. Constitution was far from a program or a theoretical construct; it expressed a people's yearning for independence, republicanism, and community participation in government. Supporters of the American system argued that it synthesized Montesquieu's *Spirit of the Laws* and Rousseau's *Social Contract*. In short, the United States had actually implemented democracy and was therefore an excellent example to imitate.

In his 1962 book, *Les Etats-Unis devant l'opinion française, 1815–1852* [The United States Before French Public Opinion], René Rémond demonstrates how the United States became a political "myth" for the French. French republican writers presented the United States as a country that had known neither military dictatorship nor a restoration and yet had succeeded in extending republicanism over a vast territorial expanse and a large population. In the United States the revolution had succeeded. In 1817 Claude-Henri de Saint-Simon wrote in his *Lettres à un Américain* [Letters to an American] that the Americans had created a new political and social civilization. In 1824 the Marquis de Lafayette visited the United States, and his trip stimulated the publication of many works that increased the popularity of the American political system. In 1826 and 1827, encouraged by French republicans, the *Revue Américaine* [American Review] appeared, edited by Armand Carrel. To French republicans, the United States appeared a sterling example of republican life.

Many Italian exiles also admired the American federative model. One of the most important of these exiles, the intransigent republican Luigi Angeloni, advocated the application of the American example to Italy. In 1818 he wrote: "As far as I am concerned, I will always insist that the kind of government which is most suited to Italy is the one which exists in the United States of America, which, most certainly, is the best which up to this point has proved capable of ruling a State." Other Italian exiles such as Amedeo Ravina and Gioacchino Prati expressed similar ideas.

German scholars have noted that after 1815 the U.S. Constitution was in vogue in Germany as well, and that the writings of Benjamin Franklin were very popular. It should also be remembered that the free-trade zone known as the *Zollverein* was seen as a means of liberating the Prussian economy from Austrian domination, much as the Americans had freed themselves from British economic hegemony. Lafayette encouraged the German economist Georg Friedrich List to visit the United States. As soon as he arrived in 1825, List praised the country for its successful transition from an agrarian and pastoral country into an industrial and commercial one. In 1827 he published *Outlines of American Political Economy* and *Appendix to the Outlines of American Political Economy*, preface to his great work *The National System of Political Economy*, which appeared in 1841.

In England the United States was viewed as the country that had realized democracy. British radicals proposed American-style electoral reforms on the grounds that the United States had a voting system of the most advanced type. In 1817 Jeremy Bentham published his *Plan of Parliamentary Reform*, in which he argued that American representative democracy was the only acceptable kind of democracy for a civilized country. His theory of representative democracy as necessary for the greatest happiness of the greatest number had reference to an American model. "Look to America" became his constant admonition to the British in attempting to convince them to accept a radical reform program. Bentham employed the American example because the Americans faced their problems in a democratic manner and because, having issued from the womb of British institutional structure, the United States could serve either as a guide or as a warning to the British ruling class.

European democrats interpreted American democracy, and especially federalism, as an example of the continuous progressive development of a people. Resting on a bourgeois social base, these democrats counterposed the American model to the conservatism of the nobility, which they alleged blocked the historical progress of civil society.

Luigi Compagnoni, who published the *Storia dell'America* [History of America] (1821–1824), emphasized how the American system was built on a foundation of John Locke and the French philosophes, and saw as its characteristics religious tolerance and the separation of church and state; but he also cited "equality of conditions" as the fundamental feature of American civil life. Alexis de Tocqueville would make the same point in his *Democracy in America* (1835).

Helping to explain the interest in these models after 1815—the end of the French revolutionary period and the Napoleonic Wars—is the implicit understanding that European society was undergoing not only a political crisis but an economic and social transformation as well. Both confusion and differences of opinion existed with regard to these different "models," but they were a response to political realities in the different countries. Other thinkers, however, refused to use existing forms of government as working models and, following a long tradition in Western thought, suggested solutions for society's ills on the basis of more speculative considerations.

THE UTOPIANS

Influenced by the writings of Plato and Sir Thomas More, the Utopians rejected the existing system in favor of idealized models. Indeed, the term applied to these political theorists comes from the title of More's book *Utopia,* which means Nowhere. In their egalitarianism, both the American and the French Revolutions revived interest in forms of government that could eliminate poverty, give dignity to work, and create true equality.

Since existing governmental models had failed to satisfy these concerns, these revolutions stimulated the search among writers—ranging from the pamphleteer to the sophisticated intellectual—for ideal governmental structures. These writers offered a variety of solutions, including Christian communalism, collectivization, and communism, to resolve these problems. Already during the most radical period of the French Revolution, William Godwin had addressed the ideal of political perfection in *The Inquiry Concerning Political Justice and Its Influence on General Virtue and Happiness* (1793). Godwin both rejected monarchy as corrupt and criticized the French Revolution for the means by which it implemented its ideals. Godwin's work demonstrated an anarchistic quality, declaring property, law, government, and marriage obstacles to liberty. He advocated a community organization whose members could act together on the basis of reason and their consciences.

During the Restoration (the period following the Congress of Vienna in 1815), the Utopians rejected politics as an expression of force and aspired to peace and harmony. Because they emphasized the moral renewal and social renovation of the community rather than giving primary importance to political forms, they were classified as socialists. Robert Owen, Charles Fourier, and Claude-Henri de Saint-Simon were the most innovative Utopian thinkers of their day. Indeed, their ideas were carried beyond Europe, extending as well to the foundation of communal settlements in the United States during the nineteenth century and even had echoes in the hippie communes of the 1960s and 1970s.

Robert Owen (1771–1858)

Born of modest circumstances in the Welsh city of Newtown, Robert Owen went to work in a textile factory. Before he was thirty, he had made himself a successful businessman and had bought the famous New Lanark mills in Scotland. There he increased workers' wages, radically improved working conditions, and built cooperative villages near his factory where his workers and their families could lead a more comfortable life. Because Owen was an industrial manager with practical experience in the problems of production, his criticism of industrialists and merchants as selfish was taken seriously. In short, his utopianism was grounded in reality.

Owen began publishing his essays in 1813. In *New View of Society: On the Principles of the Formation of Character,* he argued that physical conditions determined a person's character; this principle provided the basis of his faith in the improvement of working conditions. He implemented this principle at New Lanark and further pursued it by demanding social legislation and publishing the *Report to the County of Lanark* (1821), a plan to put the unemployed to work.

Owen's experience with improving the condition of workers led him to argue that society needed not a political revolution but a new social organization. Only by ensuring decent conditions for workers could industry be harnessed to provide vast riches for mankind. To rebut charges that he was a dreamer, and finding no support for his ideas from the British government, Owen decided to found a community that would both illustrate his ideas and form the nucleus of the new society that he advocated. In pursuit of his vision, he went to the United States, where he founded New Harmony in the state of Indiana in 1824.

Owen described the system by which he proposed to alter humanity and society in his *New View of Society.* Owen advocated a socialistic system in which profits would be limited, competition eliminated, and a symbiotic relationship established between agriculture and industry. In this way, private interests would be reduced to a minimum, working conditions would be improved, and the struggle between employees and employers would end. These changes would produce a joyous society free of poverty, crime, and punishments. In Owen's socialist commune, Bentham's principle of the greatest good for the greatest number would thus materialize.

The key to Owen's plans was the cooperative village, which he outlined in great detail. Consisting of 1,200 acres in the form of a square, the village would be equipped with public kitchens and communal meeting rooms. Each family was to have its own apartment, but education and work were to be pursued in common. By emphasizing social matters, Owen intended to criticize the political orientation of the British government, which did not interest itself in the condition of the working classes, and the Anglican Church, which neglected their education. This lethal combination of poverty and ignorance fostered by state and church destroyed the British populace, and only a concentration of energies to correct the social failings of governments could reverse the trend.

In spite of the spreading popularity of Owen's ideas, he failed to achieve his goal of transforming society through the cooperative village.

Karl Marx appears to have been correct when he stated that the Utopian dream of altering society by creating working examples of ideal communities was doomed to failure. But Utopians such as Owen hoped to publicize the political problems created by the accelerating industrial transformation of European society. Large landowners were no longer the center of political life; the industrial city, with its capitalists, its workers, its machines, and its products, had become the central expression of a new social reality. And this new reality had to be taken into account if new disorders were to be avoided.

Charles Fourier (1772–1837)

In analyzing modern society, French Utopians took increasing industrialization as their starting point as well. The crises produced by industrialization, they argued, were economic in origin, but the consequences were primarily social because they affected growing numbers of workers and consumers. Changing economic policies and altering human relationships would create a just society and bring about happiness, they believed, although their solutions frequently seem confused and unrealistic and for that reason were labeled "Utopian." They rejected the aristocratic principles of an earlier age in favor of new economic and social solutions designed to produce a just and humane society in the industrial era.

Born into a commercial family in Besançon, Charles Fourier, like Owen, engaged in business activities. He published *The Theory of the Four Movements* in 1808, a work that aroused scant interest and that Fourier viewed as badly done and incomplete. Its importance, however, lies in Fourier's enunciation of a "theory of the social movement" to contest the repressive policies implemented by the European states of the Restoration era. In opposition to the "social chaos" feared and denounced by the restored Legitimist princes, Fourier argued in favor of "social prosperity" based on the "harmony of the phalanx."

Fourier criticized existing society for having failed economically and socially. The French Revolution, he argued, did not help the poor. Production was subordinated to the interests of landowners and the commercial classes, and parliamentary systems did not represent the majority. The solution, he argued, was a new society founded on truth and justice, united by similar passions, by character, taste, and instinct, and based on equality of the sexes. Fourier believed that he had discovered the laws that governed human behavior. Critical of free enterprise and the profit motive, he advocated forms of collective living that would produce a harmonious social order. In the society he imagined, everyone could act according to his or her own will and reach an equilibrium with society. The attainment of this equilibrium would be entrusted to the will of illuminated, capable, and honest leaders operating within a well-defined structure.

In 1822 Fourier published the *Theory of Social Organization*, which advocated associations of families and would reward individuals "in proportion to [their] capital, work, and capacity, reconciling inequalities of wealth and character." He criticized liberalism (the theory that the market and society should be left free to operate according to their own rules) and self-defined liberals who misunderstand the concept of liberty and whose theory of liberty contradicts the right to work. Under the liberal system, the poor lack both political and economic liberty while wealth is concentrated in a small number of hands. In seeking solutions to these problems, Fourier praised Owen's research but criticized the social forms he suggested, because Owen believed that people should have an equal share of goods and ignored agriculture.

Fourier defined the kind of association he had in mind in *Le nouveau monde industriel et sociétaire* [The New Industrial and Societal World] (1829). In this work he described the agricultural phalanx or "phalanstery," a large building with dormitories and dining halls surrounded by a field of about 1,000 acres to permit agricultural activity. All members would be free to work and to dedicate themselves to the activity that best suited them. There was to be division of labor, but also the possibility of changing occupations, and a minimum subsistence level was to be guaranteed to all. Different phalansteries, each headed by an elected leader, would help each other and engage in public works. According to Fourier, the phalanstery's very structure would combat hunger, unemployment, and poverty.

Fourier's ideas of social organization put him more squarely in the mainstream of socialist thought than his contemporary, Saint-Simon, who was also considered a socialist forerunner.

Claude-Henri de Saint-Simon (1760–1825)

A fighter for American independence and adventurous traveler, Saint-Simon was the prophet of a new world founded on science. This belief led him to emphasize the role of industry and to apply industrial criteria to the organization of society. In 1814 he founded the journal *Industrie* [Industry], and five years later he began publishing *L'Organisateur* [The Organizer] in collaboration with two disciples, who became famous in their own right—Augustin Thierry and Auguste Comte. The first issue of *L'Organisateur* contained a parable on the uselessness of the royal family and nobility, for which he was tried. In 1821 the first volume of his *Système industriel* [Industrial System] appeared, followed by the *Catéchisme des industriels* [The Industrialists' Catechism] (1823). Discouraged by poverty, which he always fought, Saint-Simon attempted suicide in 1823. He was persuaded by his friends to resume his activity, and launched the newspaper *Le Producteur* [The Producer]. He died in 1825, the same year that his posthumous, uncompleted, *New Christianity* was published.

Saint-Simon's thought contradicted the prevailing reactionary ideas of the Restoration era. After Napoleon's fall, the Legitimists favored an aristocratic government, which would enforce the three fundamental principles they considered necessary for social order: religion, morality, and justice. Thus, the Legitimists argued, the most important governmental posts should go to the nobility of the old regime, particularly the émigrés, who were most concerned with these issues and who knew how to combat the nationalistic ideology unleashed by the French Revolution.

Saint-Simon opposed this faction and advocated the formation of an opposition party composed especially of landowners, who were the most threatened by Legitimist theory because it forced them to defend the revolution's expropriation of land from the church and nobility. In 1819 he modified this view by proposing that the opposition "party of producers" be composed of people who contributed to the public utility through their work.

The eighteenth-century philosopher the Marquis de Condorcet influenced Saint-Simon. A believer in the theory of progress, Condorcet had predicted the coming of an age during which man would achieve perfection. Saint-Simon identified that epoch with the age of industry. Economic and social changes were creating an industrial system that had rendered obsolete both the feudal aristocracy of the old regime and the French Revolution's protagonists, the petite bourgeoisie and small landholders. As a result, he believed, industrialists would compose the future ruling class.

In order to achieve this position, however, Saint-Simon argued that the industrialists had to gain the support of the working classes by improving their lot. But in effect, philanthropy was the technique by which the government of the industrialists could achieve a mass consensus; even a just means of distributing the wealth, on which Saint-Simon insisted, was but a necessary condition of the industrial system's efficiency, which required getting the support of good workers. In fact, in Saint-Simon's scheme, the workers took a backseat to the employers, who had superior education and experience and who worked with their brains instead of their brawn. In short, Saint-Simon expressed an ideology for pervasive industrial development, and he believed that the time had arrived for the industrialists to become conscious of their importance as a class and to unite in a political party to attain the privileges that their role in society conferred upon them.

It has been observed that Saint-Simon described the industrial society of the future in a manner that favored the private entrepreneurs and that it is consequently a paradox to consider him as a forerunner of the French socialist school. The same may by said of his disciple Auguste Comte, who preached the coming importance of hierarchies.

Saint-Simon's thought is also marked by a profound religious ferment. A religion of fraternity and love is the new society's engine, he said in *New Christianity*. It was time to leave aside the modern, corrupt Christianity of the clergy and return to the love and brotherhood that had characterized early Christianity. Saint-Simon argued that returning to Christian origins would produce a social religion that would improve both the physical and the moral condition of the masses.

It should be emphasized that Saint-Simon's disciples—Saint-Armand Bazard, Barthélemy-Prosper Enfantin, B. Olinde Rodrigues—elaborated on the social implications of Saint-Simon's doctrines, diffusing them in a series of lectures in Paris in 1828 and 1829 (published as the *Doctrine de Saint-Simon: Exposition* [The Doctrine of Saint-Simon]). According to them, relationships between workers and employers could become ideal in the "organic" society preached by the master, with everyone being rewarded according to their capacities. Above all, "association" must prevail over individualism.

This concept of "association" comes from Saint-Simon, whose disciples were instrumental in expanding and spreading his philosophy. In the political debate that occurred in the five years preceding the July Revolution of 1830, Saint-Simon's followers stressed the negative consequences of industrialization—the alienation caused by increasing mechanization and the deteriorating condition of the workers—even while defending industrial society.

The thought of the three most important Utopians of the Restoration period reveals such profound doctrinal differences that the divergences may be greater than the convergences. What unites Owen, Fourier, and Saint-Simon, however, is their effort to understand and address the new economic and social realities of European society caused by the rapid industrialization of the early nineteenth century. To the existing political models admired by "realists," the Utopians counterposed new social systems designed to end the injustices of their era. In that endeavor they imagined new, organic, and harmonious associations of citizens working together to overcome the frightening dislocations of the new industrial age.

2

EARLY LIBERALISM

The quest to understand social and economic realities and to discover ideal political forms were not the only dominant themes of the Restoration period in Europe. The years between Napoleon's fall and the revolutionary agitation that shook the continent up to 1832 witnessed the enunciation of the central political doctrines that characterize the modern period. These included, among others, modern conceptions of liberalism and democracy, nationality and revolution, and class politics. Immediately after 1815 liberalism appeared to be gaining support among political thinkers. Soon, however, the question of nationality was raised for Italians, Germans, and Poles, and in industrially advanced countries such as Britain and France the drama of the working class began playing out.

Like many other developments in Western history, the extremely influential current of political thought known as liberalism had its origins in the eighteenth-century industrial revolution. According to the reigning economic theory before the industrial revolution, mercantilism, the prosperity of a state depended on its wealth as measured in precious metals such as gold and silver. The larger the proportion of these metals a state possessed, the greater its strength and influence. An important axiom of this theory, however, was that the world's wealth was limited, and therefore an increase in one state's proportion of the riches necessarily decreased the proportion of another's. Since industry and trade were prime methods of accumulating wealth, governments regulated commerce and encouraged and subsidized production but assumed that they could not be successful at this endeavor unless industrialists produced high-quality products. As a result, in return for its support to employers, the state mandated stringent rules and regulations to which the recipients of this aid had to adhere. In this manner governments ensured the production of quality goods that would be in demand in foreign lands, allowing them to recoup their investments, accumulate bullion, and become more powerful.

The industrial revolution shocked this system. New methods of production influenced cotton first of all, and this "inferior" and cheaper material quickly won preference over the longer-lasting wool. The new industrialists chafed at the government-imposed rules and regulations originally designed by the mercantilist system to ensure quality and a greater share of markets. Key mercantilist axioms—such as limited world wealth and the necessity of producing high-quality goods to obtain a greater share of the world's economic pie—became obsolete. Governments, however, were loath to change, and industrialists whom technological developments had freed of their dependence on subsidies called for an end to the onerous system of rules and regulations and demanded that the government get out of their economic lives. This wish produced a new economic theory based on free enterprise, as illustrated in Adam Smith's classic *The Wealth of Nations* (1776).

Known as "Manchester" liberalism, the theory of freedom from government interference had an enormous impact in economics and all other spheres of human activity, for the "spiritual freedom" of humanity was the underlying assumption of liberalism—not only economic but also social, moral, religious, intellectual, and political. Liberals believed in a free individual who must have the capacity for unencumbered development. Since the greatest danger of interference in the lives of individuals came from governments, liberalism emphasized political liberty as the essential prerequisite for liberty in all its phases. This concern explains why liberalism as it developed in the first part of the nineteenth century assumed the form of monitoring and checking governmental activities from its parliamentary vantage points. For the same reason, the primary political struggle occurred between parliaments and monarchs, the legislative and executive powers. Because wealth was required in order to be elected to parliament and to participate in political life, and since early liberals fought to keep governments from interfering in their economic activities (which generated their wealth), they were perceived by the lower classes and many intellectuals as representatives of the rich protecting their own interests. Liberalism, however, must be distinguished from conservatism, the defense of those groups whose members already have privileges. Indeed, during this period, the two movements were identified with different social classes—liberalism with the bourgeoisie and conservatism with the aristocracy. Committed to the spiritual progress of the individual in its broadest sense, liberals believed in change and reform. Carried to the extreme, liberalism leads to radicalism—which, indeed, frequently occurred. Complex historical conditions help to explain why British liberals were generally attracted to moderate forms of liberalism, pragmatic alterations in the political system, gradual reform, and custom and tradition; a preoccupation with abstract rationalism, principled declarations of social equality, rapid innovation, and revolution more often characterized French liberals.

In the aftermath of the French Revolution and Napoleon, British liberalism had an important influence on the continent, but the French revolutionary tradition remained robust and made many converts in Europe as well. An interesting case is that of the United States, where both the British and the French versions of liberalism had a great impact. As might be expected, American liberalism derived from the British, based on customary freedoms from arbitrary government. Indeed, Edmund Burke, who condemned the French Revolution, defended the American Revolution as the defense of traditional British freedoms from the British Crown's attempt to abrogate them. At the same time, French rationalistic liberalism also penetrated America, especially through the efforts of Thomas Jefferson, American ambassador to Paris and cultivator of the prerevolutionary Enlightenment scene in France. Embodied in the Declaration of Independence, this French element permeated American liberalism along with the British. The impact of French rationalism helps explain why, in the United States, the term "liberal" is practically synonymous with "radical," unlike in Europe, where "moderate" is the synonym for liberal; the early British and French traditions appear to have been enshrined in the traditions of the American Republican and Democratic parties.

Historically, liberalism has been all of the above. Over the decades liberalism has demonstrated an enormous capacity to change and to adapt to the times while seeking to keep its fundamental premise of individual liberty in focus. This evolution, detailed in the present chapter and in Chapters 5, 6, and 18, allowed liberalism to emerge as the dominant world ideology of the twentieth century.

EARLY CONTINENTAL LIBERALISM

In his 1748 masterpiece *The Spirit of the Laws*, the French philosopher Montesquieu wrote that there is no liberty unless the legislative, executive, and judicial branches of government are separate. According to Montesquieu, the British constitutional system enshrined in law the principle of separation of powers, and he cited that form of government as the one that most respected liberty. German philosopher Immanuel Kant (1724–1804) had also discussed the concept of liberty, which he made the basis of morality, since duty could not exist without liberty. However, although liberty was a fundamental principle in Kant's thought, he indicated no specific governmental application of the concept.

The theme of political liberty reemerged powerfully on the European continent between 1810 and 1812, at the height of Napoleon's power, in Madame de Stäel's circle, which gathered in the Coppet castle in Switzerland. These thinkers—who included the influential Benjamin Constant—believed that it was not enough to define Napoleon's regime as despotic, nor to label the emperor merely as one who denied liberty, in the manner of French poet and writer François-Auguste-René de Chateaubriand. Elaboration of a liberal governmental system was necessary in order to oppose the Napoleonic system. At the same time as these discussions, the Spanish Cortes meeting in Cádiz defined liberal governments as those that adhered to the principle of separation of powers. This Cortes produced the famous Spanish Constitution of 1812, which drastically reduced the power of monarchs and strengthened that of parliaments; this constitution became a liberal shibboleth inspiring several revolutions during the early nineteenth century. In addition, Napoleon's Spanish opponents who inspired the famous guerrilla uprising against the emperor proclaimed themselves "liberals." In Prussia the period following the humiliating defeat by Napoleon in 1806 witnessed a vibrant reform movement that attempted to reconcile the state's prerogatives with individual liberty. A major figure in that country, Wilhelm von Humboldt, argued that the state should have only a minimal role in society. According to historian W. M. Simon, "Although the word had not yet been invented, Humboldt was in fact the classic German 'liberal.'" The Prussian reformer believed strongly that the constitutional state must be preceded and prepared by the "ennoblement of its citizens' character," and he advocated the reform of education, especially at the primary level. The British, active in Spain and all along the anti-French front, denounced military aggression and pressed the English limited monarchy as a constitutional model.

In the British system two houses based on different social orders—the House of Lords and the House of Commons—shared legislative powers, creating an equilibrium lacking in the Spanish constitution. This feature appealed to Napoleon's opponents, cognizant that early French revolutionary unicameralism had contributed to the excesses of Jacobinism. They supported British bicameralism as a compromise, a political understanding between the aristocratic elite in an "upper" house and the bourgeois elite represented by a "lower" one.

Even before his "restoration" as king of France, Louis XVIII, on May 2, 1814, promised the French a constitution. Louis modeled his "Charter" on the British system, with two houses. The sovereign retained not only the executive power but also the right of legislative initiative and final approval of the laws; he also chose his ministers and headed the civil administration and the army. At the time, however, this constitution was interpreted as a compromise—the "golden mean" conciliating the royal authority enshrined in the old regime with the liberty of the French "nation," which had emerged during the revolution and whose pure political form was embodied in the republic.

During the Hundred Days, even Napoleon recognized that French intellectuals had taken a "fancy" to constitutions and could not avoid conceding one that supposedly represented the entire nation's interests. Napoleon consulted Benjamin Constant, whom he had expelled from the Tribunate in 1802, and explained that he wished to be a constitutional monarch who presided over public discussions of issues, a free press, free elections, and a government responsible to parliament. Constant drafted a document that was modeled on the English system and, after discussions and modifications, was promulgated on April 22, 1815, as an "additional" act in order to maintain the fiction of the continuity of imperial institutions. Napoleon's action illustrates the widespread demand for constitutional guarantees.

Notwithstanding the importance of the German philosophy of the period, the new ideals of freedom of the press and of speech had their epicenter in England and in France. The "liberals" defended civil liberties and elaborated liberal principles. They viewed "liberalism" as fully capable of ensuring individual liberties. Behind this defense of constitutional liberty was the affirmation of the individual as a moral entity, the desire to guarantee individual rights against political abuse, and the need to ensure representation for the cultured classes.

From the linguistic viewpoint, then, during the last years of the Napoleonic period, the distinction between a "liberal" and a "servile" party, made originally in Spain, signaled a new political orientation that was concerned primarily with defending public and individual liberties. Following the polemics at the Congress of Vienna, the noun "liberalism" was opposed to "absolutism," "conservatism," "obscurantism," and "servilism," depending on the circumstances. Recent studies have emphasized that "the political concept" of liberalism in the first half of the nineteenth century was utilized in debate with other ideological categories, creating uncertainty and ambiguity with regard to the term in the different European languages.

Despite the changeable significance of the word "liberalism," two prevalent concepts emerged from it. The first, ethical-utilitarian, defended individual initiative, respect for private property, and the free market; the second, juridical-constitutional, emphasized the importance of the division of powers and the independence of parliaments in their dealings with governments. The first significance was identified with the

British milieu of Jeremy Bentham and the economists who followed
Adam Smith; the second characterized French liberalism, which found in
Benjamin Constant its most famous exponent during this era.

BENJAMIN CONSTANT (1767–1830)

Born of a Huguenot family in Lausanne, Switzerland, Benjamin Constant
studied at Oxford and Edinburgh. In 1794 he met Madame de Staël, who
encouraged him to come to Paris, where he entered politics and became a
naturalized French citizen. Napoleon named him a member of the
Tribunate but, as mentioned earlier, expelled him from that body in 1802.
In exile Constant composed a number of important works, including a
novel, *Adolphe* (published in 1816). With the fall of Napoleon he returned
to France, first supporting the Bourbon restoration, and then collaborat-
ing with Napoleon during the Hundred Days. His activities during
Napoleon's brief return caused him to flee to England during the "second" Bourbon restoration. When he returned to Paris he joined the liberal
opposition, and in 1819 he was elected to parliament. During this time,
Constant produced a great number of essays, which he collected and published in four volumes as the *Cours de politique constitutionnelle* [Course of
Constitutional Politics] (1818–1819, 1820). His works remain very much
alive and continue to be studied and commented upon.

Constant himself wrote that the core of his work was the defense of liberty. By liberty he meant the triumph of individuality over both political
authority and the masses that claimed the right to rule over the minority.
For Constant, neither social nor political authority had any right to suppress the individual.

Constant argued in favor of liberty as a conquest of modernity. Liberty,
he said, is linked with the development of the human soul, and therefore
to defend liberty is to defend morality. As a consequence, public institutions are bound to respect individual liberty in the religious, literary,
industrial, and political spheres of human activity. This guarantee is so
critical that it must be sanctioned by a constitution. In his *Principes de politique applicables à tous les gouvernements représentatifs* [Political Principles
Applicable to All Representative Governments] (1815), Constant made
the point that constitutionalism ensured to all citizens freedom from arbitrary rule, which meant the right to personal security, freedom of thought,
and respect for property. Liberty was also the foundation of public and
private morality, individual dignity, and collective wealth; as a result, all
human associations must have liberty as their goal.

A glance at Constant's works allows us to understand the intellectual
consistency that he maintained in the face of sweeping changes that
occurred between 1795 and 1820, despite apparent contradictions. The

permanent and most characteristic feature of Constant's thought was his faith in the "constitution" as a document marking the passage from an illegal to a legal political system. As the state's fundamental law, the constitution is the means whereby the separation of powers and a guarantee of liberty for all citizens is written in stone; it is the only way of making authority legitimate. According to Paul Bastid's 1966 study, *Benjamin Constant et sa doctrine* [Benjamin Constant and His Doctrine], Constant made only a formal distinction between a constitutional monarchy and a representative republic because both forms of government are constitutional. The real difference is between these two models and an absolute monarchy, which does not respect liberty. Therefore, if a moderate republican becomes a defender of constitutional monarchy, no contradiction arises. Political judgment depends upon individual conscience, which, however, always condemns the abuses of the executive branch.

Though Constant cited Britain as the country that best limited the arbitrary power of the sovereign, he understood that France could not repudiate its revolutionary past. The French Revolution not only represented a break with the tradition of absolute monarchy but also had revolutionized French society, had set opposing interests one against another, and had given impetus to fresh ideas. To advocate a literal restoration of the old regime, which could never be reconciled with the principle of national sovereignty, was absurd. According to Constant, necessity imposed adapting French political institutions to the history of the French people.

Just as it was impossible to restore the despotic monarchies of the old regime, so it was for restoration of the democratic republics of antiquity that had so influenced Enlightenment thinkers. In considering this theme, Constant refuted thinkers such as Jean-Jacques Rousseau and Gabriel Bonnot de Mably, who had proposed rule by direct democracy through virtuous popular governments. Constant opposed this model because it renewed the authority of social bodies only at the price of liberty. In ancient Greece and Rome, citizens exercised their political rights in a direct manner, participating in the administration of the executive power. For Constant, this method was the essence of ancient liberty—the subjugation of individual to *collective* liberty. The modern principle of liberty, however, was new: It meant freedom to express one's opinion; the independence to come and go as one pleased, the ability to choose one's own religion, and the right to decide one's own actions. Whereas the goal of the ancients was to spread social power among social groups, that of the moderns is to protect private property by means of representative institutions.

Intoxicated by the ancient examples that they had sought to replicate, the Jacobins had aimed at austerity and equality, but their political construction had collapsed. With all due respect for the ancients, Constant wrote, modern civil liberties must affirm themselves because the progress and changes over the centuries oblige governments to bow to individual independence and mandate that representative assemblies arrange for the just regulation of liberty.

During the Restoration, Constant concluded that a solid political organization was necessary to contest the reactionary organizations headed by Legitimists. He opposed the reactionary party that wished to suppress the Charter (the "Ultras") because the revolutionary ideal of liberty had favored a political party that would include the great majority of Frenchmen. He advocated the formation of a parliamentary party to defend the libertarian idea.

Benjamin Constant's ideas were crucial in that they strengthened the constitutional convictions of his fellow liberals.

FRENCH LIBERALS

Inspired by Constant, a younger generation of Frenchmen founded a liberal party in the early and mid–nineteenth century. Full of enthusiasm, these liberals defined themselves as romantics, and the two terms became identified with one another in France. The liberal newspaper the *Globe*, published by youngsters barely over twenty, illustrated from its first issue on September 15, 1824, the link between liberalism and romanticism—in literature they had liberated themselves from the classical rule of the past, and in politics they had adopted constitutionalism and a practical program to implement it. The *Globe* was supported by other newspapers that presented bolder political and literary themes under the direction of Armand Carrel and the historian François Auguste Mignet. The young Louis Adolphe Thiers defended the French Revolution from conservative attack in 1823 in the first volume of his *History of the French Revolution.* Mignet, in his own history of the French Revolution, asserted that a new era had begun in 1789 because the revolution had changed the nature of political power in France and had transformed the nation's essence by substituting the rule of law for arbitrary government and by replacing social privilege with civil equality. This almost religious faith in the value of liberty imparted the characteristics of a political party to French liberalism. Furthermore, the liberals' high cultural level ensured that literature and philosophy, history and poetry, were marshaled in the defense of liberty. Mignet and Thiers brought a liberal vision to history and the revolution; François Guizot and Pierre-Paul Royer-Collard examined the liberal nature of the representative system; Victor Cousin attributed philosophical importance to liberalism. And the *Globe* viewed art and literature as free expressions of the human spirit.

All liberals strongly demanded respect for the "constitution," but they restricted the political leadership to those groups that already enjoyed social or economic responsibilities. French liberals identified "administration" with the management of private or public affairs. They believed that people who had competence in the private world could effectively move into public service. Thus the right to vote, based on wealth, became for liberals a certain method of selecting the political leadership.

Following the example of the French, other European liberals elaborated their own doctrine based on the idea of liberty. They viewed liberty as the defense against absolutism, as the struggle against feudalism, and as the antidote to foreign domination. They identified the struggle for independence of oppressed nationalities with the concept of liberty: The abolition of internal tariffs and tolls and the relaxation of economic restrictions was called liberty; the suppression of slavery became a crusade for liberty.

But in mythologizing liberty these liberals ignored the problem of equality and social justice. The French tradition counted no powerful utilitarian influence of the sort that Jeremy Bentham's ideas exercised on the British; as a result, although French liberals had an important following on the continent before the 1848 revolutions brought the "social question" to the fore, after that date it was British liberalism that created the models to follow by taking social issues into serious consideration and by integrating them into its thought system. Following the French model during the Restoration, European liberalism, identified with Constant and his disciples, had reached a compromise between reaction and revolution and their respective political forms—absolute monarchy and popular democracy.

3

HEGEL:
FROM CIVIL SOCIETY
TO STATE

Liberalism, the movement that appeared triumphant at the end of the wars of the French Revolution, had its counterpoint in Georg Wilhelm Friedrich Hegel (1770–1831), a thinker whose influence beyond his lifetime was incalculable.

At the beginning of the nineteenth century the structure of a state, understood as its juridical organization, seemed determinant to many observers. This structure permitted the normal functioning of civil life—restraining diverse social forces, assuring the general welfare, managing public finances, and legitimizing the governing elite's rule over the majority. Kant had understood that justice provided a state's foundation, and that civil rights assured the liberty of its citizens; to this Fichte had added the concept that the state was the organ of collective security and therefore had an objective rationality. Hegel, however, viewed the state as the entity that overcame the conflicts of civil society by synthesizing objective social reality with the individual.

As a young man Hegel watched French revolutionary developments with sympathy. He pursued a university career, dedicating himself to philosophy and political thought. In 1807 he published his most famous philosophical work, *The Phenomenology of the Spirit,* and later he produced a number of other influential works. After he died in 1831 his students published several other works drawn from his lectures.

THE FRENCH REVOLUTION:
IMPORTANCE AND LIMITATIONS

Although a sympathizer of the French Revolution, Hegel came to criticize it primarily because of his own conception of the state. A salient example of this attitude appears in his *Philosophy of Right and Law* (1821), in which he attacks K. L. von Haller (author of *Restoration of Political Science*) for his "most blatant attempt to banish reason from the state." Rejecting the reactionary criticism of the revolution, Hegel emphasized its great merit: the elimination of the feudal monarchy and the anachronistic remnants of the middle ages. However, to accept the fundamental value of the revolution was no reason to accept blindly the revolutionary ideologies of liberty and equality. For Hegel, these were abstract terms upon which a modern functional state could never be constructed and which could themselves generate a new type of feudalism.

The dominant political thinking during the French Revolution had placed great emphasis on rights and allowed private interests to reign supreme over the general interests represented by the state. This philosophy allowed individuals to dominate the collectivity, greatly damaging the general welfare. Jacobinism believed in popular insurrection, citizen consensus, and universal suffrage. As a result, it could never formulate an organic theory of the state; the state had to exist first of all as a public authority superior to civil society, private interests, and the welfare of individuals. The private citizen is also an integral part of the state; he or she lives in a civil society but gains social dignity within the context of the state. Whereas individualism views the state as the result of a conscious and voluntary joining of single elements, Hegel believed that the whole precedes its parts and makes them significant. Thus, although the French Revolution had ended an intellectual and political era, its ideology was poorly suited to a modern world that required political institutions capable of creating an organic whole.

Hegel's political thought must also be viewed as part of the early nineteenth-century European—and particularly German—revulsion against Napoleon's imperialism and as favoring national liberty—two concepts that, ironically, coexisted uneasily within French revolutionary thought. For Hegel, the national state had the clear duty of defending a country's independence, and with it all the traditions of a people. Only within a national state can the individual avoid being downtrodden by foreign oppressors and remain capable of maintaining the institutions and liberty that are the expression and the spirit of the people. Thus, for the Germans to organize themselves in a civil society while the French lived in a political state would be absurd.

CIVIL SOCIETY

According to Hegel, civil society is an institution of collective life that is not to be confused with a state. Civil society embraces all public services, meets the needs of individuals, and is regulated by laws. The state, however, exists on a highly different plane because it provides moral goals to civil society, gives consistency to individual motivation, coordinates economic interests, and increases the effectiveness of essential administrative services. Above all, however, the state makes civilization rational. Although, in a certain sense, civil society is diametrically opposed to the state, there is also a crucial relationship between them similar to the connection between economic and moral life. Economic activity is linked by a series of institutions, associations, and organisms within which the individual lives his daily life; morality is fully actuated within the state because it is the state that develops a cultural mission, provides the ideals for the people, and increases national power.

For Hegel, England was an example of a country in which collective life remained strictly limited within the sphere of civil society. The prevalent economic form in that country was a utilitarianism based on the principle of laissez-faire, the idea that the economy would regulate itself if left alone. Without doubt, British civil society guaranteed that the citizen's property would be safe and, through numerous intermediate bodies (from private associations to local communities) allowed the citizen to express his personality. But the powerful feudal residuals that remained within British political life could be seen in the aristocratic oligarchy's domination of the parliamentary system. According to Hegel, Britain had not yet achieved the true dignity of a state.

In his political essay "Concerning the English Reform Bill," written in 1831 for the official publication *Preussiche Staatszeitung* [Prussian State Newspaper], Hegel explicitly refused to consider the English form of government as a political model, proposing Prussia instead in that role. The respect of continental Europeans for England was the direct result, he felt, of repeated declamations in favor of English liberty, but British legislation was based on a hodgepodge of liberties and privileges granted by kings and parliaments in particular circumstances. The British constitution preserved only original private rights. If in a country private interests and financial gains prevailed, Hegel argued, the decay of both the political order and the state would soon follow.

In Hegel's political thought, the habits of a people constitute its ethic, which in turn becomes part of a body of public law requiring duties; these duties are thus rooted in the consciousness of a people. Representatives of the historical school of law, from Gustav Hugo to Karl Friedrich Savigny, taught that every people imparts a particular imprint to its own laws and possesses its own constitution. In 1814 Savigny had objected to the suggestion of implementing in Germany a civil code similar to the Napoleonic Code on the ground that laws are not arbitrary legislative constructions but founded on the morality of each people and develop historically with that people. Similarly, for Hegel, political structure cannot be divided from the habits and tendencies of a people; in other words, state and law are intrinsically linked, and one cannot exist without the other.

Some of these concepts may be observed in Hegel's discussion of Prussia. Prussia did not include all of Germany and had not even been able to defend its borders successfully against Napoleon; but it did react to its defeat in a positive manner, it had a clear administrative orientation, and it seemed to follow a rational line of development. In short, Prussia could aspire to becoming a real state by following a constitutional policy. For Hegel, this last idea signified something different from what it did to most people: Possessing a constitution did not mean the same thing as writing one, as the French had done so often over the previous twenty-five years. Hegel made two major points about constitutions: They developed not over months but over centuries, and they should emphasize respect for the social equilibrium rather than express concern for a theoretical separation of powers. In this view, he resembles Edmund Burke, whom we discussed in the Introduction.

There is a view that Hegel traced the political lines of the philosophy of law by idealizing the political structure of Prussia. It also can be said that his starting point was his rejection of the British *political* model even if in his doctrinal elaboration of a modern state he considered English civil society to have positive aspects. Hegel recognized that although the influence of the British oligarchic aristocracy must be criticized, the positive aspects of English society that were to be found in the complex interplay of institutions, traditions, and functions also merit notice. These positive elements included the British constitutional tradition, local self-government, respect for humanity, and commercial development. But even though he acknowledged these positive features, in Hegel's mind they did not outweigh the "enormous" confusion in public law or the supremacy of laissez-faire economics in British civil society. He stated in *Philosophy of Right and Law* (1821) that where liberty of industry and commerce prevail, there is the possibility for the individual to share in the general wealth; but along with the facility of accumulating wealth there is the hard truth that the great masses of people will lose out, because civil society is never rich enough to eliminate the excessive poverty of the lower classes.

Though Hegel admired German life and the Prussian political construction, he believed that—owing to its despotic nature and its failure to consider civil rights in a proper perspective—Prussia remained unable to conciliate government power with the liberty of its citizens. The issue went beyond conceding universal suffrage to an "often violent and irrational" people. Only precise norms and moral goals could confer upon the Prussian political system the dignity of a state and a modern consti-

tutional value. In a constitutional government, Hegel argued, the power
of royal officials must be limited and laws applied equally to all citizens,
whereas in a despotic monarchy the actions of the ruler threatened the
goods and the lives of individuals.

FROM CIVIL SOCIETY TO STATE

In his considerations on civil society, Hegel did not attack the idea of
social stratification; on the contrary, his defense of the different roles of
classes in a well-balanced society justified it. Nor did his distinction
between civil society and state lead him to question private property,
which, indeed, he considered an indispensable condition of civil life. In
fact, for him private property created a reciprocal relationship between
civil society and state, because property marked the line between individualism in society and the limits of the state's absolute power.

With regard to state power, Hegel differs radically from many political
philosophers of his time, as well as modern ones: There is no room for an
organized political opposition. He believed that government policy could
be criticized, but he rejected the concept of an opposition party that
strives to attain power. This idea was so important because Hegel
recoiled from all doctrines that view the state as an entity that is interested only in enforcing laws and managing common interests and is not
otherwise concerned with the civil actions of its citizens. Hegel could not
imagine the state as a mere spectator observing internal struggles and
consenting to the formation of political groups, because this scenario
transformed the government into a party organization, against which an
opposition party might erect itself. In this case there would be neither
security nor stability to political life, which would be reduced to a continual struggle of parties for power. For Hegel, such a construction hardly
qualified as a state. In Hegel's terms, a state is a juridical entity with its
own national, moral, and cultural goals—not a governmental instrument
in the hands of an aristocracy or a mob.

For Hegel, the transition from civil society to state is marked by the end
of particularistic conflicts as they are absorbed into an organic and stable
harmony of the different social orders. The concept of an opposition
remained for him a degenerate form of feudal society and could never be
considered as a positive political element of a strong state endowed with
a rational structure. The antagonisms characteristic of opposition parties
must be assimilated into an organic public interest, which can be the
expression only of a national and popular conscience. Monarchs personi-
fied this unity by designating the head of a government and by maintaining the principle of government's responsibility to the sovereign, not to
the parliament. Hegel believed that administrators must prevail over

politicians and that state managers, as representatives of the state's hier-archical authority, must place social and general interests above private and individual interests.

The emphasis on the importance of national states taking shape in Europe during the early nineteenth century made this *Rechtsstaat* (state of law and right) theory attractive because it represented the supreme authority and the collective interests of citizens. Political philosophy thus evolved into the doctrine of the state, but, as Ernst Cassirer pointed out, it was not Hegel's fault if his concept of the state later became transformed into the idealization of power (*The Myth of the State*, 1946).

Hegel presented the state as a rational organization founded on institu-tions and endowed with sovereignty, not as an all-powerful construct. If in civil society the private sphere and particular interests prevail, in the state it is the public sphere and the general interest that are supreme. Hegel acknowledged that the different houses of parliament have the task of ensuring the political existence of civil society and give the power of decision to the monarch, but it is the *Rechtsstaat*, with its constitutional structure (*Verfassung*), that embodies the history and the moral life of its citizens and that confers dignity upon a people.

4

JACOBIN EQUALITY AND NATIONAL LIBERATION

After Napoleon's fall the Jacobin strain in European thought reemerged. New Jacobins reiterated the principles of 1793, demanding the just reordering of society by ending social inequalities that they believed derived from the private ownership of property.

In fact, according to Robespierre, the right of the masses to liberty, security, and assistance limited property rights. Robespierre had been guillotined in 1794, and the revolution ended soon thereafter. Gracchus Babeuf, however, asserted that the revolution must continue because the wealthy had retained control of society while keeping the poor enslaved. According to Babeuf, the revolution aimed to destroy inequality, thus ensuring to all members of society an honest existence. In order to pursue his aims, Babeuf headed the "conspiracy of the equals" against the Directory, but he was captured and executed in 1797. After his death, public debate on his egalitarian ideas ceased, but Jacobin secret societies wishing to overthrow the existing order and to implement those principles remained active.

Restoration Jacobins shared a number of ideals. They believed that the transition from an old regime to a new order could be achieved only through revolution. Arguing that humanity moves progressively toward greater equality, they criticized existing institutions because of their irrationality. Convinced internationalists, they had faith that new revolutions would not be confined to one country alone, but would spread. They fused political and social behavior, advocating the rights of all citizens to participate in political life and to share economic wealth. Jacobins believed in the revolutionary mission of the petite bourgeoisie and the lower classes, both of which were excluded from politics. They worshipped the French Revolution and particularly idealized the Convention and the Mountain, the most radical elements the revolution had produced.

Conferring the leadership on an elite provided, in Filippo Buonarroti's belief, the only hope for victory in the new revolution. In other words, democracy could triumph over tyranny only by establishing a revolutionary dictatorship—in the felicitous phrase of J. L. Talmon, "the origins of totalitarian democracy." This concept introduced a dictatorial principle into class action, which, through Marx and Lenin, became a cornerstone of modern socialist and communist thought.

Even the Italian patriot Giuseppe Mazzini believed in the need for a popular revolution, but his "popular revolution" was more than anything the armed insurrection of the Italian people to achieve independence; the real revolution would begin with the convocation of a republican convention. Already in his 1833 *Istruzione generale* [General Instructions] he wrote: "Young Italy distinguishes the insurrectionary from the revolutionary phase of the Revolution. The Revolution begins only following territorial liberation, with the gathering of a national council; this latter is the State's only fount of authority" (Giuseppe Mazzini, *Scritti* [Writings] II:51).

Mazzini differed also from Buonarroti because of his concept of nationality. Rather than deriving his ideas from a social class, Mazzini viewed human progress as a historical law tied to nationality and to God's will. For Mazzini, individuals and nations had a special "mission" within God's larger design for human improvement. In order to fulfill this plan, which conferred upon nations dignity and duty, each nationality needed its independence. As a result, empires such as the Austrian and the Turkish—which dominated existing nationalities—repressed their God-given missions, thwarted God's will, and were destined to disappear. Mazzini condemned both class warfare and the dictatorial principle, advocating instead a democratic republic, after liberation, as a means of implementing social reform.

FILIPPO BUONARROTI (1761–1837)

Filippo Buonarroti, a naturalized French citizen who had a troubled political career, was the theoretician of Jacobin ideals of social justice and equality. Buonarroti has been described as the first "professional" revolutionary because of his influence in the creation of secret societies in the nineteenth century. Indeed, he is *the* founding father of modern underground revolutionary groups, having a major impact on such twentieth-century revolutionaries as the communist Vladimir I. Lenin.

Born in Pisa, Buonarroti studied law, and at the outbreak of the French Revolution he went to Corsica and founded a newspaper advocating Italian liberty. Returning to Italy in the aftermath of the French invasion, he made contact with Italian supporters of the revolution. A follower of Robespierre, Buonarroti was arrested in Paris when the Jacobin period ended. Upon his release in 1795 he joined Babeuf's "conspiracy of the equals," only to be arrested once again after Babeuf's defeat. After he was freed, he conspired against Napoleon. With Napoleon's fall, he founded a secret society, the Society of the Sublime Perfect Masters, which aimed at creating an egalitarian world. Expelled from Switzerland because of his conspiratorial activities, he settled in Brussels in May 1824. He returned to France after the 1830 July Revolution and participated in several conspiracies designed to touch off an Italian revolution, briefly allying and then breaking with Mazzini.

Buonarroti published the book on which his reputation as a political thinker rests, the extremely influential *Babeuf's Conspiracy for Equality* (1828) in Brussels. In this work Buonarroti breaks with tradition by maintaining that there are only two fundamental political systems: the aristocratic and the egalitarian. This division is also true of political thinkers, who either support the small number of people who employ others and favor freedom of industry and commerce (the aristocratic system) or who support a complete reformation of existing society in order to improve the conditions of the overwhelming majority of wage workers and the public good (egalitarian system).

For Buonarroti, altering a political system did not mean to transfer power from one caste to another or to ensure the success of one form of government over another, but to change the social order. Given this situation, there can only be two political parties. One advocates the exclusive control of society by a class favored by fortune and education; the other believes in the participation by everyone in the exercise of sovereignty as a condition of social peace and therefore defends the causes favored by the people. The revolution thus marks the passage from the selfish aristocratic system to the democratic egalitarian system.

What makes Buonarroti's thought especially significant is that he did not have an abstract conception of equality. On the contrary, for him equality meant a social order that conditions the freedom and property of individuals to the will of the people and that impartially distributes wealth and education. The idea of equality is the basis of society because it is decreed by nature and acknowledged by reason. Equality is violated in society by people who exploit the existing differences in wealth and power. Instead civil institutions should limit the wealth and power of individuals.

Buonarroti traces the phases of the French Revolution and affirms that the real republic, one capable of satisfying the demands of the people, is the egalitarian republic whose founding principles may be discerned in the 1789 Declaration of the Rights of Man in France. In order to become a social reality, such a republic must be "popular." A popular republic means one in which the people are moving toward social justice.

Anticipating Marx, Buonarroti was familiar with the utopian ideas of Owen and Saint-Simon but rejected them because he believed that they rested upon the goodwill of people, ignored the ambitions of social groupings, and neglected the force of political power, with which he had become all too familiar in his life. Appealing to Jacobin political ideals and egalitarian principles, Buonarroti also criticized political models, ranging from constitutional monarchies to federal republics of the American type.

Buonarroti wrote his book thirty years after Babeuf's execution. He witnessed the profound socioeconomic transformation of Europe and the concomitant changes in the mode of production. He deplored the unspeakable conditions in which wage workers toiled. In any system of that kind, he wrote, the great majority of people would constantly be subject to hard work, misery, ignorance, and slavery. These altered conditions of European society help to explain why Buonarroti went beyond Babeuf's social and political themes. In the published texts of the "conspiracy of the equals," there were no references to the unlimited freedom of industry and commerce, the working class, overburdened laborers, wage-earners, or natural liberty, terms that characterize Buonarroti's writings. His polemic against the laissez-faire English economists, completely absent in Babeuf's writings, is an argument against the new merchant and industrial capitalists, who demanded the widest possible liberty in the development of industrialism. Buonarroti's program for a new social order is aimed at urban workers who favored the ideal of social justice.

Buonarroti's concept of a "revolutionary dictatorship" as a necessary instrument in achieving social equality was the most fertile aspect of his thought. This idea justified the use of force by a provisional authority that must rule until an armed insurrection gains the final victory. Anticipating Lenin, Buonarroti believed it necessary that a small minority of virtuous revolutionaries promulgate laws enforcing equality to the mass of citizens, victimized by excessive labor and rendered ignorant by shrewd and crafty oppressors. The concept of a civil dictatorship may be deduced from Robespierre's example, but since Buonarroti discusses power during an insurrection and revolution, another source appears to be Napoleon's successful military dictatorship.

In addition to Buonarroti's wider importance, it is crucial to recall that he was also an Italian patriot who hated Austria and the reactionary nobles associated with it. But the national and international elements of Buonarroti's thought merged, as they did in the many secret societies he founded. Although Buonarroti influenced Italian republicans, it is necessary to distinguish him from Giuseppe Mazzini, the most famous of that breed.

GIUSEPPE MAZZINI (1805–1872)

Born in Genoa into a Jansenist family, Mazzini received a law degree in 1827. He joined the *carbonari,* the secret nationalist society found in much of Italy and France during the period. Arrested by the Piedmontese police in November 1830, he was first imprisoned and then exiled. In Marseilles he formed a new secret society that demanded an Italian republic, which he called "Young Italy," and he founded a newspaper by the same name (1832–1834) in which he published important articles. He planned and executed an invasion of Savoy, which failed in January 1834. While in exile in Switzerland in 1834, he founded "Young Europe," designed to unite the nations of the continent. After nearly a decade in London, where he built English sympathy for the Italian cause, the revolutions of 1848 shook Italy. He went first to Milan and later to Rome, where he was asked to lead the Roman Republic after the overthrow of Pope Pius IX. When French troops restored the Pope, he again went into exile and continued his revolutionary activities in Europe and especially in Italy. Italy finally united when, after a bold invasion, Giuseppe Garibaldi handed southern Italy over to the Piedmontese despite Mazzini's advice. With a death sentence still hanging over his head because of the 1834 invasion of Savoy, Mazzini secretly traveled to Italy in February 1872, and he died at Pisa the next month.

Mazzini's primary contribution to political thought is his emphasis on insurrection and on the revolution of the people in order gain their liberty against an oppressive political authority based on overwhelming military force. Mazzini advocated insurrection, but believed that if the Italian revolution were to succeed, it must coincide with a general European revolution. Mazzini's revolutionary process consisted of three parts: conspiracy, insurrection, revolution. Conspiracy was the moment for plotting, common to all secret societies, when instructions were given to prepare for imminent insurrectionary action. The insurrection would break out at the appointed moment and would be implemented by means of guerrilla bands. The revolution would achieve the aims of the association by proclaiming first of all an indivisible republic in the entire territory of a nation and then convening a constitutional convention.

Both insurrection and revolution must have the people as their protagonist. According to Mazzini, the "people" are the primary element of revolutions, which "must be made by and for the people." More important, in contrast to Buonarroti's belief, revolutions "cannot be the monopoly of any single social class." The people as a whole—not one class—must be associated in a pact that promises equality of conditions and progressive development. Mazzini sought to mobilize the people through emotional slogans. As he argued against one class as the repository of revolution, he insisted on a republic as the only form of government within whose context the people could implement a truly democratic society. In working out these ideas, Mazzini hoped to avoid the degeneration of national revolutions into civil wars among different classes.

Completing Mazzini's thought system was his democratic conception of the nation. In fact, he merged the idea of "nation" and "people." In 1832 he defined "nation" as "the universality of citizens speaking the same tongue, enjoying equality of civil and patriotic rights, and associated in the common endeavor of developing and perfecting the social forces and activities of those same citizens." According to Mazzini, equal rights, realized through universal suffrage, and the development of "social forces" that liberate labor "permit people to become the People." From the nation-people emerges Mazzini's idea of a democratic popular nation.

As already mentioned, Mazzini organized an expedition of Italian exiles and foreigners (above all, Poles) designed to touch off an insurrection in the Kingdom of Sardinia. This expedition was planned to be the spark that would set off a European revolutionary conflagration, a tactic echoed in the twentieth-century "wars of national liberation."

Mazzini's expedition failed, but the collaboration between the Italian and the Polish democratic opposition was expanded into the Europe-wide organization called "Young Europe," which included Young Italy, Young Poland, Young Switzerland, Young Germany, and Young Austria. A group of young revolutionaries signed the document setting up the organization on April 15, 1834, with the aim of creating an alliance of peoples to contest the alliance of kings, and Young Europe became the first European democratic organism. This appeal signaled the end of the old-style secret society and the emergence of means of communication for the diffusion of national and social ideals. Exile organizations were charged not only with intensifying links with the homeland but also with building an international movement composed of national opposition groups. The protocol instituting Young Europe was the birth certificate of this new international thrust.

Mazzini developed an intimate understanding of the social problems of the British working class and broadened his concept of "people" by insisting on the essential function of workers and artisans in modern society. He founded the Union of Italian workers and a newspaper, the *Apostolato Popolare* [Popular Apostolate], to spread his ideas. He argued that the "people" consisted of workers, laborers, and salaried persons, and that when analyzing society, it was necessary to take into consideration the development of industry, the introduction of new machinery, production, competition, capital, and consumption. In addressing the most numerous, and poorest, workers ("*Agli operai italiani*"), he exhorted them to cooperate. Mazzini believed that the people had been "awakened to the idea of their own rights and of their own power," as the riots for higher wages in Europe confirmed, and that they demanded an improvement in their existence through progress and democracy.

Answering criticism in his newspaper on April 15, 1842, Mazzini wrote:

> The term "worker" does not have for us any of the indications of class usually connected to the word. It expresses only a particular occupational branch, a type of work, a particular application of human endeavor, a certain function within society—nothing else. . . . One day we will all be *workers,* that is, we will all live from payment for our work in whatever field we may labor. But this will be in the future, and the present is different. There exist in Italy, as everywhere, two classes of men. One class possesses, exclusively, the elements of what is necessary for work—land, credit, capital; the other class has nothing except its labor. . . . Those who belong to the first class fight to increase the luxuries and superficialities of life for themselves; the second class struggles to live.

This situation necessitated a social revolution in order to unite the people in a single body, Mazzini concluded, given that the nation consisted of all citizens.

Mazzini's founding of the Union of Italian Workers widened the horizons of Italian laborers, crucially influencing the democratic and national development of mutual-aid societies and social legislation. But his emphasis on the social and political equality of the citizens of a nation had another important effect: Mazzini reexamined the theories of Saint-Simon and Fourier and their disciples as well as the communistic ideologies of Babeuf's followers, such as Etienne Cabet, author of the *Crédo communiste* [Communist Creed] (1842).

From reflections on the people as a social unity and from a European outlook regarding the workers' movement emerged the seminal essay, "Thoughts upon Democracy in Europe," published in the British weekly *People's Journal* (August 1846–April 1847). In this essay Mazzini argued that the increasingly insistent demand of the masses to participate in governments and to remove control of the decisionmaking apparatus from the hands of the privileged minority could be defined as the democratic tendency of the times. No longer a utopia or a dream of political writers, this tendency toward equality had become a powerful reality in all Europe. Mazzini defined democracy not as the liberty of all "but as a government freely consented to by all." The people did not wish that "others" guide them, but that government be in the hands of the best individuals of wisdom and virtue, as determined by the people.

In the last part of his essay, however, Mazzini refuted the communist system: "Clearly, a system of *absolute* equality in the distribution of products and labor is unjust, practically impossible, and ultimately leads to the evil which we wish to eradicate. It negates all value to talent, virtue, energy, sacrifice, and to the importance of the quality of work." He added:

> With Communism you must have an arbitrary domination of chiefs having the entire disposition of the common property: masters of the mind by an exclusive education; of the body by the power of deciding upon work, the capacity, the wants of each. And these imposed or elected chiefs, it matters little which, will be, during the exercise of their power, in the position of the makers of slaves in olden times; and influenced themselves by the theory of interest which they represent—seduced by the immense power concentrated in their hands—they will endeavor to perpetuate it; they will strive by corruption to reassume the hereditary *dictatorship* of the ancient castes (vol. 36, p. 102).

According to Mazzini, with a communist regime instead of the government of the proletariat the result would be the dictatorship of the communist political class. Several months later, Marx, invited to London by the German Communist League and the English Fraternal Democrats, believed it necessary to answer Mazzini's criticisms in the second section of his *Manifesto*. In reality, Mazzini distinguished among three types of republics. The first was the American federative republic, based on "bourgeois individualism," exclusively political, ruled according to majoritarian principles, and interested only in defending the rights of the individual. The second form was the communist republic—authoritarian, based on the concept of absolute equality, and opposed to "property." This type of republic was characterized by tyrannical tendencies that produced the violation of individual rights. Most interested in the "needs" of the people, the communist republic addressed the economic side of life, imposed "duties" on its citizens, and ended up with a government that owned and possessed everything and distributed "everything which existed—land, capital, means of work, products, with every individual forced to work for a certain number of hours and receiving in return what his individual needs demand." The third type was the national democratic republic, to be based on representative democracy, led by persons responsive to the rights and duties of citizens elected by the people, advocating "the association of labor with intellect and capital," oriented toward raising the "entire sphere of men's lives." This democratic type of government assured that the right to vote "must point to the individual's participation in the management of the political world."

According to Mazzini, the democratic national republic must abolish all kinds of aristocracy and privilege and encourage association as an antidote to bourgeois individualism; it must modify existing society not by destroying the principle of authority but by substituting the authority that flows from the consensus of the majority for authority born of despotism. This democratic consensus issuing from the majority is, for Mazzini, the inviolable rule leading to progress.

The theoretician of collaboration among nations and of an alliance among peoples, Mazzini fought throughout his life for the political independence of nations. If Mazzini may be credited with awakening national sentiments, he can in no way be considered a theoretician of twentieth-century nationalism. For Mazzini, nation was intimately linked with humanity; one nation could not oppress another because the improvement of humanity was its final goal. As the champion of the nation, Mazzini opposed any nationalism that advocates hegemony and racial superiority. Mazzini defended "nationality," but not "nationalism," which he viewed as "jealous" and "hostile." He also condemned imperialism, which he defined as the expansion of a state limited only by its own force. Against "a narrow nationalism," he wrote, "re-attach the nations to the laws of progress, to humanity, to God." He added, "I abhor the usurping and monopolising nation, conceiving its own grandeur and force only in the inferiority and in the poverty of others; but who would not welcome with enthusiasm and love that people which, understanding its mission in the world, should found its security upon the progress of all surrounding it, and should be ready to sustain against the oppressor the course of right and eternal justice, violated in the oppressed?"

Mazzini thus appears as the implacable opponent of oppression, whether exercised by nation or class. By adopting modern methods for national liberation while avoiding the trap of class warfare—the "totalitarian democracy" mentioned by Talmon—Mazzini demonstrates himself a modern thinker. As he wrote in 1846: "The union of the democratic principle with representative government is an entirely modern fact." And in the post–Cold War world, Mazzini still seems to have something to say both to emerging nationalities and to established powers.

5

Democracy, Society, and Liberalism

During the Restoration, Legitimist writers such as Louis de Bonald considered the question of society in a manner opposite to that of earlier liberal thinkers. In his *Demonstration philosophique du principe constitutif de la société* [Philosophical Demonstration of the Constituent Principle of Society] (1827), Bonald argued that societies produced three types of governments: democracies, representative governments, and monarchies. He criticized representative governments as inherently unstable, and he advocated instead absolute monarchies; but he condemned democratic forms of government both because the people exercised political power and because they were at the same time subjects. These attacks produced a number of defenses of democracy, the most interesting of which viewed democracies as expressions of complex societies retaining the ability to guarantee individual liberty and equality.

ALEXIS DE TOCQUEVILLE (1805–1859)

The most penetrating analysis of modern society's democratic tendency was undertaken after 1830 by Alexis de Tocqueville. Descended from a noble Norman family, Tocqueville became a judge in 1827. Out of political favor following the July Revolution (1830), Tocqueville left for the United States to study its penal system. He resigned after his return to France in February 1832 and began writing *Democracy in America* (published in two parts in 1835 and 1840). After the overthrow of Louis Philippe, in April 1848, he was elected to the Constituent Assembly and in June 1849 was named foreign minister. After Louis Napoleon's coup d'état of December 2, 1851, Tocqueville was arrested, then released. He again dedicated himself to writing and in 1856 published *The Old Regime and the French Revolution*. He died on April 16, 1859.

Tocqueville disagreed with the political program of the French liberals, a compromise between reaction and revolution, represented by their support of Louis Philippe's Orleanist monarchy. He viewed the agreement as doomed because it had no basis in existing French society. More generally, Tocqueville accused the French ruling class of denying that the people had any capacity to handle their own affairs. His view of contemporary politics colored his writing.

In his classic *Democracy in America*, Tocqueville faults the French governing elite for having undervalued the importance of democracy and for having made a fatal error in refusing to guide it. As a result, a "democratic revolution" had occurred within French society without having left traces in the legislation and ideology, which would have channeled that development in a positive direction. In explaining his views, Tocqueville addressed a point previously made by Benjamin Constant, which was that the French revolutionaries had attempted to implement a difficult dream, the *"égalité des conditions"* [equality of conditions, or civil equality].

Tocqueville stated that it was precisely the existence of this civil equality that attracted his attention during his American trip. Furthermore, he continued, in America this equality influenced much more than politics and laws; it dominated civil society and government as well. "Equality of conditions" in the United States justified not the revolutionary Jacobins who had fought for equal rights during the French Revolution but those who had seen in the American Revolution a political process leading to democracy. This view explains why Tocqueville argued in favor of a moderate democratic republican form of government even though Louis Philippe's bourgeois monarchy seemed triumphant.

Tocqueville warned the bourgeoisie that its success promised to be ephemeral: The struggle between aristocratic and bourgeois elites would bring victory to the lower classes because, just as the nobility had been excluded from governing the nation, society's evolution would force the wealthy to cede their preeminent position to other social classes. Once equality before the law had been recognized, it was no longer possible, in practice, for control of the government to rest in the hands of a minority that based its power on wealth just as the previous ruling class had based its position on birth. Popular participation in public affairs, freedom of expression in politics, universal suffrage, decentralization—all were essential elements of American democratic organization; wealth thus did not guarantee the French bourgeois minority any permanence in power. Democracy would affirm itself not on the basis of the "legal" nation—with its restricted ballot—but on the "real" nation based on the vote for all citizens.

Tocqueville believed that society had not reached an equilibrium with the bourgeois victory because of the continuation of a powerful social process. Far from being the story of the third estate (the bourgeoisie), French history since the twelfth century was the relentless history of democratic development. Tocqueville insisted that in France and elsewhere, not one significant event in the previous 700 years had been resolved if not in favor of democracy. This "irresistible revolution," imbued almost with a religious quality, had destroyed feudalism and defeated kings—and it would certainly not retreat before the wealthy. Given that future societies would inevitably be democratic, the real function of rulers was to adapt democracy to different times and places; this task made necessary a new political science for a renovated world, and hence Tocqueville's interest in the United States.

According to Tocqueville, the Americans had discovered the formula for establishing a democratic society in which individual initiative harmonized with the collective needs of the state: local self-government. For Tocqueville, democracy was not an abstract collection of principles and institutions embodied in the U.S. Constitution, but daily practice. He thus championed the empiricism dear to Americans rather than the ideological method favored by French political writers who, when studying America, tended to focus on the Constitution. To sum up Tocqueville's beliefs: In a democracy, liberty necessarily issued from democratic practice, not from the constitutional concessions of a monarch or other rulers; liberty allowed each citizen to aspire to any public office without regard to wealth.

These reflections come from *Democracy in America*'s first part, published in 1835. Some scholars have professed to see a major difference between this section and the second, which appeared five years later. In fact Tocqueville wished to register his disapproval of both French democrats who championed the Jacobin tradition and Babeuf, who preached direct democracy, the community of goods, and state direction of social policy. Tocqueville entered into polemics with French Jacobins, democrats, and socialists. For example, Louis Blanc, despite having written a favorable review of *Democracy in America*, defined democracy as a political system that would end individualism, destroy the concept of competition, control the labor supply, and put the means of production in state hands. Blanc reiterated these ideas in an influential piece, "L'organisation du travail," which appeared in his journal, the *Revue du progrès* [Review of Progress], in 1840. Tocqueville disagreed with these views and reaffirmed his belief in liberty, representative democracy, and, in general, in institutions that protected individual initiative.

In 1856 Tocqueville published his second masterpiece, *The Old Regime and the French Revolution*. This book is most notable for its descriptions of both sociological conditions of the old regime and the social forces producing the revolutionary conflagration. It is the tale of the French road to democracy and, together with *Democracy in America,* compares American political forms to the new French political structure. It is the story of two great countries grappling with the same theme: how modern societies move toward democracy. For Tocqueville, the major dilemma was to achieve democratic progress while avoiding tyranny. His answer was to accommodate minority opposition movements in the American style.

In the United States the opposition had renounced violence because it could utilize the press, persuasion, and liberty of association in order to communicate its program to the majority. Administrative decentralization and frequent recourse to elections guaranteed the opposition's freedom of action. A distinctive characteristic of American democracy allowed diverse opinions to flourish, favored intellectual growth, and invested the opposition with a dignified role in political life. In a democratic political system, the opposition could protest against social injustices and the abuse of power. In the United States the opposition played a positive role because it prevented situations from stagnating; while the mobility of democratic societies allowed nations to progress toward moral and intellectual growth, the opposition generated the energy to do so. Moreover, the opposition did not attack the fundamental principles of the political system because it was an integral and necessary part of that system.

Thus Tocqueville understood that the essence of a society is its daily operation and—as John Stuart Mill wrote to him in 1840—he clearly identified stagnation and gridlock as the greatest dangers faced by political systems.

JOHN STUART MILL (1806–1873)

If Tocqueville's greatest contribution was his analysis of society's influence on governmental forms and the irresistible direction in which politics seemed to be evolving, practical liberal programs owe much to the ideas expressed by John Stuart Mill in his *Principles of Political Economy,* published in London in 1848. Coinciding with the revolutions of that year, the work was an instant European success. To those who believed in liberty and liberalism, Mill said that a liberal political system could not survive without producing concrete solutions for existing economic and social problems. Military means could certainly restore order, but a return to the Orleanist constitutionalism that had existed during the July Monarchy in France (1830–1848) was no longer possible. The uprisings had a number of causes, but they were not the result of the activities of a few agitators. The restricted suffrage, based on wealth, and the economic crisis of 1846–1847 had merged political and economic causes. According to Mill, only political liberalism combined with economic reform and attention to social needs could protect human dignity.

Mill set forth his further ideas on liberty in his famous *Essay on Liberty* (1859). He also argued, in his *Considerations on Representative Government* (1863), in favor of fuller parliamentary representation, and in *The Subjection of Women* (1869) he declared himself in favor of women gaining the right to vote.

The *Principles of Political Economy* remains his most important work. In this book Mill cites labor as the economy's most important component because it is indispensable to the production of goods and services. Production also requires capital and land and is affected by human, natural, and technical aspects such as competence, soil fertility, and machinery.

In his work, Mill examines the social aspect of political-economic life, which he believes derives from the relationship among labor, capital, and land. He also studies the question of the distribution of income derived from profit and investment. Whereas income distribution came about in the past in a spontaneous manner among workers, capitalists, and landowners, in industrial societies it is necessary to distinguish between capitalist and working "classes." The working class is strictly conditioned by wages, which depend on labor supply and demand for labor and on the relationship between population and capital. Given that it is very difficult to prevent wages from continually dropping, Mill favored a minimum wage and a guaranteed job on the grounds that everyone had a right to live.

Mill rejected communism, which he regarded as the equal division of private property; indeed, he maintained that communism could not be achieved in a civilized society because it completely extinguished liberty. He admitted that the workers of his day could not choose their occupations and had only limited freedom of movement, but he identified in the most advanced countries a steady increase in wealth and material prosperity. This progressive movement was the result of improvements in production and technology, which would have a cumulative positive effect on the economy and on living conditions. He believed that the increase in national wealth and the growth of cooperative movements would lead to the formation of powerful intermediate classes, which would in turn result in higher and better-distributed wages. Thus for Mill the problem of an equitable distribution of national wealth was intimately linked to the problems of the working class.

In his *Principles*, Mill also confronted the question—dear to liberals—of the government. He reiterated the liberal position that government had certain necessary functions, such as the protection of individuals from violence. But he also argued that governments had to deal with the larger issue of public interest. Though the individual remained the real defender of his own interests, governments must increase wealth by means of the tax system. Taxation had to be proportioned to the economic state of individuals and must avoid punitive rates that threatened savings and production. In other discussions Mill greatly expanded the validity of government among liberal thinkers by arguing that human beings should help one another. For that fundamental reason, the government must take the lead in charitable activities, supplanting private charities, promoting important research, and building a nation's infrastructure through vast public works programs.

Clearly, Mill's *Principles* represents an important departure from the liberalism of the old school. The older liberalism condemned government intervention in the economy and gave space only to private initiative. Given that social problems and economic needs were linked, the new liberalism recognized the impossibility of governing without addressing economic realities and without elaborating a "philosophy of society." Mill therefore called for a radical alteration of liberal philosophy: Government must direct its attention to monetary and production issues, resolve the needs of commerce and industry, implement an equitable taxation system, and confront the problems of wage labor. In short, economic effects arose out of the ordinary workings of government and could not be ignored.

Government intervention in the economy, however, intimately involved another aspect of liberal philosophy—the fear that government activism might destroy individual liberty. After Louis Napoleon's destruction of the Second Republic in France (1851) and his imposition of a dictatorship, liberals felt an urgent need to respond. Mill's answer appeared in his famous essay begun in 1854 and published in 1859, *On Liberty*, which was rapidly translated into other European languages.

In this essay Mill stated that the central issue of civil affairs is the relationship between governmental political authority and the liberty of the governed. In order to combat despotism—the major worry of the time—European states chose the method of popular elections of representatives to limited terms. According to continental liberals, when those who govern are responsible to the people, who can revoke their mandate, society can trust and regulate governmental authority. But in practice, Mill wrote, the "people" who exercise power are not the same people who are governed. The will of the people frequently means the will of those persons who know how to impose themselves on the "people."

Accentuating this problem, Mill emphasized that the tyranny of the majority is an evil against which the collectivity must defend itself. The despotism of the majority is particularly insidious because it works through public laws and public officials; it results in a social despotism that is also the worst type because, in effect, the morality of a nation derives from the interests and sense of superiority of the dominant class or group. Mill believed it imperative to fight the tendency of public opinion and of society to impose ideas on individuals by limiting the ability of the collectivity to affect personal independence. Thus when the government is considered the representative of the public interest, personal liberty will always be subjected to government encroachment. From here the debate begins between those who encourage the government to get involved in every issue where it can do good or remedy evil and those who argue that any social evil is preferable to enlarging the sphere of governmental action.

This consideration led Mill to enunciate his famous principle designed to resolve this debate: It is only legitimate for the government to use force against a person when that force is necessary to prevent the person from injuring other members of the community. Each individual must have full and absolute liberty of opinion in every field. A society that does not unconditionally and absolutely respect these principles cannot be free, no matter what its form of government.

In enunciating these ideas, Mill was responding to the observations of several British journals that had addressed the dilemma afflicting the French Second Republic (1848–1852). If the executive and legislative powers remained separate and acted only within their own sphere, the result was paralysis; too much democracy and universal suffrage, however, could result in Caesarism. Mill rejected both immobilism and the dictatorship of the majority (Louis Napoleon had exploited the issue of universal male suffrage to come to power and reinstituted it, after its limitation by the French Assembly, after his 1851 coup d'état) and elegantly resolved the question by sanctifying the right to dissent. In practical terms, Mill supported mechanisms to ensure parliamentary representation for political minorities that were not represented in a two-party system.

Mill also examined the general issue of governmental forms in his 1861 *Considerations on Representative Government*. He began with the premise that political institutions exist because of human will. They did not spring into existence full-blown but have a historical foundation and are the result of national customs and characteristics. The best political institutions are those that not only meet this criterion but also promote the honesty and develop the intelligence of a community and encourage ever-increasing participation in political life.

Therefore, according to Mill, the best form of government is representative government, because it not only enshrines the principle that sovereignty belongs to the whole community but also affords every citizen the opportunity to participate effectively in local and national affairs. Representative governments aim not only at obedience and order but also at fostering everyone's progress without interfering with individual liberty of action. This is a very satisfying result, Mill wrote, since citizens or classes that are left out of the constitution and forced to obey authority without a voice in their own destinies will inevitably harbor resentment. In this manner, Mill in effect called attention once more to the theme that the old liberalism must be modified—representative government alone could completely satisfy the demands of a common social life.

Mill identified regimes of the type that Louis Napoleon had set up in France as the negative model to be avoided at all cost. Making use of the plebiscite, Louis Napoleon curtailed freedom of the press, exiled opponents, and imprisoned opposition leaders. From the viewpoint of political theory, Mill had already denied the right of the majority to trample the freedom of those who did not agree with it, and thus Louis Napoleon's methods were illegitimate. Mill defended the right of the people to participate in electoral consultations but denied that political questions could be decided by appealing to the masses; in order to prevent such a development, he believed, the management of public affairs must remain the province of a cultured and liberal minority.

This last idea undoubtedly reveals contradictions in Mill's political thought. The enduring value of his thought system, however, is his strong belief in and defense of "liberty." And though this principle remains the most important for Mill, his insistence that social and economic questions should not be ignored and that liberty necessarily means governmental intervention to correct societal and economic problems, made a crucial contribution to the modern evolution of liberal thought.

MID-CENTURY LIBERALISM

The major concern of British liberals during the mid–nineteenth century was the battle for reform of the electoral system. Before the Reform Act of 1867–1868, fewer than 1 million citizens, of more than 5 million of voting age, had the right to vote. With about 2.5 million people eligible to vote after that reform, liberals were obliged not only to organize themselves in such a manner as to reach many more voters but also to pay stricter attention to public opinion. No longer could popular associations be ignored, nor could promises made at election time be flouted. Theory now held that it was not enough for a liberal government to be interested merely in receiving a majority; it also had to be interested in ensuring that it represented public opinion. In his work *On Parliamentary Government* (1867–1869) Alpheus Todd wrote that a government must be "responsible to the people," indicating that ministers were responsible both to parliament and people.

In a work published in London in 1867, the *English Constitution*, the brilliant writer Walter Bagehot, rather than taking a theoretician's outlook, examined the practical operation of the British system. There are, he argued, two equally erroneous interpretations of the British constitutional system. The first described British political life as being founded on the separation of powers (legislative, executive, judicial), each supposedly operating in its own sphere and not interfering with the others. The second view presents an equilibrium based on "checks and balances." For Bagehot, however, the importance of the English political system is its flexibility and, in moments of crisis, its extreme simplicity. Its secret is in the link between executive and legislative branches through the cabinet, not the separation of powers. In the past, the Crown chose the ministers, but now the head of the majority party in the House of Commons must be named prime minister. Since this majority is elected by the nation, the prime minister may choose the ministers and is authorized to govern the nation. Even though the House of Lords has many important functions, it must defer to the Commons. In short, cabinets should be responsible to a democratically elected House and their mandate to govern should be dependent on their ability to command a majority there.

Bagehot did not like the idea of universal suffrage and feared a "dictatorial or revolutionary sort of government" in the Napoleonic style. A presidential government may be more efficient, but the entire political and economic system of a country could not, according to Bagehot, be consigned to a single person. Appropriately, at the British system's core was a free government based on persuasion, and sovereignty was invested in the House of Commons; the fate of that chamber determined the fate of the country.

If British liberalism managed to adapt to new social realities after 1848, it did so thanks to a return to its utilitarian roots in Bentham's thought. French liberals reevaluated Constant, but they proved unable to present a coherent liberal doctrine in opposition to Louis Napoleon's regime, which had transformed itself into the Second Empire (1852–1870). On dominant themes such as the vote, decentralization, public education, and Italian independence, a liberal such as L. A. Prevost-Paradol wavered. French liberals discussed "necessary liberties," but they dared not elaborate a clear economic and social program for fear of being identified with radical democrats. As a result, before 1870 they timidly opposed the growth of institutional power at the expense of the individual, they failed to consider the problem of society in all its ramifications, and they did not accept the growing demands of the lower classes.

Italy, which had been unified under the aegis of liberals, implemented the policies that the disciples of Camillo Benso, Count of Cavour, believed had been the master's (Cavour died at age fifty-one in 1861). In control of the government until 1876, the party that professed to follow his ideas, the Right, extended Cavour's free-trade policies to the entire peninsula; imbued church-state relations with a liberal coloration by diminishing the church's power but guaranteeing its liberty; and protected individual rights. As in France, however, Italian liberals distinguished themselves from radical democrats, represented in Italy by Mazzini's followers.

6

LIBERAL DEMOCRACY

In France, after the fall of the Second Empire, the establishment of the Third Republic, and the Paris Commune (1870–1871), liberal receptivity toward radical democratic ideals increased. French liberals discussed the desirability of basing governments on a majority consensus, meeting the needs of lower-class citizens, guaranteeing freedom of association and expression, and instituting a graduated income tax. The major reason for this change was that liberals hoped to avoid a repetition of the Commune, a bloody experiment in which the lower classes had attempted a radical social revolution. They began to favor governments supportive of reform, of social legislation favorable to workers, and of a fiscal program that would be fair to all classes.

Charles Renouvier was a republican writer famous for an 1848 pamphlet advocating as much equality as possible without depriving citizens of their rights (the *Manuel républicain de l'homme et du citoyen* [Republican Handbook of Man and the Citizen]). He had dropped out of politics during Napoleon III's reign but became prominent once again in 1872 as editor of a political journal, *La critique philosophique, politique, scientifique, littéraire* [Philosophical, Political, Scientific, and Literary Criticism]. Although he believed in a philosophy of revolution, he condemned violence because insurrections produce dictatorships that prolong themselves indefinitely in the name of an ideal. According to Renouvier, democratic radicals must harmonize the legislation of the Third Republic with the principles of 1789. Renouvier became the theoretician of a "democratic state"—a political system open to lower-class aspirations and new scientific tendencies. This system would be brought about by the alliance of the middle class with the proletariat to combat both dictatorship and clericalism. Renouvier inspired a new radical group that organized itself in the French Parliament after 1876. The French democratic radicals resembled British liberal democrats. Among the adherents of the

French radical group was the old socialist Louis Blanc, whose electoral program included demands such as obligatory and free primary education, local self-government, a graduated income tax, and freedom of the press and of association.

In Italy as well, prominent members of the "Right" (a liberal party) advocated policies that would extend the suffrage, widen the social base of the ruling class, pay attention to social problems, and encourage the lower classes to achieve better living conditions through their labor and savings. Not surprisingly, however, the most important liberal democratic elaboration came from British thinkers. After the Reform Act of 1832, the Reform Act of 1867–1868 had expanded the suffrage among city dwellers. Discussion about extending the vote in rural areas continued, and in 1884 a new reform widened the suffrage there. Naturally enough, liberal political leaders had to increase their initiatives, and they soon realized that state intervention in social affairs could not be avoided. They accepted state action in eradicating infectious disease, delivering social services to the poor, and providing public instruction; even the passing of legislation protecting workers on the job was not seen as creating obstacles to private initiative or threatening individual liberty. Thanks to Mill, liberal theory had accepted state action in favor of progress and to encourage citizens to participate in public life. By the 1870s Thomas Hill Green elaborated liberal democracy into a comprehensive theoretical construction.

LIBERAL DEMOCRATS

A professor of moral philosophy at Oxford University, Thomas Hill Green delivered an important series of lectures from 1879 to 1889, posthumously published as the *Principles of Political Obligation* (in *Works*, London, 1886).

Influenced by the German philosophers Kant and especially Hegel, whom he interpreted in a liberal democratic vein, Green stated that institutions should produce a free existence. Green also hoped to harmonize government action with individual needs and to amalgamate ancient and modern thought in a humanistic vision. State action should infuse progress with morality. In order truly to understand Hegel, according to Green, it was necessary to return to the Greek concept of the "polis." Society must be governed by means of laws, institutions, and traditions capable of ensuring economic well-being and of appreciating the work of previous generations; society improves because the number of individuals conscious of their contribution to the general good increases.

The optimism of the honest middle-class citizen who believes in the moral progress of society pervades Green's philosophy. The social consequences of galloping industrialization troubled him little, and he did not fear the impoverishment of the working classes because he counted on state action to come to their rescue. He was confident that through appropriate legislation, the state will combat abuses and attenuate social tension.

In order to discuss this issue, Green examined the role of the general will and natural law in European philosophy from Spinoza to Rousseau. He affirmed that it is not necessary for the sovereign power to be coercive, but only to express the "general will"; it is up to the individual to judge whether a law has been formulated for the common good, because it is citizen consent, not force, that is the basis of a state. The state is not an aggregate of individuals under a ruler but a society in which rights are defined and harmonious.

For Green, while the state possesses certain rights that permit it to deal out punishments, to promote morality, and to defend property, there are also private rights that belong exclusively to the citizens. These are the right to life and liberty. Society must guarantee the citizen the ability to act according to his or her capacity. Moreover, the rights of the citizen also involve the relationship between an individual and other members of society. With the concept of "political obligation," Green aimed to provide a justification for the new tasks of the state in social life and to tie the concept of liberty to the state; it is no accident that the same idea implies obedience to the state as a moral duty.

In examining the political developments of his time, Green counterposed the concept of "commonwealth" as "society" to that of "ruler" as "Caesar," thereby attributing great significance to the idea of consensus. The state's power is not an arbitrary one resting in a single person but one that can be justified only by a constitution. Green had a clear conception of the state and opposed plebiscites of the Napoleonic type, authoritarian government on the model of Otto von Bismarck—the Prussian chancellor who had united Germany and who had remained in power until 1890—and popular rule based on fraternal cooperation as advocated by the French anarchist thinker Pierre-Joseph Proudhon. Green viewed persons within the context of their society, enjoying a common style, traditions, and habits; they must be intelligent citizens who are loyal to the society in which they act, even if they advocate radical changes in social institutions.

For Green and his school, the transformation of social institutions must be held within constitutional limits. Although a constitution is a document originally based on tradition, it can be modified through reason and is flexible enough to deal with the changing necessities of society and to be altered by modifications of a progressive legislature.

Another thinker of the liberal democratic school, John E. Acton, pointed out that during the French Revolution liberty had been the watchword of the middle class, and equality that of the lower class. He warned against exacerbating tensions between these two classes. He admitted, however, that the emphasis on civil liberties had not provided benefits for the masses, because laws had been promulgated primarily in favor of the upper class. Precisely for this reason, it was essential to broaden the scope of liberal principles; this task meant to stop stressing abstract liberty and to talk instead about "democratic freedom." For Acton and other British liberals, liberty in the concrete signified balanced and judicious consideration of a country's problems.

In short, liberals must take care to understand the general effects of their decisions and can ignore the characteristics of American democracy—as interpreted by Tocqueville—only at their peril. Good government is government by the entire population, which defends liberties guaranteed by institutions. In this sense the extension of the suffrage to workers was a recognition that political institutions are part of a wider social construction. Thus society acquired a fundamental role in the operation of government and illustrated the inadequacy of previous liberal theory. Ideas originating in radicalism, philosophical idealism, constitutional law, and economic free trade all came together after 1870 in a new conception of the liberal democratic state, which allowed liberalism to adjust to the changing needs of an industrial society.

THE LIBERAL PARTY

Liberal democracy soon became the official doctrine of the Liberal party in England. Beginning in 1877 with the foundation by Joseph Chamberlain of the National Liberal Federation, the party put itself on a modern organizational course. Until then liberals had voted for candidates with liberal opinions; now, though, the party established a caucus charged with creating a party machinery and a concrete government program in case of an electoral victory. Chamberlain affirmed the necessity of opening up the party administration and leadership to the people at large, not just the wealthy, as a way of welcoming the masses to liberalism. Since the vote had been granted to the urban masses, party leadership could not remain in the hands of the few, so he advocated creating a party parliament to establish guidelines for action and to keep open communication with the voters.

For members of the Liberal party, parliaments remained the seat of political debate. On the national scale, two great parties, one running the government, the other in the opposition, would have the tasks of legislative initiative and criticism. If, at the end of the legislative assembly's life, elections gave a majority to the opposition party, the roles would be reversed. Alternation in parliament and in government was the guiding political principle of liberal democrats. Achieving this goal meant the liberals' recognition of the fundamental role of public opinion, the necessity of improving the living conditions of all citizens, and the complete integration of the lower classes into the country's political life.

LIBERAL SOCIETY

Despite this theory and the existence of liberal governments in Western Europe at the dawn of the twentieth century, the lower classes had clearly not acquired the real liberty conferred by economic well-being. In the name of individual rights, this kind of liberty remained the privilege of a well-off minority. For liberals it was no longer sufficient to admit this problem in principle and to incorporate it into their theory; they had to construct an effective liberal state in which there would exist full juridical and social liberty, and in which each individual could realize his or her full potential and lead a dignified life. But in this principle of respect for private liberty and recognition of "public" liberty that extended benefits to all individuals lurked a certain contradiction. It was this dilemma that liberals sought to resolve by sanctioning public intervention in social relationships.

David G. Ritchie's *The Principles of State Interference* (1891) maintained that the individual and the state are not antithetical, nor are their respective powers in inverse proportion to one another. Liberal theory implied the opposite: in reality the individual exists in his or her relationship with the community and lives as a member of a political body. According to Ritchie, the argument employed against governmental intervention—that government is in the hands of a dominant class or group—loses its force as government becomes more popular.

Moderate liberals feared that if everyone had the right to vote, the majority could repress the cultured minority; but at the same time they recognized that it was no longer possible to prevent citizens from fully participating in political life. Political forces had to find their equilibrium in parliament. In England, the method of having two large parties, which could guide public opinion and smooth over political conflicts, was confirmed, and the focus shifted to the idea of a liberal society that would ensure the civil cohabitation among classes and groups. In this society, it was hoped, universal suffrage would not permit a proletariat bent on expropriating the rich to come to power.

As usual, in England the battle over the concept of a liberal society occurred on pragmatic grounds, over government programs presented in parliament. The conflict may be traced by following the fate of the Home Rule Bill for Ireland from William Gladstone's speech in the House of Commons in 1886 to Winston S. Churchill's 1909 discourse on "Liberalism and the Social Problem." In the parliamentary discussions, liberalism acquired a very wide significance—the right to a job was placed on the same plane as the right to individual liberty and property.

In a famous essay entitled *Liberalism* (1911), L. T. Hobhouse emphasized the importance of liberal society. According to him, the human personality is not formed from the outside by placing restrictions on it but from the inside with the state having the task of creating the best possible conditions for its development. Associations should be free because every person's spiritual development depends not on what is done but on the will with which it is accomplished. The state's task is to ensure freedom of expression, individual liberty, contractual freedom, liberty of association, and the right of assembly. At the same time, each individual must ask himself how a society in which everyone demands the right to disobey laws he deems unjust can survive. Hobhouse believed that extension of the state's power must proceed in step with the ability to resist abuses. Social legislation itself must allow for resistance to the state's arbitrary power.

We see the state actively intervene in favor of the poorer classes, Hobhouse wrote; it provides education for children, protects public health, checks on the purity of food, institutes old-age pensions, and organizes the labor market. The state cannot ignore charity and justice and remain indifferent. In a truly liberal society, according to Hobhouse, the state's job is to create conditions in which all its citizens are able, through their own efforts, to obtain everything necessary to their physical well-being. The right to work and the right to a living wage are every bit as valid as the right to individual freedom and to property—they are prerequisites to good order in society. A society in which honest people of normal capacity are unable to maintain themselves through useful work is evidently a society that is badly organized. Solidarity should prevail in a free society, and the government should represent the general will of a nation; as a legal and moral entity, the state's duty is to ensure that general interests prevail above particular ones.

Hobhouse also reaffirmed the intimate connection between liberty and equality and hoped that the state would have recourse to coercion as infrequently as possible. In fact, there are many forms of collective action that do not involve coercion at all; for example, the state can provide certain services without forcing anyone to take advantage of them. The fundamental point is that the good of the entire community involves each of its members, but we cannot force anyone to do anything for his or her own good. This principle is valid not because we are indifferent to people's well-being but because it is not possible to promote good through force. What then is the answer to the question of whether or not it is possible to create good people by means of the law? Hobhouse responded that it is impossible to force people to be moral because morality is the very act of being free.

While liberal democracy flourished in England, French thinkers also propounded the concept of a liberal society. In a work entitled *L'Etat moderne et ses fonctions* [The Modern State and Its Duties] (1890), Paul Leroy-Beaulieu, like his British counterparts, discussed the thorny relationship of state and society. He argued that society is much more vast and fertile than the state, because the number of groupings that society includes is almost infinite; these are the associations, spontaneous creations that contest the coercive force of the collectivity (the state), which—because members belong to different associations—become interdependent. French liberals struggled to understand the new relationship between the individual and the state within a liberal society. They believed that the state had to foster social development at all levels. If the temporary delegation of authority by the governed characterized the modern state, they reasoned, legal sanction for governmental action clearly resided in parliaments. For French liberals also, the political structure of liberal society could only be parliamentary.

In Germany, a country characterized until the end of World War I by the trappings rather than the reality of a parliamentary system, British liberalism also had influence. Georg Jellinek's works were much read at the time, especially his *System der subjektiven öffentlichen Rechte* [Theory of Subjective Public Rights] (1892). Coming on the heels of Bismarck's dismissal (1890) and the hope for greater dignity for the individual vis-à-vis the state engendered by this event, Jellinek's work asserted that the citizen had certain "public" rights that conferred the ability to act freely, including in public affairs (*"status activae libertatis"*). Furthermore, Jellinek insisted, this area of liberty must be recognized by the state. In a 1910 work entitled *Allgemeine Staatslehre* [General Theory of State], Jellinek elaborated on the effects of these principles so as to present the conciliating function of public law in new terms.

For Jellinek, state sovereignty is exercised over people who are free, even if freedom has no legal sanction. Law regulates relationships among free subjects endowed with rights and between subjects and the state; because the state functions on behalf of the general interest, its rights cannot be seen as irrelevant to the rights of individuals or of society. Furthermore, the same principle means that the state's powers are limited. State authority must not impinge on the individual's "free zone," must be continually justified, and must be strictly regulated by law. Writing in a country with a powerful state apparatus and in which individual rights were less developed than in Britain and France, Jellinek was interested in defining the state's limitations. For this reason, he emphasized that because of the individual's rights, the relationship between state and individual could not be resolved in the state's complete favor. Constitutions codify individual rights with regard to state power, and respect for "individual public rights" must characterize all forms of government. More than the British or French liberals, Jellinek emphasized the law as a necessary limit on government; but for him, as for other liberals, liberty always limits authority.

MODERN LIBERALISM

In order to understand the significance of the "liberal society" concept, it is necessary to study liberals of the early generations. Early liberals posed the problem of liberty primarily in terms of government. They supported the principles of the separation of powers and constitutional balances against monarchies, which were still relatively powerful. When the problem shifted from government to society, from political to social institutions, the issue of liberty took on a different hue. The separation of powers no longer sufficed to guarantee liberty. The answer to assuring liberty in the modern world could be discovered by examining civil society—by emphasizing its complex division into political parties and associations, and by reinforcing the concept of representative institutions.

The insistence on the liberal-society model included a recognition of the bourgeoisie's right to guide an intellectually and economically advanced society. But considering past dissensions among high, middle, and petite bourgeoisie, liberal thinkers implicitly recognized the middle bourgeoisie's hegemony over both the old privileged classes and the emerging ones. It merited this role because of its cultural superiority and its openness to the resolution of social problems. As a political outlook, therefore, liberalism presented a middle-class bourgeois ideology capable of assuring European society a civil evolution that could improve the condition not only of its own class but of all classes.

Rather than to rethink the theoretical terms of the concept of liberty, liberals stressed the utility of living in a society ruled by representative parliamentary government. For the middle class, this system supposedly assured continual development, and for the lower class, an increased standard of living. Culture, now accessible to the poor through education, would smash the barrier separating the cultured from the illiterate, and people of high quality, whatever their social origins, would rise to the fore.

The political institution that would bring liberal society into being remained parliament. Liberals viewed this institution as capable of implementing constitutional guarantees of individual and public liberty. Concerned with parliamentary efficiency, liberal writers proposed reforms to expand the vote, to limit the number of parties, and to check on the behavior of parliamentary deputies. In line with these considerations, liberal thinkers also believed that if a war erupted among the

European powers, military exigencies would likely overwhelm liberal principles. This fear contributed to the pacifist tendencies of many liberals—their preferences for neutrality and mediation of diplomatic issues. Thus opened the wide gulf—characteristic of the years before World War I—that separated pacifistic liberals from nationalists who glorified war.

7

THE CLASS STRUGGLE: SOCIALISM, COMMUNISM, AND SOCIAL DEMOCRACY

Liberalism, the theory that had challenged absolute monarchy, began by justifying the rule of the few, but by the end of the nineteenth century it had developed sufficiently to include large numbers of people in the art of government. Throughout the century and stretching into the twentieth, however, the industrial workers—a class created by the accelerating industrialization of Western society—challenged liberalism and liberal democracy for supremacy.

The term "labor" assumed doctrinal importance during the early part of the century. With the expansion of industry came increasing conflict between employers and workers, and labor took on a social in addition to an economic dimension. Swiss author Simonde de Sismondi stated in his 1819 *Nouveaux principes d'économie politique* [New Principles of Political Economy] that mechanical labor had replaced manual and individual labor, thus profoundly altering the relationship between wages and profit to the detriment of workers. For many thinkers, workers had to remove themselves from the mechanics of the free market so dear to liberals, because it gave employers complete power to make decisions about wages and the methods of production. In this case, a new social organization became necessary.

After 1830, workers' demands for improvement of their lot began to find justification on the doctrinal plane: They had to associate in order to fight for their rights, for increased wages, for a reduction of working hours, and above all, to defend their condition. Labor and association were the main themes developed by the early working-class movements, the British Chartists and French Socialists, in those countries in which industrialization had proceeded the furthest.

BEGINNINGS:
FROM ASSOCIATIONISM TO SOCIALISM

The British associationist movement known as Chartism was the first organic attempt by workers to demand better economic treatment and active participation in political life through the vote. Chartism had its origins in the trade unions that workers struggled to create in order to fight the long hours, low salaries, and misery that afflicted them during the early industrial revolution.

In 1836 a group of working class leaders founded the London Working Men's Association, which quickly gained support during the following year owing to an economic depression. In 1838, encouraged by Francis Place, a radical member of Parliament, association leader William Lovett drafted a list of demands that became known as the People's Charter. The Charter made six important requests: universal suffrage, equal electoral districts, abolition of property requirements to qualify for Parliament, salaries for members of Parliament, the secret ballot, and annual parliaments. Although these points were hardly original, their significance lay in their political sponsorship by a workers' organization.

The Birmingham Political Union, a group that had distinguished itself in the battle for political reform in 1832, proposed that the Charter be presented in Parliament as a national petition designed to influence public opinion. This public opinion, in turn, could also be utilized as a revolutionary threat should the government refuse the demands. Confusion between the Charter's two functions remained a persistent source of weakness, because the proponents of parliamentary opposition—led by Lovett—and those of radical coercion represented by Bronterre O'Brien and Feargus O'Connor dueled for control of the movement. In 1839 the division among Chartist leaders, tactical errors, and a botched hint at mass agitation nullified the potential force that a million signatures might have had on Parliament: In July Parliament refused to discuss the petition by an overwhelming vote of 237 to 44. This setback provoked militant leaders to set a date for a general strike, but disillusionment among the rank and file and government reaction defeated the proposal. Despite an attempt by O'Connor to revive the movement through a new People's Charter that garnered over 3 million signatures, Parliament again crushed the petition by a devastating margin in May 1842.

Chartist leaders continued their protracted battles, and the movement floundered into 1848, when, for all intents and purposes, it ended. Besides the reasons already cited, the first mass workers' movement had been done in by the failure of British radicals to understand that solutions to the problems raised by the industrial revolution had to be found within the core of an increasingly mechanized society—the factory—and that their demands had to go beyond a generic reform program and criticism of privilege.

Movement in this direction came in France from within the republican movement, influenced by the ideology of democracy that arose during the "July Days" of 1830, which brought Louis Philippe to power and galvanized opposition to his government. Organized around the newspaper *La Tribune*, republican leaders hoped to attract the lower and middle classes, artisans and workers, into their orbit. Republican thinkers believed in "the people" as the source of all authority, and fought privilege of all kind in the name of popular sovereignty. They advocated the association of all popular forces, especially workers. Because the French penal code of the period prohibited political discussions at public meetings without government permission, republicans pressed for the right to organize and to meet freely in the hope of gradually changing the makeup of society. Ignorance and weakness, they believed, caused all society's ills; freedom of expression uncovered abuses, and freedom of association corrected them.

Two crucial periods may be distinguished in the evolution of this movement. In the first (1831–1832), a generically popular organization prevailed, the *Société des amis du peuple* [Society of the Friends of the People]; the second period (1833–1834) witnessed the prevalence of the more egalitarian association *Société des droits de l'homme* [Society of the Rights of Man]. This association represented a change in political orientation from an emphasis on republicanism to a concern with social issues. On January 1, 1833, *La Tribune* published an issue aimed at workers and affirmed that republicans and proletarians had the same aim—to ensure that the wealth produced by society be shared by the greatest number. Concerned by growing agitation among workers, the government cracked down on workers' organizations that had republican tendencies. The result was an insurrection in April 1834, put down with military force and resulting in the dissolution of republican organizations and the arrest of republican leaders. Since legal opposition was rendered impossible, republicans established secret societies with egalitarian and socialist programs infused with an aversion to social inequities. Between 1835 and 1840 the French republican movement underwent a theoretical radicalization in a socialist direction.

Two of the major leaders in this development, Armand Barbès and Auguste Blanqui, demanded a radical social revolution favoring the workers, who possessed nothing. They blamed inequality on property, which they deemed responsible for causing social differences and impeding the revolutionary ideals of liberty, equality, and fraternity. In support of their ideas, they founded the secret "Society of the Seasons," which touched off a failed insurrection in Paris in May 1839.

In June 1840 Pierre Joseph Proudhon (discussed in Chapter 8) published his famous pamphlet, *What Is Property?* He answered his question with the famous line, "Property is theft." He meant that property belonged to everyone, but that a bourgeois minority had taken it from the majority and had used it as a tool to dominate political life, just as earlier the aristocracy had consolidated its power by eliminating commoners from holding public office and from performing public service. Though the originality of Proudhon's thesis was immediately questioned, the importance of his work lay in his justification of revolution and his emphasis on the eradication of privilege, equal rights for everyone, and the rule of law—all on behalf of the lowest and poorest classes. In fact, for Proudhon, abuses characterized his age. The worker did not "own" his value and could not dispose of it freely; nor would even a manyfold increase in production bring any relief, because society's structure ensured that any such increase would immediately be appropriated by property holders.

Thus, after 1835 socialism in France emerged as the economic and political alternative to capitalism. Authors from this period may be considered the precursors of several schools of socialist thought, from syndicalism to collectivism to Christian democracy; all refused to accept the existing Orleanist economic structure and highlighted the miserable state of the working classes. Their criticism frequently assumed a literary and romantic tone and they were viewed as "utopian" or "romantic" socialists, as they passionately promoted association among workers in order to achieve their demands for higher salaries and improved working conditions—and production without capitalistic profit. Karl Marx provided an organic theory of the function, aims, and strategy of the class struggle.

THE CLASS STRUGGLE COMES OF AGE: YOUNG MARX

Born in Trier, Germany, Karl Marx (1818–1883) was early influenced by Hegel's ideas. In 1843 he emigrated to Paris, where he met Friedrich Engels and made contact with French and other European revolutionary exponents. With Arnold Ruge, he edited the *Deutsch-Französische Jahrbücher* [German-French Annals], in which he expressed his communist beliefs. Expelled from France, he emigrated to Brussels, where, between 1845 and 1846, he split from the radicals Bruno Bauer and Max Stirner, founded the society of the "German Democratic Communists," and prepared a work containing his exposition of historical materialism,

The German Ideology. In January 1848 he and Engels wrote *The Manifesto of the Communist Party,* published in London. In 1849 he moved with his family to London, where he remained until his death. He devoted himself to studying political economy and the relationship between labor, capital, and value, which found expression in *The Critique of Political Economy* (1859). In 1864 he became secretary of the International Workingmen's Association. The first volume of his magisterial *Capital* appeared in 1867, and the second and third volumes were published posthumously by Engels in 1885 and 1894.

Marx challenged the prevailing orthodoxy among French revolutionaries as soon as he arrived in Paris. The reference points for those revolutionaries remained the decade 1789–1799 and the radicals who dominated those years, Robespierre and Babeuf. In his article "On the Jewish Question," appearing in the *Deutsch-Französische Jahrbücher* (1844), Marx argued that although the French Revolution had destroyed feudalism, it had substituted bourgeois capitalist society in its place. As a purely political event, the French Revolution had not liberated humanity from the constraints of property and had not given political power to the proletariat. In another article in the same journal, "Contribution to the Critique of Hegel's *Philosophy of Right,*" Marx identified the proletariat as the only class capable of modifying the social order and of achieving social revolution. As the class that seeks to emancipate itself and become the champion of universal rights, the proletariat stakes its claim to general supremacy.

On the changes in Marx's thought between 1844 and 1846, *The Economic and Philosophic Manuscripts of 1844* (written in 1844 but not published until 1937) have an important place. The basic idea in these writings is again the concept of class, which Marx used to criticize a number of important thinkers, including Hegel, Adam Smith, David Ricardo, Rousseau, and Proudhon. According to Marx, the proletariat was born when the bourgeoisie's utilitarian spirit fired up the industrial revolution, which resulted in the replacement of the medieval corporations by the division of labor in the factories. Marx argued that Hegel's dialectic of thesis and antithesis could be employed to describe the modern relationship between the two social classes: the contrast between rich and poor and between exploiting and exploited classes. He viewed all history as the history of class struggles. Because of the new industrial organization of society, in the nineteenth century the bourgeoisie oppressed the proletariat, but the proletarians would become the major actors on the economic, political, and social scene.

As it appears in *The German Ideology,* the idea of "class" in Marx's thought is linked to a general theory of history. In the first chapter Marx criticized the philosophy of Ludwig Feuerbach and stated that there is a stage in which, in the evolution of production, one class, consisting of a majority of the population, carries practically the entire weight of society. This class constitutes the ruled class and gradually becomes conscious that it is necessary to revolt in order to put society on a new basis. Standing in antithesis to this class is the ruling class, a spiritual and material entity that controls the means both of physical and intellectual production; ideas are thus also expressions of the dominant relationship in society. Certainly contrasts within the ruling class may exist among intellectuals and politicians, but these disputes evaporate when the class as a whole is in danger. Although the ideas of the dominating class are presented as existing independently of the material conditions of production, they are not. For example, the aristocracy favored conceptions of honor and loyalty, which were important when the aristocracy dominated society, but when the bourgeoisie prevailed, so did its ideas of liberty and equality.

Marx believed that the separation between city and countryside determined the first great division of people into classes, but the industrial revolution destroyed the artisan class and created the proletariat. In present society, he said, proletarians have no control over production and must modify the existing social structure.

According to Marx, in the new society individuals will acquire liberty within their community and workers will become once again associated and "socialized." Only with the emancipation of the proletariat through a social revolution will it be possible to achieve fraternity. In arguing against Proudhon, Marx made the statement that the antagonism between proletarians and capitalists is a class struggle and will end in a social and political revolution.

The term "class" had come into wide circulation in Europe after 1830 in France, Britain, and Germany; its significance in Marx's thought is that he employed it as the premise for his philosophy, as the key in his analysis of capitalistic society's energetic force, and, above all, as the dynamic element in the resolution of current political and social problems.

For Marx, the class struggle between proletariat and bourgeoisie was the crucial lever causing change in modern society. Owners of capital and large landowners constituted the bourgeoisie, founded on the capitalistic mode of production. The essential preconditions for the existence and domination of the bourgeoisie were the accumulation of wealth in private hands and the formation and increase of capital. The modern state was nothing more than an association that administered the business affairs of the bourgeois class. Of all the opponents of this class, only the proletariat constituted a truly revolutionary entity. The proletariat must at the same time organize itself as a class movement and develop a class consciousness in order to fulfill its mission.

Marx believed that the proletariat as a political and social class had not been contemplated by the forms of government instituted during the French revolutionary period. The body that had been so praised by French radicals and democrats, the Convention (1792–1795), could not serve as a model for future revolutions because it had proposed equality among citizens in only an abstract manner. Other national governments that had been cited by various political thinkers as functioning political models were conditioned by bourgeois economic considerations, given their status as political expressions of the current mode of production, and were thus uninterested in working-class issues. Marx criticized the method of proposing existing governmental forms as political "models" because they were only systems created by bourgeois groups to maintain their power. These groups well knew that models could not be transferred from country to country because economic conditions varied. In fact, Marx criticized the institutions of all countries, but devoted himself to studying England, where the industrial transformation had advanced furthest and where the division between workers and employers was greatest.

Marx had little consideration for thinkers such as Fourier and Owen who had proposed theoretical schemes to improve conditions for the working class and who sought to establish a peaceful harmony, based on justice, between the classes. Labeling these socialists "utopians," Marx criticized them for failing to confront the issue of political power for the proletariat. Workers must create a new communist society, Marx firmly believed. In Marx's opinion, neither the Chartist movement in Britain nor the various socialist societies qualified as such a party.

Marx joined the concepts of "class" and "party" in order to revolutionize the existing social and political structure: The proletariat had to participate in the political struggle through its own party and, conscious of its own strength, battle the bourgeoisie for power and install communism. As for the problem of nationality, it was subsumed in an international vision of the working class.

The formative phase of Marx's thought is condensed, elaborated, and clarified in the *Manifesto of the Communist Party,* one of the most important texts in the history of European political thought, to which Marx remained faithful throughout his life. Commissioned by the Communist League in London to draft that organization's theoretical and practical program, Marx (and Engels) produced a German version that went to press shortly before the French Revolution of February 24, 1848, followed by a French translation in June and an English translation in November 1850.

According to the *Manifesto,* the bourgeoisie has had a revolutionary role in history, but by transforming small artisan enterprises into the factory of industrial capitalism, the bourgeoisie concentrated therein masses of wage-earning, exploited workers. Because of the precarious and uncertain nature of modern life and employment, the oppressed and impoverished workers begin to unite in order to defend their wages. The bourgeoisie responds by breaking their organizations, but of all the opponents of the bourgeoisie, the proletariat remains the only truly revolutionary class. Crushed by the bourgeoisie, the propertyless proletariat cannot rise and liberate itself without destroying the entire superstructure of official bourgeois society. Thus the necessity of a revolution and the violent overthrow of the bourgeoisie.

The *Manifesto*'s second section, in part, answering Mazzini, concerns Communist relationships with other parties. What distinguishes Communists from other proletarian organizations is that they defend the common interests of the entire proletariat, regardless of national issues, against the bourgeoisie and "always and everywhere represent the interests of the movement as a whole." These features make the Communists "the most advanced and resolute section of the working class parties of every country," while, on the theoretical side, they have "the advantage of clearly understanding the line of march, the conditions, and the ultimate general results of the proletarian movement." Three points guide the proletariat's political action: organization of the proletariat as a class; destruction of bourgeois supremacy; and proletarian conquest of political power. This program coincides with the evolution of property, according to Marx. The French Revolution destroyed feudal property in favor of bourgeois property; now it is necessary to abolish not property in general but private bourgeois property. This kind of property, having been transformed into capital and thus the antagonist of wage labor, must be changed into common property belonging to all members of society. In this manner, property, having become social property, sheds its characteristic as class property. At the same time, labor must be a means of improving life; in a communist society, labor would be incapable of being transformed into capital, money, or landed property and therefore can never become bourgeois property.

In order to achieve these changes, the proletariat must elevate itself into the ruling class in order to centralize the means of production in the hands of the state, that is, in the hands of the proletariat organized as the dominant class. The means may vary from country to country, but the aim is to end political antagonism and the role of government as an instrument of oppression against the working class. According to Marx, only in this manner will it be possible to stimulate a new kind of associationism in which the free development of each person will be "the condition of the free development of all."

In the third part of the *Manifesto*, Marx criticizes existing socialist literature as confused. In the fourth, he discusses the relationship of the

Communists with other existing opposition parties and pledges that "Communists everywhere [will] support every revolutionary movement against the existing social and political order of things." He concludes with the stirring statement, "Working men of all countries, unite!"

The *Manifesto* is a political document that put its stamp on an era. Marx's conclusion is clear: Communism is the only true socialism because communism fights for the working class, organizes itself as a political party to battle capitalism, aims to wrest political power from the bourgeoisie, and supports all workers' parties regardless of nationality. In asking all workers to unite, Communists "openly declare that their ends can be attained only by the forcible overthrow of all existing social conditions." The *Manifesto* reflects the predicament of European exiles who were victims of reaction and repression and who anxiously awaited the imminent outbreak of a revolution that would have overthrown existing governments and radically transformed society. Much more than a "catechism" for the Communist League, the *Manifesto* helped to create a class movement by summarizing the revolutionary program of international communism. In doing so, Marx's work proved a portent for the future.

"STATE SOCIALISM": RODBERTUS AND LASSALLE

In his *Manifesto* Marx drew a distinction between socialism and communism, which was not primarily preoccupied with national political issues. A glance at the political rhetoric of the 1848–1870 period reveals that the term "socialist" was applied to people who demanded "social reforms" in order to "socialize" property, who wanted new national and local institutions, who hoped to "change" society; they championed working-class aspirations and denounced "bourgeois" governments who defended the interests of the rich. Their language generally counterposed polemical terms almost as mathematical binomials—"workers-owners," "wage earners–capitalists," "labor-capital," "proletarian-proprietor," "revolution-reaction," "popular classes–bourgeoisie," "equality-privilege."

The economic struggle between capital and labor, profit and wages, originated in the different social concerns of bourgeoisie and workers, but these contrasts were also presented as a struggle between existing capitalist-type governments and possible future governments favoring the proletariat. In order to impose these social-proletarian governments, it was necessary to mobilize the popular forces of society to protect workers against the abuses of the dominating classes. After 1848, the idea of state intervention to protect the interests of the collectivity of a nation became widespread, especially in Germany. The rapid development of German industry, the flow of peasants from the countryside into big cities, the lowering of salaries—all conspired to intensify the requests of workers for state intervention to improve their lot.

German philosophical culture, heavily influenced by Fichte and Hegel, favored this increasing appeal to the state to improve the well-being of civil society. German intellectuals supported the demand for state intervention in economic life to regulate not only production but also the relationship between owners and workers. According to their view, the state should be granted ample powers to act in the interests of society. In order to protect workers from exploitation, in other words, the state had the right to restrain the industrialists.

Karl J. Rodbertus (1805–1875) was the spokesman of such a "state socialism." In his "social letters" (*Sociale Briefe*), written in 1850 and 1851, Rodbertus stated that if labor is the real source of value, then each worker must receive the equivalent of his labor so as to enable him to provide for his own sustenance. Salaries should be calculated according to the difficulty of the work and the time needed for production of an item. In addition, legislation should guarantee workers employment and adjust wages to the cost of living. The process of implementing these principles would necessarily cause a crisis of capitalism and result in the transferring of ownership of the means of production from private to collective hands. The state could guide this process, if it aimed at a socialist society. By improving the lot of workers and prohibiting capitalist exploitation, the state could produce changes in the structure of society and avoid the damage caused by revolutions.

Rodbertus owed much to Hegel's philosophy and to List's economic thought. He was convinced that "state socialism" would resolve many problems of the working class. Rodbertus even professed to accept the monarchy, if this form of government backed the people's cause, and he ended by supporting Bismarck's policies because of their seeming sensibility to social problems.

To block bourgeois parties from taking control of the labor world, socialist leaders proposed founding workers' parties capable of defending their members' interests. With this concept in mind, on March 23, 1863, the first German workers' party, the Allgemeiner Deutscher Arbeiterverein (ADAV), came into existence under the leadership of Ferdinand Lassalle (1825–1864). Lassalle and the other founders believed that only a workers' political party could develop a consciousness among workers of the rights they possessed and allow them to evolve into a political force. Lassalle himself had studied at Berlin and had spent time in Paris, where he mixed with revolutionary elements. He participated in the German revolution of 1848 and spent a year in jail as a result. Convinced that Hegelian philosophy justified social change, he began to organize the working class. Tried for his activities, he soon became the principal figure in German socialism.

He subsequently incurred Marx's ire because he favored a national organization of German workers—a contradiction of Marx's internationalism. In 1861 he published a two-volume work, *System der erworbenen Rechte* [Theory of Acquired Rights], which he followed with other important writings appearing in 1863 and 1864.

In his works Lassalle incited workers to participate in politics and to constitute their own autonomous political force. He argued that even progressive liberals could not defend worker rights because no commonality of interests existed between capital and labor. Moreover, the initiatives of private groups and the occasional sympathy of bourgeois parties would never suffice to end the poverty of the masses; it was necessary for the proletariat, by its votes, to pressure the state to intervene. For example, Lassalle did not believe in consumers' cooperatives, which, because of their competition, would lower salaries for the workers themselves, but he favored extension of credit to workers so that they could enter the field of production. Accordingly, Lassalle's program rested on two fundamental points. First, workers should fight for universal suffrage, which would allow them to vote and pressure the government to help the masses. Second, state subsidies must stimulate development of producers' cooperatives, which would eventually transform the entire economic system from a capitalist into a cooperative one. Why should the state pursue this course? In Lassalle's opinion, it was in the state's own best interest to do so, because by protecting workers from exploitation and identifying itself with the good of all society, the state would earn the consensus and support of a large part of the masses.

According to some observers, Lassalle's friend Rodbertus influenced him; according to others, Lassalle was influenced more by French socialist Louis Blanc's ideas on producers' cooperatives. In fact, Lassalle made his own contribution. He wished to end liberal democratic domination of the workers and did not hesitate to link up with Bismarck, who needed popular support to achieve national unity. Nor should it be forgotten that national workers' parties of the kind championed by Lassalle were indeed the most popular type of organization chosen by workers in Germany and elsewhere.

In his history of German social democracy, Franz Mehring noted that for Lassalle theory and practice were not two concepts but one and the same, and they translated into thought and action on behalf of a class that in Germany had no influence on the legislative process. Lassalle's statement before the court against the charge that he had stimulated the workers to hate the rich is a spirited defense of the role of the working class. He argued that the state was duty-bound to help improve the lot of the workers and to uphold their rights. He contended that science had been utilized to further bourgeois political and economic privilege. Lassalle hoped instead to bring science to the aid of the working class because he identified it with the interests of humanity in general and believed the working class incapable of developing into a new privileged caste.

Although the corpus of Lassalle's work is not vast, the idea that the German working class must organize itself as a national association, and the conviction that the state must have an important role in stimulating the public good gave the socialist movement a clear orientation, in the opinion of British historian G.D.H. Cole. By supporting the working class the state could break the "iron law of wages" (the idea, associated with economist David Ricardo, that wages, on average, could only rise to sub-sistence level) that ensured the misery of workers; continuing state action could also achieve political and social equality by emancipating the masses from the grip of capital. Unlike Marx, who believed that history pro-gressed in fits and starts, Hegel's philosophy inspired Lassalle to view history as the progressive realization of justice and liberty.

MARX'S *CAPITAL* AND
THE FIRST INTERNATIONAL

Before formulating a specific theory of class government after the *Manifesto of the Communist Party,* Marx thought it essential to overturn the economic theories of the bourgeoisie, which were founded on capital, and develop a proletarian economic doctrine based on labor. A firm believer in the strict interconnection between politics and economics, Marx criti-cized the capitalist political economy that underpinned the political econ-omy of bourgeois governments. Marx conceived his doctrine as an eco-nomic and political program in anticipation of the coming to power of the proletariat.

In analyzing the economic structure of European society, Marx began from a historical premise summarized in the Introduction to *A Critique of Political Economy,* written in 1857 but not published until forty years later. Marx wrote that feudal social forms dissolved only in the eighteenth cen-tury, and a transition to bourgeois society also occurred in which social relationships became instruments in private hands.

In 1859 Marx's *Critique of Political Economy* appeared; this is the work that presented "the economic doctrine of the proletariat." Elaboration of such a philosophy was crucial, Marx believed, because without a theoret-ical analysis of capitalism a revolution was impossible. In this work he provided the nucleus of his economic determinism. He argued that pro-ductive relationships constitute the economic structure of a society—that is, the base upon which the legal and political superstructure is erected and to which social consciousness corresponds. The means of production of the material conditions of life shape the social, political, and economic processes of life. At a certain point, however, the productive forces of society enter into contradiction with existing social relationships, and it is then that an era of social revolutions begins. In sum, with the alteration of society's economic base comes a rapid change in its superstructure, which is the visible legal, economic, and political expression of a society.

Marx's criticism of bourgeois political economy is divided into three sections, written at diverse times: merchandise, money (that is, its circulation), and capital. In the first two, he described the bourgeoisie—defined as the persons who possess merchandise and desire money—and rejected bourgeois economic thought because it begins with production and aspires to riches. In 1867 Marx finally finished the third section, which appeared as the first volume of *Capital*. In this work Marx hoped to present himself as a "scientist" examining economic problems and attempting to understand the ideological function of bourgeois economy.

Capital continues the discourse on political economy and opposes the cycle goods-money-goods to that of money-goods-money. Marx explained that the simple circulation of goods begins with sales and ends with purchases; the circulation of currency as capital begins with purchase and ends with sale. In the first case, money is ultimately transformed into a good that serves as "use-value." In the second, the buyer spends money in order to cash in money as a seller, the motive being the exchange value itself; the result is the circulation of money as capital with an increase in value—surplus value. The circulation of money as capital is an end in itself, since the one who possesses it (the capitalist) seeks only an increase in value: He buys at a low price in order to sell at a higher one. But the capitalist finds on the market merchandise consisting of the mental and physical entirety of a person, which he is able to buy—labor.

The worker works under the capitalist's control, which means that the capitalist owns the worker's time; therefore the worker's product belongs to the capitalist who pays the daily value of a person's labor. Surplus value is the difference between what the product is worth and the wages paid, and belongs to the capitalist; surplus value increases in the most advanced phases of capitalism when the capitalist has to introduce machinery in order to increase production, and the exploitation increases. Marx presents the theory of surplus value as the key to explaining bourgeois society and as the reason for the accumulation of capital in the hands of the few.

According to Marx, accumulation leads to a centralization of capital, allowing industrialists to increase the scope of their activities. But as capital is accumulated in fewer and fewer hands, the workers' situation worsens, whatever their wages. This development determines an accumulation of misery that mirrors the accumulation of capital; the result is polarization—wealth on one side, poverty on the other. Marx described in colorful language the differences in the mode of existence of both poles.

Convinced that capitalist production generated its own negation, Marx argued that a collapse was inevitable. After the crash, capitalism would be replaced by a social economy based on cooperation and on the collective possession of the land and the means of production; expropriation of the few by the many would follow inevitably the expropriation of the many by the few. Marx cited passages in the *Manifesto of the Communist Party* stating that a proletarian victory was inevitable because the proletariat was the only revolutionary class. Even his current work, *Capital*, had a revolutionary function; by application of its principles, it was to sound the death knell of capitalism by shortening the time needed for the proletariat to end the capitalist era and to impose "social property."

The critical literature on the first volume of *Capital* is enormous. According to some observers, such as Joseph Schumpeter, the book is a scientific treatment of the economy, not society. Others, such as Raymond Aron, consider it a work of political economy that is simultaneously a sociology of capitalism and a philosophical history of humanity's conflicts. It is important to note, however, that in *Capital* the economic theory of capitalist evolution and the coming of collectivism is viewed as a political theory, even if a specific form of government is not described. Once in possession of the means of production, the proletariat will impose a classless society and establish a new social community and will no longer need the power of the bourgeois state.

In the realm of practice, Marx worked primarily through the First International, established in London in September 1864. As the most influential member of a subcommittee charged with planning policy and drafting a constitution for the organization, Marx reiterated the principles announced in the *Manifesto*. By fighting Mazzini's influence, he blocked efforts to turn the International into a friendly association of mutual-aid societies. Marx believed in an international workers' party organization, not in a more accommodating organization on the model of Lassalle's national workers' party. He insisted that the constitution refer to an organization capable of liberating the working class and of establishing a common direction for workers. For Marx it was essential that national workers' parties could take unified action on issues of general interest proposed by the central committee. Even if he favored a highly centralized party organization, from a tactical viewpoint Marx carefully avoided alienating other working-class theoreticians such as Proudhon. Marx did not reply to an attack that Proudhon made on authoritarian communism, for example, convinced as he was that communism followed scientific laws of evolution and that revolutions did not occur spontaneously but must be planned. On these points, Engels was very influential, but it is important to distinguish between the two men. Engels, the son of an industrialist, was influenced by the factory model. In a great socialized "factory," the autonomy of subordinates cannot be allowed, because each unit follows a production plan; a noncapitalist planned society will extend its discipline to all economic and social sectors. Capitalists and bourgeois politicians will no longer manage the "factory," but worker representatives keeping in mind the collectivity's interests will.

Despite the tactical concessions that Marx made in the International's constitution, the differences with representatives of other workers' viewpoints remained profound. At the congresses of Brussels (1868) and Basel (1869), it became clear that the real issue was between mutualism (mutual-aid societies) and communism. Mutualism meant local associations and decentralization; communism spelled the centralization of power in the hands of a proletarian government.

In short, within the European workers' movement, Marx distinguished among dialectical communism, the state socialism of Lassalle, and Proudhon's mutualistic socialism. According to Marx, communism must avoid social reformism, because only communism represented the revolutionary will of the proletariat for the conquest of power and a classless society.

SOCIAL DEMOCRACY

Although the Marxist outlook rapidly made converts, divisions soon appeared that pitted theoreticians against practitioners of the class struggle; in the beginning, the disputes involved communists versus Lassalle and his followers, but they soon took on more ideological substance, which threatened to alter Marxism itself.

In August 1869, in Eisenach, Wilhelm Liebknecht and August Bebel founded a German workers' party (Sozialdemokratische Arbeiterpartei, SDAP). When the defeat of the French Commune in 1871 revealed the limit of violent revolutionary political action, the talks began about fusing the SDAP with Lassalle's ADAV. At the same time, the term "social democracy" came into vogue in several European countries besides Germany, where in 1864 the newspaper *Der Sozialdemokrat*, edited by J. B. Schweitzer, had appeared.

As previously discussed, Lassalle's followers believed in supporting workers' associations and in asking the state to pass social legislation. The Eisenachers concentrated instead on working-class unity and criticized the Lassallians for their conscious or de facto dependence on the Prussian government. In the 1874 elections, however, the two groups supported each other on the second ballot, initiating the process of unification. After police repression had brought the organizations closer, on December 15, 1874, parliamentary representatives of both groups agreed on the class struggle as the central focus of unification, which finally came about in May 1875 on the basis of the Gotha Program. After 1890 this unified party became known as the German Social Democratic Party (Sozialdemokratische Partei Deutschlands, SPD).

The Gotha Program, which was the fruit of compromise and the object of a famous critique by Marx, incorporated all the principles insisted upon by the followers of Lassalle. The document stated that the working class understands that the common aim of all workers in civilized countries is the international brotherhood of peoples, but that it struggles for its own emancipation within the context of the national state. Given this situation, according to the program, the German workers' party aims to achieve a free state, a socialist society, the end of the wage system and the exploitation it generates, and the cessation of all social and political inequality by all legal means. These demands could be accomplished through producers' cooperatives aided by the state and under the democratic control of working people. These cooperatives should be established in such numbers that they will lead to the socialist organization of all industrial and agricultural production. The program also demanded a series of general reforms designed to put the state on a more solid moral and spiritual footing; these included compulsory, free, and equal education, a "normal" working day, limits on working hours and conditions of women and children, and state surveillance of working conditions in industry, as well as in artisan and domestic endeavors. Appealing to the concept of "scientific socialism," the new organization formulated an original political project: Civil society meant a workers' society governed according to democratic principles. If the state became the workers' state (*Volksstaat*), all honest people must rally to it. This free state of the people must support not only democratic reforms but a new social structure, better conditions for workers, and true economic justice.

Between 1875 and 1890, further differentiation occurred within the German working-class movement as a result of divisions with anarchists and of a consensus against them on the part of Lassallian and Eisenacher social democrats. Both socialist groups distinguished themselves from the anarchists, who demanded the end of state authority and denounced "legalitarian socialism." Anarchists charged that the socialists wrongly relied on a peaceful and gradual conquest of political power and wrongly believed that increased wages and decreased hours really made a difference in workers' lives. Socialists emphasized worker organization and stressed that they had no faith in spontaneous revolutions, passionate appeals to the masses, or individualism. In addition, Bismarck's antisocialist legislation of October 1878 marked a turning point for German workers. As illustrated in socialist writings of the time in the newspapers *Volksstaat* and *Sozialdemokrat*, the party organ after 1881, the crisis caused by the laws was defused by faith in a future people's state that would assume a socialist configuration under worker direction. August Bebel, a leading exponent, explained that despite its internationalism, the party defended the German fatherland.

Thus, until the Erfurt Program of 1891, socialists conceived of the socialist state in terms of a "social democracy," with power in proletarian hands, although that term would soon assume a different connotation. Linked to German industrial development and the formation of an urban working class, this idea reached full fruition when it seemed that German economic expansion could not survive foreign competition without state support. Nor was there any reason to abandon this conception, given the party's widening support during these years—from 300,000 votes in 1881 to over 500,000 in 1884 to 760,000 in 1887. An ideological bond formed between the notion of a socialist workers' party and a socialist state of the people, with the leadership of the socialist workers' party elected by a national congress imagined as the future government of the new state of the people. Rules adopted to govern the party could produce a new kind of representative state, if applied to the country's political life. If the principle of worker representation was respected, a kind of proletarian parliamentarism could be achieved; the parliamentary idea could be adapted to future socialist society—if the working class could implement a radical transformation of the state by ending capitalist control of existing society. Even Engels had to confront the issue of the state after Marx's death in 1883, and as faith in the doctrine of an imminent capitalist collapse receded, he admitted that the state could serve a mediating function.

Hence what has been called a compromise between Lassallians and Eisenachers represented in reality an adjustment to German conditions, necessitating alterations in ideology to confront the challenge of government despotism on the one hand and of anarchism on the other. Party functionaries and union leaders would find a place within a social democratic state structure, which would also resolve the dilemma of ending exploitation of workers while continuing to stimulate the country's economic growth. Even the representative system was acceptable, so long as those representatives were elected by workers.

Europeans studied, discussed, and criticized the principles of social democracy, because this ideology soon appeared as a counterpoint to liberal democracy. In Britain the formation of the Labour party clarified ideas within the workers' movement, because this organization aimed at reducing the power of capital in social affairs. In a social democratic society, the theoreticians of this movement argued, workers must be assured the necessities of life, that is, a just wage, accident insurance, old-age pensions, decent housing, and free education for their children. Widely accepted by British social democratic thinkers, these ideas found expression in a monumental work published by Beatrice and Sidney Webb, *Industrial Democracy* (1897). Mostly gradualist, British socialists viewed the society of the future as "socialized" and anticipated the idea of economic planning. Their proposals included mutual aid to sustain strikers, collective contracts, political mobilization for favorable legislation, a minimum wage, and safe working conditions in factories.

In France socialists struggled to agree on a common program. Jules Guesde's Parti Ouvrier Français [French Workers' Party] (POF) clung to its maximalist positions, holding out for complete victory, while Paul Brousse's Parti Ouvrier Socialiste Révolutionnaire [Socialist Revolutionary Workers' Party] (PSOR) faced accusations of "possibilism" (striving to achieve what is currently possible) because it seemed to accept the notion of reforms. Both organizations talked about social democracy but were imprecise about the kind of society they hoped to achieve. A declaration of principles elaborated for the 1892 elections advocated the conquest of public power and greater local autonomy, implying the possibility of a democratic transformation of the existing political system. Because socialists of this persuasion believed it possible to achieve socialism gradually through reforms voted into law, they were known as "reformists."

In Italy socialists hoped to found a workers' party, but disputes divided a party that excluded nonworkers (even those who were socialist), a "socialist league" consisting primarily of intellectuals, a regional "revolutionary" socialist party, and a Lombard workers' confederation. They disagreed on the significance of democratic socialism and on the proper relationship with bourgeois democrats. Amid myriad difficulties, these elements came together at Genoa in 1892 to found the Italian Socialist party, whose leaders agreed that socialist action to erode the bourgeoisie's power occurred daily in the work of agricultural leagues, cooperatives, and local administrations.

In brief, European socialist movements favored autonomous proletarian activity to end the bourgeois wage system, but the exact nature of a social democratic society remained elusive. "Possibilist" socialists limited themselves to asserting that in such a society people could live according to the principles of equality and justice. This outlook sanctioned a legalitarian method of achieving their aims, and they rejected revolutionary action in favor of a simple reform policy. However, it fell to a German thinker, Eduard Bernstein, to elaborate a clear, integrated political project that respected the postulates of both socialism and democracy. In accomplishing this aim, he set off a crisis within the socialist movement.

EDUARD BERNSTEIN (1850–1932)

Born in Berlin, Bernstein participated as a youth in the activities of the socialist workers' party founded at Gotha in 1875. In 1881 he became editor of the party organ *Sozialdemokrat*, published in Zurich because of German antisocialist laws. Expelled from Switzerland in 1888, he went to London, where he collaborated with Engels and wrote for the party's theoretical review *Neue Zeit* [New Time], founded and edited by Karl Kautsky. As he explained in his memoirs, published in 1920, during his London exile Bernstein studied and reflected on the British trade union movement. His considerations led him to revise Marxist theories, fully expressed in his fundamental book *Evolutionary Socialism* (first published in German in 1899). His views, which had an affinity with reformism, gained many adherents and produced a movement within Marxism known as "revisionism." Within two years Bernstein had returned to Germany and had been elected a deputy to the Reichstag. His ideas caused great debate and consternation, not only in his homeland but worldwide.

From 1896 to 1898 Bernstein published a series of articles on the problems of socialism in *Neue Zeit*, which he elaborated for *Evolutionary Socialism*. Bernstein argued that some fundamental Marxist tenets had to be revised because the collapse of bourgeois society clearly was not imminent and because the "proletarianization" of the middle classes had not occurred. In politics, he wrote, democratic institutions affirmed themselves; workers fought capitalist exploitation and bourgeois privilege ever more successfully. Labor legislation, the increasingly democratic nature of local political administrations, the reaffirmation of unions and cooperative organizations—all signaled a profound social evolution. Social democracy's great task was to prepare the working class for democracy and to accomplish a democratic transformation of the state. Bernstein looked to the British social and political scene but also referred to the introduction to Marx's *Class Wars in France* written by Engels in 1895 a few months before his death. It appeared, according to Engels's interpretation of Marx, that it was possible for socialism to achieve power through the skilled use of universal suffrage. Bernstein used Engels's interpretation to urge a realistic adjustment to a new historical reality that did not lend credence to the concept of an imminent and inevitable "collapse" of the bourgeois system. Bernstein thus interpreted the coming of socialism as an evolutionary necessity, not as an inevitable revolutionary development.

Bernstein understood that the violent language of many socialists frequently served as cover for a reformist orientation, and he expressed the difference between theory and practice that afflicted the socialist movement. In private, socialist leaders admitted that the demands of peasants and the petite bourgeoisie, many of whom voted socialist, could not be ignored. Also, from a cultural viewpoint, the supremacy of morality and law over economics was generally acknowledged, another contradiction of Marx.

In the preface to the French translation of Bernstein's book, which was published with his consent and enjoyed a wide European circulation (*Socialisme théorique et socialdémocratie pratique* [Theoretical Socialism and Practical Social Democracy], Paris, 1900), Bernstein reiterated the importance of ideological forces—that is, the "superstructure"—in society's development. Criticizing what he considered a sterile dogmatism, he asked that the European socialist parties not only conform their words to their actions but also help to construct a modern civil society characterized by the expansion of the middle classes.

According to Bernstein, industrial production is a characteristic of the modern world, but in bourgeois society the profits from that production flow to those who possess capital, not to those who do the actual work. The real "producer" lives as a dependent wage earner and never escapes that condition; for that reason the attainment of socialism is a necessity for the proletariat, which must take the political reins in order to organize labor on the basis of free association. The proletariat, including as it does different social strata and groups, does not constitute a homogeneous mass, but it can find unity if the conquest of power occurs through the moral and political utilization of the right to vote. Bernstein added that the ideal of agricultural workers is to own the land they work. Furthermore, the state cannot appropriate all the means of production and manage them according to its own criteria, but must implement social democracy and consider the aspirations of all workers.

Bernstein took a critical view of producers' cooperatives, the subject of widespread literature in Britain, Germany, and France. According to writers such as Beatrice Webb and Franz Oppenheimer, producers' cooperatives were capable of infusing capitalist society with a new and diverse structure in which individual initiative would have acquired a social function. Bernstein expressed his doubts that cooperatives could gain control of the production and distribution of goods. Social democratic thought could consider the role of industrial and agricultural cooperatives but must also stimulate development of unions, the real institutions capable of breaking the capitalist monopoly and of winning a direct voice for workers in the factory. The union would allow workers to manage industrial production, but this role should not blind them from having a political vision of a society founded on representation.

For Bernstein social democracy had a precise significance: a social order in which no class predominated, that is, no class was to enjoy any kind of privilege with respect to the entire community. Social democratic society meant equal rights for all community members, limiting government by the majority; the more equality became general and became absorbed into people's consciousness, the more democracy became identified with the greatest liberty for all. The absence of privilege characterized democracy, a particular organization of society in which laws assumed a permanent quality but did not prejudice individual liberty.

Since Bernstein believed in the inseparability of social democracy and universal suffrage, Marx's phrase the "dictatorship of the proletariat" meant little. Marx believed that after the revolution the proletariat would take absolute power in order to exterminate its enemies and impose communism; but what sense did this concept have in an era when social democratic representatives operated according to the principles of parliamentary action, proportional representation, and social legislation and opposed dictatorial principles? Bernstein postulated that class dictatorships belonged to a more primitive era. The practical action of social democrats aimed to prepare the conditions to move from the existing social structure to a higher one. In sum, Bernstein believed that the passage from capitalist to socialist society must come about through modern means such as the gradual socialization of production and the progressive increase in worker autonomy.

It has been noted that Bernstein's social democracy sought to conciliate Marx and Proudhon. In reality, he hoped to attain socialism without violence, without the dictatorship of the proletariat, and without a political catastrophe. For Bernstein, socialism without democratic institutions and traditions is not possible. The goal of social democracy is the socialist transformation of property through democratic and economic reforms. Aiming at harmonizing collective production and individualism by means of a just division of goods, social democracy must nevertheless prove its validity on the political plane by transforming the representative system into a system in which the working class governs by giving parliament the task of defending worker interests. To the many socialists who continued to argue for the state's destruction because it was the instrument of class oppression, Bernstein replied that with the appearance of a social democratic society the power structure and therefore the state would be transformed. When workers could elect socialist politicians, democratic policies in favor of the working class could be implemented.

Lassalle had stated that evolution toward an improved order depended on the building of a new democratic state at the service of society; Bernstein foresaw a socialist parliament capable of eliminating political and economic inequality brought about by capitalism and a voting system based on wealth. Universal suffrage, strong unions, and socialist parties would transform society and accomplish a social revolution by making the people understand the power of participating in civil life. The "people's state" (*Volksstaat*), so much discussed by German social democrats, would be implemented as the result of a direct relationship between working-class forces and the parliamentary structure. A parliament supported by the overwhelming majority of the people would destroy the old system of bourgeois privilege and capitalist abuses and would preside over social democratic society.

Bernstein delineated a kind of society that was quite different from the model outlined by republican radicals of the nineteenth century. Social democracy presented a long-term outlook, but one that—with its conciliatory spirit—overcame the dire predictions of crises, wars, and catastrophes as the lot of Western society. Democratic socialism advocated collective prosperity and a more equitable distribution of goods; this was the kind of socialism for all citizens without capital and living from their own labor. At the same time that Bernstein published his articles and book, in France Jean Jaurès wrote in the *Revue de Paris* [Paris Review] (December 1, 1898) that in a democratic society every person must participate in the general administration of government and must have the power to designate representatives. It was the expression of the belief that parliament could be transformed into the representative institution of labor. Jaurès stimulated sociologist Emile Durkheim to devote himself to studying the social question; in a series of lectures held in Paris in 1895 and 1896, Durkheim stated that socialism aimed at a more democratic organization of society and assigned social value to labor. In Italy as well, Filippo Turati, Anna Kuliscioff, and Claudio Treves, leaders of the Italian Socialist party, had been pushing the organization in a social democratic direction since its foundation in 1892. At the national congress of 1900, a majority endorsed an explicit declaration of democratic reforms that aimed at transforming the state by parliamentary means. In that country as in others, however, this policy set off a howl of protest that challenged the social democratic concept of the class struggle best represented by Eduard Bernstein.

The polemic against social democracy, therefore, was fueled by the conviction that in order to destroy the existing capitalist political and economic order, a revolutionary plan elaborated by the working class was necessary. To adherents of this idea, the term "social democracy" itself seemed ambiguous because it implied that democrats wanted a change of government rather than a revolutionary transformation of the economic and social system. Furthermore, social democratic principles imposed a theoretical revision of Marx's thought, but this hypothesis was rejected by the German Social Democratic Party, which in fact reaffirmed Marxism. But this development by no means ended the debate, as the supporters of social democracy attempted to dominate European socialist parties, and "orthodox" Marxists staved off the attacks.

THE BERNSTEIN DEBATE: ANTONIO LABRIOLA (1843–1904)

Born at Cassino, near Naples, Antonio Labriola studied at the University of Naples, a center of Hegelian thought, and worked with the philosopher Bertrando Spaventa. In 1874 the University of Rome named him to the chair of moral philosophy and pedagogy. Originally sympathetic to the Italian moderate liberal party, he soon broke with it and converted to Marxism, after which he corresponded with Engels and other international socialist figures. He contributed articles to the most famous German and French socialist reviews. In a short period, he wrote three brilliant essays on which his reputation as a major Marxist philosopher rests, *In memoria del Manifesto dei comunisti* (1895), *Del materialismo storico* (1896) (both translated into English under the title *Essays on the Materialistic Conception of History*), and *Socialism and Philosophy* (1897). In 1902 he held the chair of theoretical philosophy, but the grave illness that would soon cause his death forced him to give up his scholarly activity in 1903.

First of all, Labriola's aversion to parliamentarism must be emphasized. He considered parliamentarism a method of making socialism palatable to the bourgeoisie. He often said that it had cost him a lot to become a socialist and that he was unwilling to become the tool of opportunistic politicians who favored parliamentary compromises. He broke off with the official socialist movement in Italy and wrote in an 1891 letter to Engels that it was necessary to "accept the flag of anti-parliamentarism." For Labriola, the defense of parliamentarism signified the defense of bourgeois ideology and bourgeois production; bourgeois political structures were unimportant, because only proletarian political organization counted.

Above all, Labriola believed that it was necessary to develop the political consciousness of the proletariat. By adopting this intransigent position, Labriola aligned himself with the critics of intellectual reformist "ambiguity" and of the reformist policies of socialist deputies. Why did reformist socialists wish to create mass parties? To get elected to parliament! Socialism was not the fulfillment of a long parliamentary movement but the beginning of a new historical era signaling a new political order. The mania to be elected at any cost with the votes of nonsocialists was incompatible with the class struggle and with the proletarian movement.

Against equivocal politicians ready to adapt themselves to "varied and multiform circumstances and conditions," and opposed to the muddled thinking of "semisocialists" anxious to adopt "practical measures," Labriola in his *In memoria del Manifesto dei comunisti* [In Memory of the *Communist Manifesto*] decisively denounced social democratic theoreticians for mistakenly believing that the collision between bourgeoisie and proletariat could be postponed ad infinitum. According to social democrats, Labriola wrote, the inevitable battle between the two would never be joined because everything frittered away in the infinite details of government and in the partial clashes of economic competition. "In other words, present society, instead of cracking and dissolving, perpetually patches itself up." And every proletarian movement that is not violently repressed would, like Chartism, peter out and flow into the trade-union movement—the "battle cry of this means of reasoning, the boast of vulgar economists and two-bit sociologists." Labriola cited the "precise and certain" expectations of "critical communism" against the reformists and wrote that social democracy can be taken to mean many things, but never revolution or communism; social democracy and historical materialism should never be confused.

In *Del materialismo storico* [On Historical Materialism], Labriola insisted that the "bourgeois phase" had ended and that historical materialism had revolutionized all the assumptions of politicians, theologians, and jurists by explicitly negating all forms of rationalistic thought. Ideas depend on social conditions, and for that reason the main determinant of history is the underlying economic structure. Since new economic structures produce great revolutions, historical materialism is the "objective theory of social revolution." Labriola wished to demonstrate that liberalism and modern democracy had their origin in the great bourgeois revolution of 1789 and that ideology had served as a weapon and an instrument to impart juridical form to the economic basis of modern society.

THE BERNSTEIN DEBATE:
KARL KAUTSKY (1854–1938)

The public debate over Bernstein's book began in Germany at the 1899 Hanover Congress of the SPD with August Bebel's philippic against social democratic revisionism. In Bebel's opinion, Bernstein negated Marxism's fundamental tenets—historical materialism, dialectics, the labor theory of value, the concept of increasing poverty. True socialists could never renounce the idea of appropriating the means of production held by capitalists, and revisionist theses in effect denied the workers' capacity to carry out their historic mission. Bebel viewed Bernstein's statements as an echo of criticisms formulated by socialism's enemies.

In the program adopted at Erfurt in 1891, German workers demanded immediate implementation of direct universal suffrage, proportional representation, social legislation, and progressive taxation, but clearly these reforms did not alter the bourgeois productive system. Clearly workers could not remain inactive while they awaited the revolution; they demanded social reforms but understood that they did not alter the class struggle's essence or modify the proletariat's revolutionary aims. While the bourgeoisie remained in power there could be at most an attenuation of abuses, but the structure of society would remain capitalist; instead the goal was to transform society from a capitalist enterprise into a socialist collectivity.

Bebel's criticism was only a warning shot across Bernstein's bow. The official defense of the party's Erfurt Program was undertaken by the person who had elaborated the theory embodied in that document, namely, Karl Kautsky. Kautsky's refutation of Bernstein's ideas, *Bernstein und das sozialdemokratishe Programm* [Bernstein and the Social Democratic Program], appeared in 1899.

Born in Prague, Kautsky studied at Vienna and was attracted by Marxism around 1880. The following year, he went to London, where he met Marx and Engels. He moved to Stuttgart, where in January 1883 he founded *Neue Zeit* with Liebknecht and Bebel. His activities as editor of this review established him as a Marxist theoretician, and a series of writings on historical materialism gained him Engels's confidence and an international reputation. A work on the French Revolution, published for the centenary of that event, increased his fame. Invited to make preparations for the 1891 Erfurt congress, he did so with the collaboration of Engels. In 1899 he not only refuted Bernstein but also analyzed the agrarian problem utilizing the third and final volume of Marx's *Capital*, which had appeared posthumously in 1894. He became the most famous European Marxist theoretician, with his works widely translated and commented upon. The confirmed defender of Marxist orthodoxy, Kautsky found his influence declining under the combined attacks of socialist right and left wings in the new century, especially after his criticism of the Bolshevik Revolution in 1918. He retired to Vienna but was forced to move to Prague with the advent of Nazism, and finally to Amsterdam, where he died.

According to Kautsky, the antithesis of the capitalist state was a Marxist socialist republic. Modern governing systems reflected the interests of the ruling class, and a socialist government would install a new socioeconomic order in which the interests of the workers would prevail. Thus the Marxist vision of society was diametrically opposed to Bernstein's moderate views, which ignored two fundamental tenets—historical materialism and the class struggle. Political tensions would unavoidably increase in proportion to the proletariat's expanding power, leading to revolution.

In Kautsky's mind, the polemic against Bernstein could not be dissociated from the position of the peasants. In 1899, in addition to the refutation of Bernstein, Kautsky published *Agrarfrage* [The Agrarian Question], an analysis of the peasants' role in the coming of socialism. In this work, Kautsky maintained that capitalists would take control of agriculture and, as in industry, destroy old forms of production, transform it, and create the need for new forms of organization. In short, the economics of agriculture and industry moved in tandem, and industry determined agricultural development.

Kautsky reiterated these themes in 1902 in *The Social Revolution*, when Bernstein's influence became more widespread. Incapable of impeding capitalistic expansion or the intensification of the class struggle and, consequently, the revolution, the reform issue had taken a new turn. Finance capitalists had decided not to give any more concessions and were inclined toward militarism. With the class struggle's sharpening, there was no other choice for the proletariat—workers and peasants—but to aim at complete power. Kautsky believed that the strike, which had become a major weapon in the workers' arsenal, would increase in importance and would become the proletariat's principal instrument of active participation in political life.

After the revolution a political system based on representation could not be excluded, Kautsky believed, so long as it was a diverse form of parliamentary rule adapted to socialism. In a *Neue Zeit* essay translated into French and published with an introduction by French Socialist leader Jean Jaurès (*Parlementarisme et socialisme* [Parliamentarism and Socialism], 1900), Kautsky disputed the notion that legislation could be passed directly by the people and endorsed representative institutions within a socialist state provided that they came under the control of the workers' party. The rigid discipline of workers' organizations must characterize the marriage of socialism and parliamentarism, which meant that socialist deputies must be simple delegates of the proletariat. As the most famous representative of Marxist orthodoxy, Kautsky demonstrated a sensitive and sometimes acute understanding of new social developments but furnished little original analysis.

ORTHODOXY VERSUS REVISIONISM

Besides Kautsky and Labriola, a host of philosophers and political activists who resented what they considered Bernstein's attack on Marxist fundamentals sought to halt the inroads that social democracy made in the workers' movement.

Perhaps the most acute denunciation of Bernstein came from a young German activist of Polish descent, Rosa Luxemburg. In *Reform or Revolution?* Luxemburg criticized the manner in which Bernstein had posed the problem: Social reform or revolution? According to Luxemburg, reform and revolution are not different methods of historical progress that can be selected at will from the "buffet" of history, like hot and cold sausages; they represent different moments in the evolution of societies and classes. The real issue is the need to evaluate a reform's substance and to judge whether it tends to favor the bourgeoisie's or the proletariat's political "pole." Thus Luxemburg rejected revisionism by drawing a crucial distinction between bourgeois and proletarian social democracy. In bourgeois social democracy, the political pole is private enterprise; proletarian social democracy has as its goal the conquest of power by the workers.

Bernstein believed in the attainment of socialism through the gradual transformation of the bourgeois state and society by means of a social democratic parliamentary majority. But, Luxemburg replied, parliament is far from the expression of the collectivity's interests—it is the assertion of society's capitalist interests. Thus parliament is not an instrument capable of ending capitalist control of society, as Bernstein believed, but a tool for ordering the juridical command of capitalism. Luxemburg concluded that although it is perfectly appropriate for workers to accept reforms and parliament in a bourgeois system, the proletariat's goal remained a revolution that would end all forms of exploitation.

The choice between "reform" and "revolution" posed itself dramatically to the socialists of all Europe after the 1899 publication of Bernstein's *Evolutionary Socialism,* with disputations and controversy reaching a high pitch in all countries. In Austria, the *Wiener Arbeiterzeitung* [Viennese Workers' Newspaper], founded by the socialist leader Victor Adler, followed the argument closely. Adler continued to write for *Neue Zeit* and remained friendly to Bernstein, but he distinguished between political democracy based on civil rights and a social democracy that could be consummated only within a socialist society. Vienna was also the center of controversy between distinct economic and political schools; when Eugen Böhm-Bawerk criticized the third volume of Marx's *Capital* in 1896, the Austrian socialists responded by rejecting all attempts at revision and declaring their loyalty to Marx, principles that they renewed even at the later appearance of works seeking to moderate Marx's revolutionary principles.

The Austrians injected an interesting aspect into the debate. The Viennese school of Marxism understood that advanced national societies exploited backward societies through imperialistic policies; therefore, a correct analysis of capitalism could not neglect an examination of imperialism. The workers of advanced industrial states could profit from imperialist expansion and as a result could be contented by social reforms and parliamentarism, but in so doing so, they stimulated the growth of great capitalist cartels.

Some defenders of Marxist orthodoxy believed that the economic benefits brought about by imperialism were responsible for the lessening of
tensions in democratic Europe, a phenomenon prominently cited by
Bernstein. This meant that the reduced tensions would prove temporary,
as the disappearance of backward areas to exploit would provoke the
crash of capitalism. For that reason, the Marxist theory of capitalism's collapse was valid and remained the basis for the future expropriation of the
bourgeoisie by the workers. In other words, the revolutionary vision of
the orthodox Marxists coincided with the notion of a capitalist downfall,
just as the end of feudal society had determined the rise of capitalism,
and the orthodox version had to be defended at all costs against
Bernstein's attempt to undermine Marxism.

The radical left also defended its revolutionary vision by excoriating
the image of the parliamentarian. According to its view, such personages
were ambitious, power hungry, unconcerned with and cut off from the
needs of their electors, and interested only in their own visibility. Rather
than championing democracy, defenders of parliament were generally
intellectuals concerned with their own privileged position. Radical leftists
used this representation to condemn the social democratic intellectual,
who, they charged, exploited the respect that ordinary people had for culture and science to bolster their own position. The French philosopher
Georges Sorel observed that social democratic intellectuals hoped to
achieve positions of command at the expense of the proletariat.
According to him, social democrats may appear revolutionary but were
"profoundly reactionary" politicians seeking to convince people to vote
them into power; and, like all politicians, they were "by nature mediocre
and reformist."

So, according to many orthodox Marxists, social democratic intellectuals who should have placed themselves and their abilities at the service of
the working class instead sought to "make it" in the world of politics,
despised manual labor, and wished to be supported financially by the
proletariat. In parliament, socialist deputies who thundered against social
injustice but who favored the "transformation" of society through
"reforms" merely masked their opportunism and guilty consciences by
their rhetoric. Socialist literature of this period is filled with attacks on
social democratic intellectuals who allegedly defended workers for the
sole purpose of being elected and enjoying the privileges distributed by
the bourgeois political system.

Perhaps the real difference between "orthodox" Marxists and "reformists" (or "revisionists") was that the former emphasized ideological rigor,
and the latter, struck by the concrete difficulties of workers and peasants,
emphasized immediate, practical results.

8

ANARCHISM

As shown in the previous chapter, the class struggle as conceived by Marx called for revolution, the centralization of all economic and political power in a workers' state, and an overwhelming dose of coercion to achieve socialism. Another school of socialist thought, anarchism, also believed in equality and the common ownership of the means of production as necessary to obtain social justice, but shunned the concentration of authority in governmental hands as a sure prescription for dictatorship. This school advocated immediate destruction of existing states and replacement of current forms of economic organization by cooperative institutions.

Just as Germany was the center of socialism, France was the heart of anarchism. After 1850 mutual-aid societies and a host of similar voluntary associations designed to smooth out the dislocations of economic life flourished in France. Most of these associations felt the influence of Pierre Joseph Proudhon, who considered these institutions capable of changing society by bringing about "the division of property [and] the independence of labor. . . . "

PIERRE JOSEPH PROUDHON (1809–1865)

Proudhon became famous at a young age with the essay *What Is Property? An Inquiry into the Principle of Right and Government* (1840), mentioned in the previous chapter. After 1848 he started effective political activities.

Since the political struggle pitted the rich bourgeoisie against the poor "people," Proudhon posed the difficult question of how to transform a political revolution into a social one. He discussed the issue in his *General Idea of the Revolution in the Nineteenth Century* (1851). He viewed revolution as the expression of society's needs as opposed to the government's desire for centralization. According to Proudhon, society must be based on the principle of equality, which meant suppressing authority; otherwise, the outcome would be dictatorship, the most exaggerated form of government. Since administrative government is authoritarian and organized to benefit the rich bourgeoisie, the antidote is popular government based on the direct participation of workers. This meant noncentralized, communal government.

Proudhon opposed administrative centralization because he saw it as the prime cause of the people's division into classes, and he envisioned a society without a constituted authority. Administration generated the police, and worship of the state created inquisitions. He equated the state and religion, since both were based on authoritarian and hierarchical principles. This equation explained why the Second Empire—created by Louis Napoleon in 1852 after he had destroyed the republic founded in 1848—sought the Church's support; Proudhon wrote in *De la justice dans la Révolution et dans l'Eglise* [On Justice in the Revolution and in the Church] (1858) that the empire's restoration masked mediocrity and brought France dishonor, which only a revolution could wash clean. He cited Rousseau in attempting to elaborate a political theory for the people based on the principles of "Revolution, Philosophy, Justice." Unequal social and economic conditions rendered current governmental forms unstable, but it was the lack of respect for justice that created inequality, rather than any natural or social precept.

Proudhon's writings against the empire made him the reference point of the revolutionary opposition. Many leftists, French as well as other Europeans, responded to his denunciation of administrative centralization and focused on the executive as the repressive agent impeding the participation of the proletarian masses in government. Condemned to three years in prison for his antigovernment views, Proudhon fled in 1858 to Belgium, where he worked on *La guerre et la paix* [War and Peace] (1861). Examining the 1859 war for Italian unification, which pitted Piedmont and France against Austria, he searched for a general reason to explain conflicts. The modern age had greatly stimulated the appetite for conquest, Proudhon wrote, but economics rather than politics caused warfare. Patriotism inspired wars, but the universal cause could be found in the rupture of the economic equilibrium. As far as Italy was concerned, he supported the proponents of federalism in that country against a centralized state. From his Italian example, he extended the federalist ideal as a good governmental principle for all countries, advocating greater powers for local rather than central administrations. In his excursion into this area, *The Principle of Federation*, he not only maintained that federalism as a political form was capable of creating the conditions of order, justice, and liberty that he desired, but he also applied the federalist principle to society. Since society was divided into two classes—one consisting of landowners, capitalists, and industrialists, the other of workers and other wage earners—he proposed an "anarchist" agricultural-industrial federation to oppose the "centralizing" state and to create equality through "decentralization."

In another work Proudhon answered a point frequently raised by the bourgeoisie: The people could make revolutions but did not know how to rule; therefore, the bourgeoisie's authority rested on its capacity to govern. In his posthumously published *De la capacité politique des classes ouvrières* [On the Political Capacities of the Working Class] (1865), Proudhon reasoned that the workers, armed with the knowledge of the division of modern society into two opposing classes, could implement a new kind of democracy. This work's primary concern, however, was that the proletariat avoid the "communist system," that is, a regime based on the dictatorship of the masses only in appearance. In reality in such a system the masses have no other function but to ensure a condition of universal servitude because they are tricked by formulas and concepts filched from the despotic states of ancient times. The characteristics of such thralldom are heavy-handed centralization, the systematic destruction of all individual and group thought considered heretical, a prying police, and universal suffrage organized in such a manner as to lend legitimacy to this anonymous tyranny and to ensure the triumph of mediocrity. In order to avoid such a fate, Proudhon promoted "mutualism"— voluntary cooperation—applied to labor, the economy, and government, and "pluralism," defined as institutional autonomy, free association, political and economic self-determination, and religious independence. Implementation of these tenets would institute his much-cherished "federalism" in the political, economic, social, and religious spheres.

Other writers of the time upheld similar ideals based on decentralization and cooperation. In Belgium Napoleon de Keyser used his 1854 study of natural law to conclude that the communes, or towns, should entrust the land and the means of production to individuals and cooperatives until this form of association became the basis of economic and social organization. In London between 1857 and 1868, the Russian exile Aleksandr Herzen published his *Kolokol* [The Bell]. Herzen believed that the peasant, not the workers, would accomplish a social revolution. Another Russian, Nikolai Cernysewkij, founded the secret revolutionary society Zemlja i volja [Land and Liberty]; he saw in the Russian village assembly (the *mir*) the primitive peasant form of modern socialization.

In French the phrase "commune" for the anarchists recalled the revolutionary events of 1793 and symbolized popular unity against oppressive bourgeois power. In the commune the origins and characteristics of popular government could be discovered; in the commune citizens would be empowered to participate in political and social life; in the commune democracy would be concretely realized. The political terminology of the left had utilized "communal" to endow different expressions with a social revolutionary energy. In France there was discussion about communal autonomy, communal authority, communal movements, communal federations, and communal programs, and many democrats defined themselves as "communalist republicans."

As we have seen, Proudhon had rejected all forms of states—the state was always bourgeois—and had proposed a federation of what were essentially communes. The Russian anarchist Mikhail Bakunin attacked the state much more explicitly as the root cause of inequality.

MIKHAIL BAKUNIN (1814–1876)

Born near Moscow, Bakunin studied Hegel's philosophy in Berlin. An adherent of the Hegelian left, he circulated among radical groups in Switzerland and France preaching libertarian doctrines. Imprisoned in Germany and extradited to Russia, he was sent to Siberia, from which he escaped in 1861. He went to London, where he met many other exiles, including Marx, Engels, Mazzini, and Carlo Cafiero, his major Italian disciple. In 1864 he traveled to Italy and gave life to the anarchist movement there.

In order to demolish the state, Bakunin had a ready plan, which he described in a letter written to Albert Richard in April 1870. If Paris rose successfully, he wrote, it would have the right to proclaim the liquidation of the state in all of its manifestations—political, juridical, financial, administrative; all the state's powers, its services, its functions, its financial solvency, would end. After destroying the means of production, buildings, and capital of all kinds, the Parisian workers would gather in associations and would reorganize the city as an independent unit. Armed and organized at the neighborhood and the street level, workers would form revolutionary district federations, the *Commune fédérative.*" This Paris Commune would signal the other French "communes" and the insurrection would begin. Communal delegates would meet in Paris, the communes would federate among themselves and create a federal revolutionary assembly; this body would organize services and the means of production and exchange in common and write a constitution based on equality—the common foundation of liberty. In order to realize his revolutionary plan, Bakunin sought the support of all who, followers of Proudhon or not, proclaimed themselves federalists in the sense that they postulated the spontaneous organization of all the communes of France. In addition to his federalism, Bakunin also propounded "collectivism," which for him signified the abolition of private property and aimed at a nonauthoritarian form of communism, but his aversion to the state remained the fundamental tenet of his doctrine.

Another famous revolutionary of the period, Auguste Blanqui, also believed in a revolution of the communes and the struggle against the state. As early as 1864, a *"blanquiste"* group convinced of their ability to touch off the revolution had coalesced in Paris. Consisting primarily of young people, it considered Blanqui "the father of the Commune" and was committed to defending revolutionary ideals. From then, the Blanquists participated vigorously in all Parisian demonstrations, agitating in favor of "the revolutionary Commune of the French workers." Blanqui fervently maintained that a small, well-organized minority could touch off a revolution with a bold stroke.

Political events seemed to verify the emphasis of theoreticians on the commune as the center of political and social life. On January 28, 1871, France signed an armistice with Prussia, and national elections that would decide war or peace took place. A majority of conservatives were returned to the new National Assembly; when it convened on February 13 at Bordeaux, it designated a moderate politician, Adolphe Thiers, to lead the government. On March 2, to their general dismay, the Parisians learned that the Assembly had accepted the peace treaty; to prevent outbreaks of protest, the government suspended liberty of the press, but to no avail. Demonstrators took control of public offices and called for an election for a city council. These events stimulated the beginning of the *"mouvement communaliste,"* which adhered to Proudhon's federalist principles, to Bakunin's anarchism, and to Blanqui's ideas of armed revolution. Elections to the city council returned about fifteen moderate republicans, an equal number of Blanquists, and twenty adherents of the International. Described as a "heterogeneous and passionate" assembly, the new "Commune" nonetheless made a series of radical decisions, convinced that it acted as the government of the people and that revolutions would have erupted in other French cities.

In a letter written on April 5, 1871, Bakunin asserted that the Paris revolution had been accomplished by the working class, a theme upon which he later elaborated. He claimed the Paris Commune as an outcome of the federalist and anarchist ideas because it had been a bold negation of the state itself: Paris, capital of political centralization, had negated the state and had fought for the emancipation of the masses. He reaffirmed his principle that a social revolution could not be decreed either by a dictatorship or by a constituent assembly. The penalty would be the reconstitution of the state, of privileges, of inequality.

The Paris Commune also forced Marx to undergo a profound reflection. He concurred that the Commune had expelled the bourgeoisie from

power and had taken important steps characteristic of a class government; these included destruction of the bureaucracy, suppression of the
standing army and its substitution by the people in arms, the end of parliamentarism and the creation of a combined legislative and executive
working group, and the election of public officials and judges. In examining the Parisian events of 1871, Marx had to confront the problem of the
management of political power by the working class, as demonstrated in
an address he made to the International's executive body on May 30,
1871, two days after the Commune's bloody suppression. The text, *The
Civil War in France,* went through three drafts that permit a close study of
his thinking on the subject. Analysis shows that for Marx the Commune
represented a decisive point in his thought; after having studied the history of the modern state from the French Revolution of 1789 to the fall of
the Second Empire, and after having traced the evolution of bourgeois
governmental forms since the eighteenth century, Marx pronounced the
Paris Commune to be the direct antithesis of these forms and a positive
example of the social republic. Essentially, Marx stated, the Commune
was the government of the working class, the political form that would
permit the economic emancipation of workers and peasants. His affirmation of the Commune as an example of the concrete form of government
that would have liberated workers and peasants confirms the important
place that the communal concept enjoyed during this period.

BEYOND ANARCHISM

After Bakunin's death in July 1876, anarchists continued to believe in a
new society born of a revolution that would destroy the oppressive bourgeois state and every other form of organized authoritarianism, allowing
proletarian social values to prevail. The Russian exile Pyotr Kropotkin
elaborated a theory of anarchism founded on individual cooperation and
spontaneous equilibrium. For Kropotkin, equality must be total and
therefore was incompatible with government. The revolution would abolish private property and constitute federations consisting of groups that
would voluntarily unite and that would be free of capitalist oppression.
The anarchist task was to awaken the masses and make them aware of
injustice, because only they could resolve the problems of production and
distribution through the creation of a just community. Ordinances would
not be necessary to keep order, because a new morality would permit the
integration of labor and society. Kropotkin considered parliamentary
regimes as defenses organized by the commercial and industrial bourgeoisie; representative government was the bourgeoisie's most effective
line of defense, despite universal suffrage and the democratic verbiage of
parties. The works that express Kropotkin's ideas most succinctly are

Words of a Rebel (1885), *The Conquest of Bread* (1892), and *Anarchism: Its Philosophy and Ideal* (1896).

Other anarchist thinkers had wide currency. Worthy of attention is William Morris, who published *News from Nowhere* in 1891. This work presents an ideal society that exists practically without government, class divisions, or social differences. In this society everyone is satisfied with his labor and poverty is unknown. In Italy anarchism took different forms, from collectivism to anarcho-communism. The most famous Italian anarchist was Errico Malatesta, a tireless political practitioner and writer who elaborated a socialist anarcho-revolutionary program in 1889. Malatesta criticized the parliamentary politics of Italian socialism and demanded "the abolition of government and of every institution which makes laws and forces others to obey them." He too wanted the organization of society by means of free associations and federations of consumers and producers.

It would be surprising if, with all the emphasis on workers, a revolutionary movement had not arisen that had as its fulcrum the organizations that the workers themselves had created: the unions. Indeed, there was a close relationship between union-based thought and visions of a socialist-anarchist society. The union was seen as the nucleus of the new society; just as capitalism had created the factories, it was believed that organizations created by workers must act to destroy from the inside the system that exploited them, and to bring about true justice. Thus the struggle began within the factories. In France the *Bourses du travail* [Labor Exchanges], institutions that included all types of workers, had so much success that they formed a federation and declared their independence from political parties. Indeed, in both France and Italy, the workers of this tendency shunned nonworkers—intellectuals and party heads.

Union leader Fernand Pelloutier drew up a battle plan. The working class had to prepare itself to manage the society of the future, but the instrument of its revolutionary action was the general strike. Pelloutier's thought is best known from a posthumously published work, *Histoire des Bourses du travail* (1902), in which Pelloutier expressed his belief that the society of the future would be based on producers, organized in free unions, who would possess the means of production.

Thanks to Pelloutier, the tendency known as revolutionary syndicalism acquired consistency. This movement accepted the Marxist premise of an exploited proletariat but was essentially anarchist. It proposed a revolutionary technique different from Marx's: The revolution, begun in the factories and implemented through the general strike, would be conducted by the workers primarily against the state, the source of social injustice. Future society would not rest upon parliamentary political structures, but must be based on the principle that labor is autonomous. Groups would associate with each other and produce goods in an autonomous manner, according to the needs of society. Property would exist only as collective property held by the workers. Manual workers and intellectuals would collaborate in a harmonic manner; cooperatives would unite in unions, and unions in federations. Once again, the new society would be a federative one, stimulated by mutual understanding and working in concert without the coercive and destructive power of a state. No state meant no dictatorship.

To prevent revolutionary syndicalism from becoming flaccid, the retired French civil servant and philosopher Georges Sorel developed the idea of a new myth capable of animating the workers and infusing them with a sense of mission. Thus Sorel presented the general strike as the outstanding "social myth" of the working class. Workers had no use for an "evolutionary" myth such as the one advanced by social democrats but desperately required one that had a revolutionary charge. In his preface to Pelloutier's book, Sorel had already judged "official" socialism as incapable of building a truly socialist society.

If the myth of the general strike prepared the ground for revolution, violence must crush the authority of the bourgeoisie. Sorel's most famous work, *Reflections on Violence* (1908), is aimed at "parliamentary socialists" who, the author believed, lacked the courage to unmask themselves as reformists pure and simple. According to Sorel, parliamentary socialists no longer believed in insurrection and only talked about it occasionally to feel important. In a complex modern society subject to myriad economic shocks, an enormous number of unhappy people are produced; it is to these individuals that parliamentary socialists appeal to in order to get elected, and they speak different languages according to the nature of their clientele and of the current discontent.

Thus, if reformist socialists hoped to harness the proletariat's electoral force to the parliamentary system in order to transform society legally, and if Marxist communism spelled authoritarianism, the anarchist and revolutionary syndicalist wings of socialism emphasized the liberating effect that direct proletarian action would have. Not only would this action destroy the bourgeoisie's political power and the authoritarian structure of capitalist society, but it would also set up federations and communes capable of governing themselves directly, producing and distributing goods in a harmonious manner, and, finally, achieving the social justice for which everyone yearned.

9

SOCIAL SCIENCE
AND POLITICS

The revolutionary burst of violence provoked by the Paris Commune set off a round of profound political reflection among both conservatives and radicals. Conservatives took heart in the Commune's failure at the hands of Bismarck and Thiers but could not ignore the popular resentment illustrated by the events of 1871; radicals rejoiced at the revolutionary force demonstrated by the masses but had no clear idea on what form a popular government would assume. As a result, after 1871 all groups, on the right and the left, were forced to reopen the debate on the legitimacy of governments, the functions of the state, and the role of classes in society. During this discussion a consensus emerged: that the empirical needs of society must serve as the starting point to orient governments. This understanding meant that a clear comprehension of how society actually worked could produce a science of politics capable of resolving social and political problems.

In considering this problem, thinkers already had a model. Between 1830 and 1842, the French philosopher Auguste Comte had published his influential *Cours de philosophie positive* [Course on Positive Philosophy], arguing in favor of a "science" of society, a study necessarily based on sociology. For Comte—father of "positivism"—society would become the center of interest for *all* science. Positivism considered sense perceptions as the only basis for observation and thought. Comte affirmed that it was essential to scrutinize society as a complex structure with competing class and group interests embroiled in economic problems and religious differences. For Comte, it was indispensable to clarify relationships between political and social forces, always keeping in mind collective interests.

In the late-nineteenth-century intellectual context, a positivist methodology applied to social realities came to be considered capable of provid-

ing basic certainties useful for life lived in common. It was from this interest in society as the sum of human interrelationships, and from faith in
science as the "positive" tool for the proper examination of existing reality, that all the "social sciences" would gather strength.

As might be expected, in this "positivist" era Darwin's ideas on evolution had a great impact, influencing sociological and historical analyses of
society. In the study of society, sociology supplemented biology and had
the task of clarifying the connections between individuals and groups,
groups and society, and society and power; as a science, it could discover
the constants of social reality and supply a true picture of society's development. Since society always had a political organization, sociology
could also provide a better understanding of the political realities in
which people historically operated. As a result, great historical syntheses
were attempted in an effort to untangle collective phenomena. Sociology
was believed capable of integrating different cultural areas that until then
had operated on different planes with diverse goals in mind. The most
representative thinker of this "positivist" school was Herbert Spencer.

HERBERT SPENCER (1820–1903)

Herbert Spencer, born in Derby, England, had received a scientific education and claimed that he stuck to scientific principles in his writings.
Although he published several early essays on statistics and economics,
he first enunciated his ideas most clearly and comprehensively in *First
Principles* (1862). Here he asserted the general importance of the principle
of evolution, believing it to be a fundamental law. In later works he
applied evolutionary ideas to biology, psychology, sociology, and ethics.
According to Spencer, the principle of evolution was the interpretative
key in all fields, because it illustrated the development from the homogeneous to the heterogeneous in the lives of both individuals and societies.
Spencer owed much to Darwin, in whose *The Origin of Species* (1859) he
saw scientific confirmation of his own ideas with respect to the evolution
of societies. Spencer had great influence on many contemporaries who
considered him the preeminent master of the social sciences.

Spencer's ideas may be found fully explained in his two-volume
Principles of Sociology (1876–1879). Spencer believed in the necessity of
applying the principle of evolution to social phenomena because evolution clarified the genesis and growth of human association. The transition
from primitive to modern society, according to Spencer, could be considered an instance of evolutionary progress because cooperative forms of
living had evolved from the tribal to the national pattern. Arguing from
the premise that "sustenance" and "defense" were the two crucial
moments in the struggle for life, Spencer stated that in a complex structure

"sustenance" involves both production and distribution, and "defense" provokes a schism between dominated and dominating classes.

The theme of the ruling class is linked to the successive structural differentiation of advanced societies, Spencer continued, created by the different functions needed to confront an ever more complex reality. Integration occurs within modern society, but it never eliminates heterogeneity. Spencer confronted the dilemma of social transformations that modify governmental powers, distinguishing two radically different forms of political organization within modern society—"military" society, prevalently authoritarian, and "industrial" society, tending toward liberalism. Military society creates a disciplined economic organization, subordinating all activities to a central power; industrial society respects citizen rights and attempts to avoid damaging the interests of individuals in the hope of increasing prosperity. In an industrial society, arbitration regulates conflicts, and free expression is essential for equitable accords. Consequently, the characterizing element of industrial society is the multiplicity and heterogeneity of associations of all kinds and sizes. Spencer insisted that empirical studies were crucial in order to understand their complicated development; furthermore, since institutions constantly change, continual research is essential for an understanding of increasingly complex social structures. This belief put social science at the center of European cultural endeavors.

Spencer's belief that societies evolve from the homogeneous to the heterogeneous, and that the law of progress induces states to develop from the military state to the industrial state, produced a clearly optimistic historical vision; indeed, he was convinced that even if it is difficult to trace the exact path of evolution, progress always prevails. But is it true that advanced industrial society ensures human dignity and tranquillity? And does solidarity manifest itself fully in modern society?

Human dignity based on the morality of the community had already existed in ancient times, as N. D. Fustel de Coulanges wrote in *The Ancient City: A Study of the Religion, Laws, and Institutions of Greece and Rome* (1864), and it had lasted as long as respect for one's ancestors and a sense of family prevailed. Human solidarity had been deeply felt in the ancient Germanic world as well, philosopher J. J. Bachofen had believed, and, according to L. H. Morgan, the spirit of solidarity had imbued ancient society as a whole. But a very influential and subtle work on a similar theme injected a different element. Henry S. Maine observed in his *Ancient Law* (1861) that the ties among men that should have been those of rights and duties had been substituted by contract law, which was frequently based on force; this development had instituted contractual relationships between master and servant, between worker and employer, intimately tied to private property.

These ideas—so closely parallel to the more properly political thought that had produced an ideology based on class struggle—led to a "cultural" justification of state intervention in favor of society's weaker elements similar to the thinking of the reformist movement in the socialist parties. German writer Otto Gierke insisted in two noted works, *Natural Law and the Theory of Society, 1500–1800* (3 volumes, 1868–1881) and *The Development of Political Theory* (1880), that new legislation had to be passed in favor of the community, precisely because laws were supposed to protect the individual. According to the "Socialists of the Chair" (academic socialists) such as Gustav Schmoller, it was perfectly legitimate for the state to intervene on behalf of the poor in order to ensure greater justice in the distribution of wealth. This concept of the state's having a role in safeguarding the interests of the poor and of workers, characteristic of German social and legal thought, greatly influenced European writers and politicians who were not socialists.

COMMUNITY AND SOCIETY

European cultural tendencies in the last decades of the nineteenth century were also inspired by the German writer Ferdinand Tönnies, whose major work was *Community and Society*, first published in 1887. Tönnies wrote that Comte, Spencer, Maine, Bachofen, Morgan, Gierke, Marx, and the "Socialists of the Chair" all influenced his ideas.

According to Tönnies, these authors had made him comprehend that in examining society it was a mistake to consider only bourgeois customs, ignoring the values of the common people of the city and countryside. Society must be analyzed beginning with the first communities and following their development until the formation of a capitalist economy. For Tönnies, this meant utilizing the methods of sociology to analyze the historical development of the diverse forms of association and integration.

Tönnies drew a fundamental distinction between "community" and "society." In a community, a person is linked to other persons, for good and bad, from birth, by a series of relationships involving custom, language, and religion; society, in contrast, signifies the coexistence of independent persons, living peacefully with one another, but substantially separate. "Community" is a positive construction, with its fundamental concept being a primitive understanding that remains solid despite the centrifugal tendencies of modern life. Community relationships have their roots in the bonds between mother and child, between man and woman, between brother and sister. Within the community there is a deep feeling of equality, and the group will always come together in response to external danger.

"Society" consists of people with limited fields of activity. No one does anything for anyone else, and no one will give anyone anything without something in return. In a society, whatever one person possesses and enjoys is possessed and enjoyed to everyone else's exclusion; no action is conceivable without some ulterior aim or without an equal return. For this reason, the value of goods that are exchanged in a society depends on the time necessary to produce them, and trade becomes a general phenomenon because everything becomes a commodity—and all commodities are for sale. Individuals act only in their own behalf, while claiming to act for society. In society, crass calculation and speculation cause the sources of morality to dry up, producing the triumph of interest and profit; religion and friendship lose value, and life in the big cities becomes totally negative.

Tönnies distinguished two types of common living: one founded on consensus and concord; and one based on arbitrary will guaranteed by legislation. It is the latter type that prevails in large cities, the "industrial city." Here wealth is capital—money that reproduces itself through use in the form of commercial, usurious, or industrial investment, the means by which the products of labor are appropriated and workers exploited. In the industrial city, the family disintegrates and a yawning gap opens up between upper and lower classes.

But this gloomy conclusion did not lead Tönnies to advocate violence. Because the class struggle destroys society, reestablishment of a community spirit is urgent; Tönnies believed that this task must be accomplished not by restoring the simple and familial communism that existed in a primitive era but by transforming it into state socialism.

SOCIAL SCIENCE AND POLITICS

French sociologist Emile Durkheim also confronted the problems of social evolution, industrial production, and the formation of great urban agglomerations in his 1893 work, *The Division of Labor in Society*. Durkheim acknowledged that Comte and Spencer had founded a positivistic science of society, but he found that their view of society fell short. Spencer believed that individualistic and utilitarian elements held society together, but Durkheim postulated morality and solidarity as the adhesive force. Durkheim distinguished between the "mechanical" solidarity of simple societies, such as rural ones, and the "organic" solidarity of complex, industrial, societies. Since solidarity is more important in industrial societies, the division of labor characteristic of these societies necessarily produces coercion because of the need to coordinate life and work and public order.

Durkheim's view of the division of labor had a political goal similar to that of other social scientists—to prevent the conflicts among social classes in industrialized society from degenerating into civil war, as they had during the Paris Commune. No longer satisfied with the functions assigned to them by tradition and the law, the lower classes aspired to take over functions denied to them, overthrowing those who currently performed those tasks. Durkheim attributed the origins of domestic strife to the manner in which work was distributed. In sum, the class struggle resulted from the disharmony between individuals and the tasks, or work, that were imposed on them against their will. Such a constriction resulted in inequality, and equality could be reestablished only through new contracts capable of bringing about consensual agreements. Advanced, complex societies aimed at introducing ever greater equity in social relationships by assuring the free development of all socially useful energies. For Durkheim, it was not necessary to study forms of government but to understand the lifestyles and value systems of complex societies and to remedy their defects.

The methodological problems of the political and social sciences were also at the center of Max Weber's interests. A member, with other progressive scholars, of the "Verein für Sozialpolitik" [Social Politics Association], Weber was also close to the "Socialists of the Chair" and was familiar with their works. Weber rejected the "positivistic" methods of both Comte and Spencer as well as historical determinism, proposing instead a more subtle methodology capable of considering the multiple processes of historical development. This method is best illustrated in his famous *The Protestant Ethic and the Spirit of Capitalism* (1904–1905). In this work Weber contended that economics does not explain religion, but religious sentiment gives rise to a new conception of society. The work's main theme is that the ethics of the most active and morally engaged classes were at the origins of capitalism. The methodological conclusions to be drawn from this work are clear and in the end similar to the general conceptions of social science already discussed: Because society changes, it is imperative to study the transformation of the general structures of society, in addition to the transformation of ideologies. Furthermore, in keeping with another theme that has been emphasized, all classes may be carriers of new moral and social values.

Weber attempted to be historically objective, but he actively followed developments in both imperial and republican Germany, keeping in mind always the ethical imperatives of the state and the political necessities of the parties. His dynamic conception of society emphasized struggle, with particular reference to "Man" (Nietzsche) and to the working class (Marx). Nevertheless, the political class remained central to his research, and he hoped that politics would be looked upon as a profession.

Keeping these aspects of Weber's thought in mind makes it easier to appreciate the political value of his *Parlament und Regierung* [Parliament and Government] (1918) and particularly the work of his full maturity, *The Theory of Social and Economic Organization* (1922). Published posthumously, this work creates a fresh, innovative sociological system for the study and exercise of power and an analysis of its negative bureaucratic consequences.

In addition to social scientists, Christian socialists also defended the rights of the masses, altering the Church's earlier hostility. They contended that the papal encyclical *Rerum novarum* (1891) had revised the Church's attitude toward the people, conferring its blessing on the social demands of workers. Following Leo XIII's teachings, Christian socialists debated the connection between civil society and religious society. Thus the economist and sociologist Giuseppe Toniolo posited a Christian politics according to which goodwill, brotherhood, and a respect for individual rights must mark human relationships.

This search became the focal point of many social scientists and illustrates how, at the end of the nineteenth century, theorists in all the fields of social science searched for ways of preventing violent breaks in society. Conflicts might erupt as a result of historical evolution, they seemed to agree, but frontal engagements between classes and a final battle along the lines of Marx's predictions must be avoided at all costs. As a complex and advanced society, Europe supposedly moved toward greater respect for individual civil rights and social exigencies. For some, the rationality of the reigning political elite would achieve that goal, whereas for others the strength of the masses would gradually modify the existing structure of European society and permit the attainment of socialism. Verbal dissension was frequently violent, and polemics raged in the press, but despite the aggressive language, the possibility of mediation among opposing groups always remained open. The conviction that armed conflict, such as that between governmental forces and the Parisian Communards in 1871, would have provoked the disintegration of the European moral and social order made many social scientists cautious.

Suggested by the social sciences and gaining wide acceptance in all cultural circles, this opinion against violence favored moderate solutions for social and political dilemmas over radical ones; these moderate solutions were the liberal democracy (on the right) and the social democracy (on the left) discussed in previous chapters.

10

THE AUTHORITARIAN STATE AND ANTIPARLIAMENTARISM

In 1848 an age of disorder that had lasted sixty years culminated in revolutions that shook the major European countries. In response to these continuous revolts a reaction occurred among citizens, political thinkers, and politicians in what can best be described as a revolt against revolution and its implications. Supporters of this view objected not to the principle of implementing the people's will but to the method of expressing and implementing its decisions, considered first conducive to disorder and then to mediocrity. The period between 1848 and the new century witnessed the elaboration of various political projects critical of the representative institutions that had emerged from Enlightenment and French revolutionary tenets. The authors of these proposals injected an authoritarian theme into the political debate not in the name of old regime monarchical beliefs but, paradoxically, with the goal of providing political constructions with a modern legitimacy.

LOUIS NAPOLEON AND CAESARISM

In France after 1850, the term "Caesarism" signified a form of government that had emerged from revolutionary disorder and was headed by a charismatic leader ruling strongly in the interest of and by the will of everyone. The head of state agreed to consult with the governed by means of plebiscites. The concept of Caesarism (from the political dictatorship imposed by Julius Caesar for the salvation of ancient Rome) promised to put an end to revolutionary agitation while avoiding both the absolutism of monarchies and the inefficiency of parliaments. A dictionary published in 1863 affirmed that the word stood for a political theory that restrained liberty but in return gave a certain satisfaction to democratic interests.

French developments after 1848 help to explain the popularity of this idea. After the expulsion of King Louis Philippe, the insurgents declared a republic. In their first presidential election, millions of voters elected Louis Napoleon, nephew of Napoleon I, as president of France. For several years disputes raged between president and Assembly over their respective powers and over the president's desire to amend the constitution to allow him a second term. On December 2, 1851, Louis Napoleon seized power in a coup d'état against the Assembly. He announced a plebiscite, which was held on December 20. He received the approval of 7.5 million participants against 500,000 opposing ballots. He went on to modify the constitution, first becoming president for ten years and then proclaiming the Second Empire with himself as Emperor Napoleon III in 1852.

Though historians typically attribute Louis Napoleon's political successes either to military repression or to the power of the Napoleonic legend, neither fully explains his electoral victories. Although he received political inspiration from both Caesar and Napoleon I, Louis Napoleon's government may be considered an example of a modern dictatorship. Louis Napoleon was neither a general nor a great administrator like his uncle; he did not come to power during war but during peace; he was an able politician who used his competence to create a favorable public opinion and convincing rhetoric to gain the consensus of those who listened to him; he made populist promises in order to achieve mass support and understood the economic necessities of an expanding industrial society. Since the demand for order originated in the psychological scars produced by insecurity, anxiety, and uneasiness, Louis Napoleon used language that imparted a sense of security and implicitly criticized the dissension, the constantly shifting factions, and the maneuvers of the legislature. As a "Caesar," he presented himself as standing above the factionalism of groups and classes and as ruling in the nation's interest—new roads, railways, monuments, and other public works symbolized the "constructive" politics of the new regime. He stimulated the country's economic development by consulting experts, supporting the foundation of new banks specializing in raising capital for industry and agriculture, and strengthening the administration's ability to intervene decisively on the local level. The intimate link between economics and politics found in Louis Napoleon's rule was a characteristic of modern Caesarism.

Louis Napoleon and his supporters claimed to be realists and frequently cited their "positivism." Even so, it is improbable that Louis Napoleon gave much attention to the works of the most famous French positivist, Auguste Comte, but they would have agreed on the positivist concept that society and power are intimately bound up with each other and that disorder is society's enemy.

AUGUSTE COMTE (1798–1857)

Convinced that the 1848 revolution in France created a favorable climate for his positivist ideas, Comte founded the Positivist Society and published his *System of Positive Polity* (four volumes, 1851–1854). Shortly after the first volume appeared, Louis Napoleon's coup took place. Comte supported the new regime, stating that the republic that he had enthusiastically greeted in February 1848 had followed its natural evolutionary course. In the preface to the second volume of his work, Comte argued that the Second Republic had spontaneously passed to a dictatorial phase, a form that was truly French. According to him, this kind of energetic government contrasted with retrograde monarchy and parliamentary anarchy. The chronic insurrection of the countryside against the city produced anarchy, he wrote; social progress and salvation could come only through "positivist" politics, the precondition of which must be the proletariat's complete rejection of revolutionary doctrines, which had now become retrograde and anarchistic.

In August 1854 Comte painted a picture of the future in volume 4 of his work—the "positivist dictatorship." According to contemporary observers, the result of this system would have been the suffocation of the bourgeoisie, of intellectuals, and of all factions, and the production of a patrician ruling group and a proletariat stamped with theological prejudices. The strongest condemnation of Comte's political vision came in John Stuart Mill's highly influential *On Liberty* (1859). According to Mill, Comte's system would allow rulers to establish the despotism of society over the individual and to impose their own opinions as a rule of conduct for others. Mill subsequently reiterated this view in an essay, *Auguste Comte and Positivism* (1863), and in his autobiography.

The policies of Louis Napoleon attempted to transform governmental views into public opinion, and then to draw his political legitimacy from that public opinion. The regime constantly had recourse to popular referendums, with an emphasis on the message; and it communicated directly with the people through newspapers in order to convince the public to support decisions already taken by the government.

Thus Caesarism emerged as a European phenomenon in the post-1848 world. After the defeat of the dreams and illusions of that revolutionary year, the idea of a responsible leader capable of liberating the people took shape. Economic and social reasons help explain this development, in addition to psychological ones: As previously indicated, a "Caesar" could foster economic growth. In Germany the political literature constantly invoked a "German Caesar." Indeed, Marx wrote *The Eighteenth Brumaire of Louis Bonaparte* (1852) under the powerful influence of French developments, quickly comprehending that the new type of government established by Louis Napoleon had important implications for any country with a class structure similar to that of France in 1848. Germany seemed to him one of the areas where the French model could be replicated. In the preface to the second edition of his book (1869), he expressed the following desire: "Lastly, I hope that my work will contribute towards eliminating the school-taught phrase now current, particularly in Germany, of so-called *Caesarism.*" Mazzini, too, warned that Caesarism threatened democracy; in June 1867 August Bebel and Wilhelm Liebknecht identified Caesarism as the common enemy of the German and the Italian people; and in 1865 the Englishman Walter Bagehot defined it as a "detestable government."

A NEW MODEL

In September 1870, after a decisive military defeat at Prussian hands at the Battle of Sedan, the Second Empire died. Louis Napoleon's fall and the proclamation of the German Empire caused a deep moral crisis in France. Those French admirers of liberal Germany represented by Herder, Goethe, Kant, and Hegel, and who had dreamed of Franco-German cooperation in building a liberal Europe saw their illusions dissipate. Ernest Renan's *Réforme intellectuelle et morale de la France* [The Intellectual and Moral Reform of France] (1871) indicates the direction taken by many French intellectuals as a result of this moral crisis.

France's current troubles originated in the French Revolution, when continual disorder and regicide had been applauded, Renan wrote. He believed that the end of Louis Napoleon's rule did not resolve French ills, the root of which lay in a misunderstanding of democracy. A country that believed in democracy and direct universal suffrage could not be governed or administered well and faced gridlock. In order to end the crisis, Renan called for strong government, a constitutional monarchy capable of engendering loyalty in its citizens. Renan looked to Bismarck's Prussia as a model—a militaristic constitutional monarchy with a strong kaiser and with a government responsible only to the sovereign and not to parliament; France should adopt the same kind of authoritarian state if it wished to reform itself intellectually and morally.

The necessity of establishing an authoritarian state, unconditioned by popular consultations and social experiments, became the dominant theme for many French intellectuals who considered themselves liberals. Renan's name, for example, was closely linked to that of Hippolyte Taine, author of a two-volume work, *The French Revolution* (1875), which he dedicated to the old regime. Taine began in a polemical manner, stating that 10 million ignorant people do not make one who is wise. Consulting the people at best makes for an understanding of the form of government it might like, not the kind it needs. According to Taine, France had run through thirteen constitutions in eighty years because it had dissolved its ancient form of organization without grasping that the political and social forms of a people are determined by its character and its past. Taine concurred with Renan in arguing that the great revolution of 1789 had ushered in a period of terrible crisis for France. From that point on, street violence served the ends of radical dogma, and radical dogma placed itself at the service of street violence.

Thus, in France and Europe, writers suggested the possibility of ending the political and moral crisis of the period by delegating greater authority to the state—as in Germany. After the Prussian victory over France, Bismarck—no admirer of the parliamentary system—had given life to an authoritarian *Reich*. In German this word signified "empire," "reign," or "state," but Bismarck had given it the sense of a strong political structure. The 1871 German constitution had created a strong emperor who was at the same time king of Prussia, had wide executive powers, convoked the legislature, promulgated laws, implemented them, declared war, and concluded peace. He delegated some of his powers to a chancellor who was responsible to him, not to the legislature. The legislature, consisting of a Reichstag elected by universal suffrage and a Bundesrat representing the German states, could not limit Bismarck's authority through votes of confidence.

A strong belief in political centralization linked Louis Napoleon's Caesarism and Bismarck's *Kaisertum*, but whereas Louis Napoleon drew his authority from popular plebiscites, Bismarck believed that authority originated from above. Indeed, an authoritarian conception of the state marked Bismarck's governmental system, which exercised an effective control of German political life. Bismarck manipulated constitutional mechanisms to prevent the popularly elected Reichstag from exercising governmental action while combining internal authoritarianism and an expansionist foreign policy to thwart the political and social forces challenging his authority.

For these reasons Bismarck's authoritarian state appealed to large landowners, great industrialists, financiers, capitalists, military officials, and, generally, people who believed in discipline and order. Since these groups saw in the authoritarian state the conciliation of industrial development, military security, population increase, and economic progress, it became a model for Europe.

The Bismarckian state also had a juridical justification, provided above all by Paul Laband's *Das Staatsrecht des deutschen Reiches* [The Public Law of the German Empire] (1876–1882). Taking the reality of Bismarck's politics as his starting point, Laband confidently argued that the law justified historical processes. As the foundation of public law, the state prevailed over particular interests. Laband argued that in the new *Reich* the state was identified, in a legal sense, with the *Volk* (people) and became the source of authority. The German Empire's constitution reflected this political and juridical reality and justified the state's power. In Laband's authoritarian conception of the state, there was no space for the separation of powers, and he attributed all state authority to the emperor, not individuals. Laband's work had a wide currency in Europe because it corresponded to an existing political reality that had victoriously affirmed itself.

HEINRICH VON TREITSCHKE (1834–1896)

Unlike Laband, some intellectuals justified Bismarck's policies primarily in terms of *raison d'état* ("reason of state," the idea that the state's interests are paramount). The most influential defender of this concept was Heinrich von Treitschke. A professor of history at the University of Heidelberg, Treitschke distinguished among three kinds of state—federal, confederated, and unitary. In Bismarck's system, he saw a new type of unitary state, a dominant state (Prussia) guiding a number of subordinate states; thus the king of Prussia headed the German nation and its army. Treitschke's essential ideas may be found in his posthumously published *Politics* (four volumes, 1897–1898), a collection of lectures to his students from 1864 to 1875.

This work consists of four parts dealing with the state, its essence, its social basis, its forms, and its administration. By "state," Treitschke meant a people legitimately united as an independent power. States not only maintain order but reveal their own historical and ethical personality; states signify the coordination of public force for defense and offense. By definition, civil society means the ordering of classes, but the state must be independent of and above single classes in order to dispense justice to all groups. Sympathetic to the "worthy" part of the bourgeoisie and the nobility, Treitschke also contended that although the lower classes included the worst social elements they also possessed energies capable of renewing entire nations.

With regard to the constitutional structure of states, Treitschke believed that the separation of powers among the three branches of government made no sense theoretically or practically. Since unity represented the essence of a state, that state was best organized in which the executive, legislative, and judicial powers were consolidated under a firm and independent hand. This reasoning also led Treitschke to argue that a strong, modern state could only be a monarchy, a governmental form that mediated between theocracies and republics. Not surprisingly, Treitschke cited the German Empire as a prime example of a monarchical form of government because Bismarck, chancellor of the empire, implemented the will of the Prussian king over all of Germany.

For Treitschke, the function of political science was to uncover the foundation of states in their historical traditions. In this sense, he maintained that a community united by legal ties that has become a permanent institution demanding full loyalty and sacrifice is at the origin of a state. The state, like a person, must affirm its identity with relation to other states, and for this reason it requires unity and independence. Therefore, *"der Staat ist Macht"*—the state is power. The defense of the state is entrusted to government, which consists of ruling groups. In this manner, the hierarchical organization of society is fixed and necessary. In fact, Treitschke had no confidence in elections, believing that the ruling class must be the aristocratic class, the personification of which he found in Bismarck.

Because the state aims at self-preservation and cannot adopt Christian morals, Treitschke makes a clear distinction between private and public morality. Diverse forms of government are strictly linked with different kinds of states. The governing style of monarchies is distinct from those of theocracies and democracies. Theocracies are obsolete, and therefore the *Kulturkampf* (the "struggle for civilization," Bismarck's persecution of the Catholic Church and party) against Church interference in public affairs is justified; democracy, for its part, spells revolution and instability, leading to Treitschke's negative judgment on democratic republics. Treitschke also opposed parliamentary governments that gave the executive power to a majority party of an elected house, on the English model. In a real monarchy, power belongs to a chancellor who implements the will of the sovereign. Again, Treitschke approvingly cited the German model—a state administration consisting of civilians dependent on the monarch and not on parliament; a chancellor sensitive to the opinions of a legislative house representing the states of the empire, and not to those of political parties.

The German historian Friedrich Meinecke—author of *Machiavellism: The Doctrine of Raison d'Etat and Its Place in Modern History*—considered Treitschke the theoretician of the authoritarian state. According to Meinecke, Prussian military might and conservative policies had been essential in the unification of Germany, but he argued that the institutions of united Germany needed further evolution in a more liberal direction. Because of the influence of Treitschke and other intellectuals, however, faith in monarchies became transformed into confidence in the power of the state.

THE EMERGENCE OF RACISM

After the proclamation of the German Empire in 1871, many German writers exalted in the unity of the German people. The concept of a Germanic *Volk* became an instrument for the stimulation of national ambition. The confusion between a strong state and national spirit may be found in Paul de Lagarde's *Deutsche Schriften* [German Writings] (1878). For Lagarde, the Germanic people possessed individual characteristics that it must develop in order to regenerate the nation, a moral entity that counted more than the state. As a result of the Franco-Prussian War that produced the German Empire, the French ceded Alsace and Lorraine, components of medieval Germany but part of France since the seventeenth century. Most inhabitants of these areas considered themselves French, but many Germans claimed to understand their ethnic identity better than the natives themselves and insisted that their German national identity must be restored to the inhabitants even against their will.

In Paris, Count Arthur de Gobineau in the meantime had published *The Inequality of Human Races* (four volumes, 1853–1855), discussing what he believed to be inborn characteristics of different races and the negative results of inbreeding; he concluded that the primacy among races belonged to the Germanic element, representative of the pure "Aryan" race. During this era, "race" was considered a scientific concept. Gobineau's work did not enjoy great popularity during his lifetime, but the publication of a posthumous edition in 1884 testifies to the increasing interest and to the continuing debate about the supposed inequality of races; the editors of Gobineau's work emphasized that the interbreeding of races could damage the national spirit. The concept of *Volk* and "race" had become linked to the issue of types of states. Strong, authoritarian states became identified with the Aryan race, carrier of civilization and morality. This idea of race facilitated an attack on certain races, a tendency represented by Eugen Dühring's *Die Judenfrage* [The Jewish Question] (1880), which condemned the Jews for their race, culture, and morals. Writers even linked national economies to the history of national civilizations. After German unification the "National-Okonomie," theorized by Bruno Hildebrand and Karl Knies, was considered the science of national development.

Thus, after German unification many thinkers went beyond Bismarck's positions. Bismarck had succeeded in unifying Germany politically; the moral unification of the German people through a profound understanding of national values and formation of a specifically German culture had yet to be accomplished. The national state defended this culture, thereby creating confusion between the military and national missions of the state. This perplexity developed into paranoia, with the German nation seeing itself as perpetually threatened by surrounding nationalities.

THE TRIUMPH OF ANTIPARLIAMENTARISM

The authoritarian state—whether based on the model of Louis Napoleon or that of Bismarck—was not the only response to the instability caused by revolutionary movements. Antiparliamentarism of the right directly criticized democratic institutions that had their modern origin in revolution and that enjoyed the support of both liberal democrats and social democrats. While leftist ideologues condemned parliaments because they supposedly represented only the interests of the rich, rightists criticized the "demagogic" nature of parliamentary arrangements. In a liberal democratic society, they argued, power is wielded not by persons of superior culture and morality but by mediocre politicians who manipulate universal suffrage and representative principles to their advantage. In practice, democracies are run by unrepresentative minority political groups skilled at achieving and maintaining control through their knowledge of the system. This is the premise of the theory of the "political class."

The antiparliamentary theme linked frequently disparate political ideologies, but from the criticism of a "corrupt" liberal democratic system emerged the idea of a state in which executive power prevailed over the legislative branch of government. Many antiparliamentary critics defined themselves as traditional liberals—not liberal democrats. They yearned for constitutional monarchies and attacked parliaments on the grounds that they were not really representative and encouraged corruption, administrative confusion, and governmental inefficiency. Italy, which hosted noted writers and practitioners of antiparliamentary criticism, produced the theoretician who formulated the "political class" concept.

GAETANO MOSCA (1858–1941)

Gaetano Mosca, a professor at the universities of Turin and Rome, elected a deputy in 1909 and named a senator in 1919, retired from politics in 1925 after a speech against a bill attacking Benito Mussolini's governmental reorganization scheme that solidified *Il Duce*'s power. Mosca published his groundbreaking *Sulla teorica dei governi e sul governo parlamentare* [On the Theory of Government and on Parliamentary Government] (1884) at the age of twenty-six. This work caused an uproar, because Mosca criticized the concepts of representation and popular sovereignty and maintained that regardless of the form of government, power is always wielded by an organized minority—the political class.

The change from constitutional to parliamentary forms of government had led to the absolute preponderance of an elective house, according to Mosca, which made and unmade governments according to majority votes, designating the ministers at its pleasure to the king. Instead, for Mosca, the Crown and the Senate must exercise a controlling function, because they represented independent political forces counterbalancing the authority of an elected assembly.

Skilled practitioners of the art of parliamentary procedure, parliamentary deputies were also men of moral and intellectual mediocrity who devoted their energies to bargaining among themselves with the common intent of remaining in power as long as possible; they governed only incidentally. They fulfilled the desires of their electorates through favoritism and corruption. Mosca saw these corrupting aspects of the Italian system of government not as an aberration but as integral to the principles of democracy and popular sovereignty. In practice, in order to ensure their reelection, deputies had to use all methods possible to gain the votes of their electors; and in order to maintain a majority in Parliament, ministers had to form political alliances with deputies who were frequently incompetent. Thus the terms "democracy" and "representation" often masked abusive concessions, unjust protection, illegal pressures, and clientelistic favoritism.

In discussing these aspects of government, Mosca formulated his concept of the "political class": In every form of government a political class exists; this class, always a minority, controls the machinery of government, exercises power, and governs; the governed do nothing more than obey the laws. Thus the traditional class division of governments into types depending on the number of people who rule—one (monarchies), a few (aristocracies), many (democracies)—should be replaced by a classification according to types of political classes. Each political class makes use of a "political formula" to legitimate its power and gain the consensus of the governed.

Mosca devoted greater attention to analyzing the political class in his 1896 work, *The Ruling Class*. In all societies, from the most sophisticated to the most primitive, Mosca reaffirmed, two classes of persons existed: the governing and the governed. The minority governing class dominates politics, monopolizes power, and enjoys its advantages; this political class guides the governed, the majority, in a more or less legal, more or less arbitrary, and more or less violent manner; it provides the governed with the material means of sustenance and whatever is necessary to ensure the vitality of political organisms. For Mosca, the concepts of "political class" and "political formulas" were fundamental in political science, because they favored an analysis of governments without being sidetracked by such notions as "people," "citizens," "majority."

For Mosca these principles were exemplified by liberal democratic regimes, typically presented as parliamentary constructions based on elective chambers claiming to represent all citizens. In liberal democracies the political power of the elected assembly in combination with the great authority of governmental agencies over employment, contracts, public works, and other favors is a major cause of decadence; even more frightening, liberal democracy tends to evolve into social democracy. In this model, not only political power but also all economic production and distribution would be in the same hands—and government functionaries would be the arbiters of everyone's livelihood and fortune. In response to these threats, Mosca favored the liberal-constitutional governmental model without any democratic "contamination" of the kind he witnessed in the representative political institutions of Europe.

Mosca's theory of the "political class" examined the nature of political forces, and his concept of the "political formula" analyzed the incidence and diffusion of political ideologies. Taken together, they opened up interesting avenues of study for political scientists because of the relationship between movements and ideas—in fact, for Mosca, it was not the creed that determined the political class's formation, but the political class that adopted the most convenient credo. Mosca's thought is often linked with Vilfredo Pareto's "theory of elites," but as an economist Pareto's starting point was production.

VILFREDO PARETO (1848–1923)

The son of a Mazzinian exile, Pareto was born in Paris but attended school in Turin, receiving a degree in engineering. Pareto's practical experience with government officials when he was directing the Italian railways embittered him. Dedicating himself to economics, he collaborated with Europe's most famous economists and in 1893 was named professor of political economy at the University of Lausanne in Switzerland.

Reasoning from the Italian situation, Pareto maintained that parliamentarism produced "statism" in politics and "protectionism" in economics (*La liberté économique et les événements d'Italie* [Economic Liberty and Events in Italy], 1898). He saw no clear demarcation between liberal and social democracy—both threaten property rights. When production comes under governmental tutelage, private interests and public life become falsified. The governing class sees nothing beyond the daily intrigues of parliamentary life, creates complex machinery to alter the "natural" distribution of riches, and seeks to convince the people that the state can improve the life of the poor. According to Pareto, governments desire centralization in order to increase the number of bureaucrats and functionaries who work for it. He believed that both liberal democracy and social democracy wind up damaging those people who work and ask nothing from the state.

Pareto opposed both liberal democratic and social democratic forms of government because the tendency of both toward statism cannot be reconciled with the individualism of a liberal economy. This is the theme of his *Les systèmes socialistes* [Socialist Systems] (two volumes, 1902–1903), an economic and sociological examination of socialist systems from the religious to the communist to the scientific. Although Pareto's historical knowledge of these systems may be questioned, the work is important for an understanding of the nature of his attack on parliamentary democracy, which he opposed less for its inefficiency and dysfunctions than for what he considered its distortion of the "natural" liberal order.

According to Pareto, in every society the upper classes constitute an aristocracy or an "elite." So long as the social equilibrium is stable, the elite in power appears competent; but elites do not last forever, so it is proper to speak of a continual circulation of elites. In Europe the rural lower classes contribute basic new components that allow elites to survive. Given this fact, it is essential to ensure that weak, dysfunctional, lazy, and defective elements are not selected during the necessary process of replacement. The phenomenon of creating new elites is, for Pareto, at the origin of great social movements, but it is also a method of judging political systems. Short-term observers see only accidental circumstances in this process, such as revolts, demands, oppression. The true phenomenon reveals that currently ruling elites try to hang onto their positions, while other elites try to expel them from power by claiming the support of the majority. When the opposition elite finally achieves its aims, a new elite emerges that, in turn, opposes the elite in power with the assistance of the majority.

According to Pareto, historians describe these conflicts as the struggle of the aristocracy against the "people," whereas they are in fact battles between aristocracies. Over time every aristocracy is replaced by another aristocracy. When a new elite comes to power in place of an old elite in full decline, there is usually a period of great prosperity. This change does not occur because of the people but because of the new elite, which imagines that it rules in the name of the people but is primarily interested in power. In order to maintain their ascendancy, elites resort to force, which is what creates social institutions. Elites unwilling to preserve their authority by force are decadent and have no choice but to abandon their position to a new elite that has the qualities they lack. As an example Pareto cited the liberal democrats; sensitive to humanitarian sentiments, only vaguely aware of the danger from social democrats, lacking a spirit of sacrifice and abnegation, unwilling to defend themselves, liberal democrats constituted an elite that manifested all the signs of decline.

Pareto's main themes are the demystification of democracy and opposition to parliamentarism. His theory of the circulation of elites appeared practically contemporaneously with Mosca's musings and were already implicit in an 1894 economic study of salaries. Mosca complained that Pareto did not mention his own theory of the "political class," but Pareto's cultural interests were different from Mosca's. Together they had a great impact. Both the theories of the political class and of the circulation of elites freed political thought from the fiction of popular sovereignty, criticizing the scientific validity of political ideologies and focusing on the negative aspects of democracy.

UNDEMOCRATIC PARTIES

The attacks on the poor practical functioning of democracy through the parliamentary system during the early years of the twentieth century invested the very principle of political participation. During the second half of the previous century, progressive political forces, envisioning the development of an informed public opinion, sensitive to social issues and foreign affairs, and capable of choosing among diverse political platforms, had successfully battled for universal suffrage. In practice, however, public affairs and initiatives remained in the hands of "politicians" who manipulated voters in unsavory ways in order to pass parliamentary legislation that did not favor the general interest.

From the end of the nineteenth century until the birth of fascism, the polemic against parliamentary corruption was frequently waged in the name of an ethical renewal of bourgeois society and of a new culture that would have imparted a new course to politics. The brilliant philosopher and theoretician of the "superman," Friedrich Nietzsche (1844–1900), was repeatedly cited as the enemy of democratic mediocrity. Frequently opinion was based on parts of his work *Thus Spake Zarathustra* (1885) and *The Will to Power* (1919), published posthumously with fragmented and false revisions by his fervently anti-Semitic sister, Elizabeth, who became a Nazi in 1933.

In the late nineteenth and early twentieth centuries, responsibility for this state of affairs was laid at the doorstep of political parties. Conservatives identified the party system with the moral degeneration of public life, and revolutionaries considered parties sophisticated bourgeois instruments for the creation of dissension within the working class. Both right and left blamed parties for sending to parliament mediocre politicians who promised reform but only protected their own interests. Local political clubs and associations mobilized to secure the election of candidates who, once elected, did not feel a responsibility toward citizens but to their constituencies. Furthermore, in order to achieve a majority, those parties participated in governmental coalitions of a fragile and equivocal nature.

From here the polemic against parties turned into a denunciation of democrats, who defended the concept of a multiparty system in the name of liberty. They conceived of this system as a guarantee of individual rights and of the general right to express agreement or dissent toward government policies. They insisted, furthermore, that from the debate expressed by parties would issue the stimulus toward progress. Instead, by recognizing the right of political associations to organize themselves into parties, democrats had stimulated social dissent. In order to increase their influence in parliament, disparate groups of diverse political extraction formed coalitions, thus damaging either the "nation" (for the right) or the "proletariat" (for the left). Stimulating studies on the formation and behavior of parties within the parliamentary context, however, were scarce before the beginning of the new century. Robert Michels, a German thinker who lived for many years in Italy, took up the slack.

THE "IRON LAW OF OLIGARCHY": ROBERT MICHELS (1876–1936)

Studying the German Socialist party, Michels revealed in a 1909 essay written for the Italian journal *Rassegna Contemporanea* [Contemporary Review], "La democrazia e la legge ferrea dell'oligarchia" [Democracy and the Iron Law of Oligarchy], the almost permanent quality of the SPD's leadership. Michels drew the inference that every organization, even if democratic, tended toward oligarchy. Furthermore, both democratic party heads and elected parliamentary leaders ended by forming unremovable castes that defended their positions more tenaciously than any aristocracy. In 1911 Michels expanded this idea in his major theoretical work, *Political Parties: A Sociological Study of the Oligarchic Tendencies of Modern Democracies*. He interpreted the political party as a new force that had entered the fray to aid the individual's struggle against the establishment. At the end of his analysis, Michels maintained that all political parties—leftist or rightist, socialist or conservative—have an oligarchic structure because leadership is a fundamental phenomenon in every kind of social life.

All parties, Michels affirmed, aim to increase the number of their supporters and wage their struggle in the collectivity's name. Before undertaking their march toward power, these organizations solemnly announce a program of liberation of the majority from the minority's yoke and stake out their claim to replace the old, unjust regime, with a new, just order. By nature, parties are formed for the purpose of defending particular interests, but they identify themselves with the totality of citizens and present themselves as acting in the name of all and for everyone's benefit.

Michels focused on socialist parties, which he knew best. They proclaim themselves to be "democratic" and criticize the bourgeoisie for monopolizing the country's social life. In examining the administrative, psychological, and intellectual relationships between leaders and masses, Michels noted the striking stability of the circle of people who lead these modern and democratic organizations. This fact should come as no surprise, Michels concluded, because although political organization is necessary to achieve power, that same organization is unavoidably oligarchic and inevitably becomes conservative when it achieves its goal. And, since the parliamentary system requires an ever-increasing number of votes in favor of a party, and consequently an ever-tighter structure, oligarchic tendencies always prevail, even in democratic parties. The iron law of oligarchy means that the minority will prevail and results in the formation of a dominant political class. This oligarchic phenomenon can be explained by tactical and technical factors that result from the strengthening of every aggregation operating in a disciplined manner on the political scene.

Thus all political parties are guided by minorities seeking to consolidate their leadership to an ever-greater degree. Because of universal suffrage and the need to appeal to all groups, all candidates put forward by political parties must endorse programs based on social reforms, and they must submit to the party's hierarchical order to gain the support they require to get elected. For conservative organizations, this submission is genuine, given the clearly oligarchic character of these parties, but the rule holds equally for socialist parties, which present themselves as either revolutionary or democratic, and are therefore not clearly oligarchic. Michels believed that the internal structure of parties may be either of the parliamentary type, yielding some political space to the opposition, or of the "statist" kind, based on authority. In the first case, diversity prevails in the leadership, and the opinions of different currents may be expressed; in the second instance, the executive prevails on the ground of efficiency as the best means of achieving the final goal. Diversity within the party leadership presages the establishment of future government coalitions, while party management by a dominant elite concentrates on the struggle for power and marginalizes party members who openly dissent from the leadership's program.

If a dominant elite that imposed an oligarchic leadership formed within a party, it was logical to suppose that this elite would attempt to impose its will on the dominant elites of other parties, and at the same time it would spur its own party to become a dominant party composed of millions of people. The contrast between political parties is thus transformed into a struggle between dominant elites who justify their oligarchic role within parties as necessary to defeat the opposing parties. A party that achieves a majority is unsatisfied with a momentary victory and aims to affirm itself as the dominant party. In this manner Michels applied the principles of Mosca and Pareto (whom he explicitly cited) to political parties and to their operations within democratic systems.

The conclusions that may be drawn from Michels's studies is that the crisis of parliamentarism and the weakness of coalition governments could be overcome only by the triumph of a dominant party that had millions of members and appealed favorably to masses of voters. In fact, both socialist and nationalist parties foreshadowed the formation of mass parties that advocated a proletarian or nationalistic society and were capable of dominating the political scene in an entire country. Such mass organizations not only must necessarily possess a dynamic character more typical of movements but also must advocate programs capable of attaining wide support among all social classes; these qualities meant that the mass party assumed the obligation of providing the nation with a new social and political order. Nationalists advocated solidarity among all social strata to achieve greater national dignity, and dreams of grandeur motivated popular nationalist movements (to be discussed in Chapter 11). Socialists appealed to workers and peasants, crushed by injustice and exploitation, to fight for the power that derived from their status as the most numerous classes. Nationalists and socialists demanded a "revolution" that clearly could never result from parliamentary agreements or political deals among disparate groups. Both right and left agreed that collaboration with governmental parties was only a shrewd expedient on the part of conservatives to bolster the establishment. The only alternative was the conquest of power through violence, direct action, and the destruction of representative institutions.

FROM DOMINANT TO SINGLE PARTIES

Implicit in the concept of the "dominant party" operating within a party system was the notion that the political leadership of a country would pass to the party leadership, which would not only choose candidates to run in elections but would also issue orders both to its delegates in parliament and to its ministers in government. In the years before World War I, the sentiment spread that only a "dominant party" could end the crisis of parliamentarism—caused by the compromises of multiparty government—establish good government, and respond quickly to the needs of the governed. Mechanisms that would give an absolute majority to parties that had only a plurality were also studied.

The creation of a "dominant party" with an absolute majority in a multiparty system would have resulted in a new type of government, because governments would be imposed by party leaderships and would not be conditioned by the continual need to obtain favorable votes in parliament. In this manner state and nation would be linked through the party, not parliament. Arrangements between dominant and minor parties would be negotiated by their directing committees, not their respective elected deputies. If it were indeed true that permanent oligarchies ran both conservative and progressive parties, as Michels argued, then the result would be the greater stability welcomed by all. A form of government characterized by the hegemony of only one party would permit a series of meaningful reforms and economic alteration of civil society. The dominant party's concrete policies would thus encompass the very structure of society rather than revolve around the concerns of other parties; public affairs would flow from the party itself.

This concept meant that the classical division of governmental forms into "monarchy," "aristocracy," and "democracy" would be replaced by a new typology: government by alternation, government by coalition, and government by a dominant party. A two-party system meant the alternation of those in power as the result of elections; a multiparty structure signified building a coalition capable of winning a parliamentary majority; and a dominant-party arrangement indicated long-term stable government. A dominant party clearly implied that the direction of public affairs would be reserved to representatives of that party, and parliaments would take a backseat. The risk, of course, would be that a "dominant party" might impose itself as a "single party," giving rise to a new kind of political system.

The one-party system that affirmed itself in Europe after World War I, therefore, did not spring spontaneously from practice unprepared by theory—the "dominant party" concept justified the single-party idea from a theoretical viewpoint. In fact, the "dominant party" doctrine allowed for the permanence in power of one organization to the exclusion of alternatives. The concept of Caesarism discussed at the beginning of this chapter was echoed in the idea that the single party would be concretized in power by a charismatic figure who, in his role as head of the government, would act in a dictatorial manner. This one-party system, however, would have as its defining characteristic not the concept of "dictatorship"— which has more remote origins—but the new relationship between government and party, embodied by the charismatic leader.

In order to justify its role the single party was bound to select its political class in a vigilant manner and at the same time cultivate its contacts with the masses. Excellent moral qualities and leadership capabilities would characterize a ruling class obliged to act in the party's, and therefore the nation's, interests. The party would be aware of the opinion of all the social strata and be ready to adopt all necessary measures to improve people's lives by establishing its presence in all public institutions. In turn, the government would discover in the party the instrument to operate swiftly and conveniently in favor of society's general interests. In a one-party system, therefore, a single party becomes a "state party," and all other parties are dissolved on the grounds that they act in a manner inconsistent with the state's national arrangement. These suppositions assumed a large dose of trust, but many people believed that such a system could bring stability and function efficiently. The single-party concept produced different kinds of governments—the Soviet Bolshevik, the Italian Fascist, and the German Nazi—which will be discussed in following chapters for their own doctrinal slants in order to understand how Europe passed from dominant-party to one-party systems.

11

POPULAR NATIONALISM

The end of the Franco-Prussian war witnessed the detachment of Alsace and Lorraine from France and their incorporation into a united Germany (1871). This event set off a debate on the true nationality of the inhabitants, given that they had been part of the Holy Roman Empire, a German-based medieval construction dissolved only in 1806 but which had lost all practical significance at least since 1648. This debate exacerbated tensions between France and Germany; French political forces demanded a war of revenge, and the Germans smoldered over their alleged mistreatment at French hands over the centuries.

In France the debate gained intensity and changed character with the Dreyfus affair. In 1894 Captain Alfred Dreyfus, a Jew, was accused of selling military secrets to Germany. He was tried and condemned to Devil's Island. His family consistently believed in his innocence and worked to reopen the case. They enlisted the aid of Émile Zola, a famous novelist of the period. Although Dreyfus was eventually retried and found guilty once again, new evidence pointed to his innocence, and the ultimately successful struggle to free him raged unabated. The case split French society, dividing supporters of the Third Republic (established in 1870) from its detractors, church and state, left and right, army and civilian government. Up to that time the drive for a war of revenge against Germany animated the left, which appealed to the revolutionary values of 1789–1794 against the premier European conservative power; now the right took over the notion of an anti-German crusade, basing the idea on nationalism.

FRENCH NATIONALISM

As the Dreyfus affair heated up, so did French patriotic furor and anti-Semitism, intimately linked to French nationalist ideology. The debate—fueled by nationalist associations such as the Ligue de la Patrie Française

[League of the French Fatherland] and reviews such as *L'Action française* [French Action]—deliberated on what should be the values of a unified French civil society, on the insidious intrigues of foreigners, and on how best to organize a true nationalist state. With the installation of a radical government and the defeat of the anti-Dreyfusard forces between 1899 and 1902 came a convergence of rightist forces with diverse origins— from Legitimism (support for a Bourbon monarchy), to Bonapartism, to moderate constitutionalism. The common values of these groups included antiparliamentarism, an overriding belief in force, a yearning for action, the primary value of authority, and respect for the notion of strong leaders. Adherents of these groups demanded not the political or social reforms requested by leftist groups but "intellectual reform" according to the views of Renan: moral and national regeneration. Their rhetoric denouncing the current "decadence" of national life and calling for "redemption" and "liberation" clearly reflected these views. The effect of this language and the intellectual appeal of this political tendency for university students, many of whom considered themselves romantic defenders of French "civilization," cannot be underestimated.

Thus, at the beginning of the twentieth century, the French patriotic movement presented itself with a modern ideological face and a fresh proposal for a nationalist society.

MAURICE BARRÈS (1862–1923) AND CHARLES MAURRAS (1868–1952)

Maurice Barrès aimed to provide nationalism with a new image. Like Charles Maurras and Italian Enrico Corradini, Barrès came to nationalism from literature. Between 1889 and 1892 he published three "ideological" novels, culminating in the three-volume *Le roman de l'énergie nationale* [The Romance of National Energy] (1897–1902). He strongly opposed Dreyfus and Dreyfus's champion Zola. In 1889 he successfully ran for a seat in Parliament on a populist program advocating the suppression of Parliament itself because of its supposed corruption and impotence.

The main points of Barrès's nationalism as they appeared at the dawn of the twentieth century are: approbation of individual and national energies; recognition that the personality of a Frenchman issues from a French "essence"; importance of tradition and of the connection to the native soil; conception of a nation as a tight-knit community having the will to work together. The fatherland, wrote Barrès in *Les Scènes et doctrines du nationalisme* [Scenes and Doctrines of Nationalism] (1902), resembles the individual in that it is the sum of a long history of effort, sacrifice, and loyalty. Our ancestors, who made us what we are, deserve respect—which means belief in our social, familial, and individual destiny. Barrès preached diffidence toward abstract intellectuals and "internal" enemies such as Freemasons, Jews, and half-breeds. He linked nationalism and economic protectionism, favoring not great industrialists but workers. He denounced capitalists as feudal financiers and great barons who crush the workers, and viewed big banking with its financial clout as a major threat for millions of human beings. In order to fight these forces, he advocated "modern corpora-tivism," a system of production linked to collective property. Without doubt, his nationalist outlook was that of rural France, tied to values of order and savings, but Barrès was also concerned with developing a polit-ical and ethical outlook that differed from those of liberalism and socialism.

Barrès's nationalism is imbued with the notions of *revanche* (revenge against Germany) and discipline. His lyricism in favor of the land and his reverence for dead ancestors reveal chauvinist intentions. Even though Barrès's view of the fatherland implied equality among its citizens, it did so to the detriment of foreigners. This fact may be discerned in his demands that the fatherland protect workers but exclude foreign workers from national work sites. However, the historically French character of Barrès's thought is also intimately linked to the French cultural milieu of the period, with writers such as Henri Bergson, who in works such as *Time and Free Will: An Essay on the Immediate Data of Free Will* (1889) announced such later, crucial concepts as "creative evolution."

Barrès formulated the idea of "organic nationalism," capable of rein-forcing patriotic sentiment and unifying the nation, with which his name is identified. He argued that national feeling outweighed individual rea-son and that the French people are the sole fount of French truth. Authoritarianism, anticapitalism, anti-Semitism, and romantic revolu-tionism also characterize Barrès's ideology, which should be considered in conjunction with the "integral nationalism" of Charles Maurras.

Maurras's "integral nationalism" conditioned the entire French right. His *Enquête sur la Monarchie* [Inquiry on the Monarchy] (1900–1909) and articles in the review *L'Action française* diffused in France the conception of a hierarchical society that respected traditional values. Unlike liberals and social democrats, Maurras attributed the decadence of France to for-eign intellectual influences and demanded a return to political stability based on a monarchical form of government. The core of Maurras's thought is founded on ethical and religious factors and on his anti-Semitic and anti-Protestant views. Peace and order, he believed, cannot be based on the electoral system, which, on the contrary, is always at the ori-gin of agitation and conflicts. Party politics are conducted by organiza-tions headed by egotistical minorities oblivious to French interests, and only by renouncing those politics can the country find tranquillity. Maurras made reference to the concept of a "Prince"—a king-dictator capable of resolving political and social issues and of responding to worker needs; this kind of monarchy could be imposed by force because of the masses' willingness to accept such methods in the name of the national interest. For Maurras, the "Prince" embodies national tradition and governs without being paralyzed by parliamentary coalitions. In short, the "Prince"—and only the "Prince"—could impose a truly national policy and reestablish peace for the French.

Maurras's most typical work, *Enquête sur la Monarchie,* aimed at the "national" transformation of France's political problems by achieving national reconciliation in the name of the country's "traditional liberties" and by means of the monarchical principle. He defended the ideal of association, identifying in the family the first "natural" association and the natural vehicle of a tradition based on morality. Behind this ethical concept, however, the idea of a "dictatorship" emerged. Already in place by 1899, Maurras's "dictatorship" ideologically opposed the "dictatorship of the proletariat" advocated by the Marxist parties. Maurras's "dictatorship" reconstituted the "natural" order by downgrading liberty, by increasing respect for authority, and by enhancing esteem for the fatherland.

Furthermore, turn-of-the-century nationalism, sporting rightist roots, also sought to develop an alternative model for society that was neither liberal nor socialist. In France this attempt failed owing to internal doctrinal contradictions. The romantic image of a harmonious and unified France during ancient times was clearly a historical abstraction, and its proponents lacked strong links to clear social groupings. Furthermore, both Barrès and Maurras belonged to a category of psychological malcontents whose paradoxical affirmations strongly resembled those of the German philosopher Friedrich Nietzsche or the Italian novelist-poet Gabriele D'Annunzio. These writers' concepts did not appeal to the masses, who could neither understand nor accept them.

In this crucial fact lay the difference between the French and the Italian political and social milieux. Italy was governed by a parliamentary monarchy, and Italian intellectuals were obsessed with the idea of a "betrayed" and "incomplete" *Risorgimento* (the movement for unification) and of a failed mission. Giovanni Giolitti, the most important politician between 1901 and 1915, governed the country sensibly and favored economic prosperity and the extension of political liberty. But the right hated him precisely because of his pragmatism and dreamed of moral renovation, grandeur, and a new political system.

ENRICO CORRADINI (1865–1931)

The primary exponent of these ideas was the Italian review *Il Regno,* founded in 1903 by the major nationalist spokesman Enrico Corradini.

Corradini, who published several novels on nationalist themes, thundered against democratic socialism, the bourgeoisie, and especially a government dominated by a spirit of concession and compromise. He condemned the "timid" policies supported by the bourgeoisie, the social democrats, and the governing liberals, insisting on greater unity for the nation and an aggressive expansionist policy designed to impart worth to Italian emigration. Italy had a civilizing function in the world, the nationalists argued, and this mission must proceed.

On December 3, 1910, Corradini organized a conference in Florence's Palazzo Vecchio that included speeches by other nationalist stalwarts on a variety of themes. The end of the conference witnessed the foundation of the Nationalist Association and of a weekly newspaper, the *Idea Nazionale* [National Idea]. In 1923 the nationalists joined the Fascist movement, which adopted many nationalist concepts, even though Corradini himself only had slight influence in that party.

The nationalist program as illustrated in *Idea Nazionale* called for the following: renewed emphasis on the genius and traditions of ancient Rome; liberation of Italian culture from foreign influence; reinvigoration of the state's authority against the centrifugal conduct of political parties; renewal of the monarchy's prestige; rededication of the Catholic Church as the premier state institution of national life; strengthening of the army as the instrument of national policy; reorientation of national energies toward colonial conquests; rejection of parliamentarism as the fount of continuing corruption; and a struggle against both socialist and Masonic internationalism—the one proletarian and the other bourgeois. These last two movements, the nationalists believed, especially threatened the nation.

As in the French case, in nationalist ideology the nation took on an authoritarian and hierarchical hue. The state had the task of seeing to the individual's well-being, and the individual had to conform to the demands of the nation as announced by a strong government ready to defend the national interests. In this way, everyday life became fused with a political system at the service of a nationalist government. As did French nationalists, Italian nationalists attacked both liberal and social democracy; and, like Barrès and Maurras, Corradini's political activity cannot be separated from his literary orientation. His novels, *La patria lontana* [The Faraway Fatherland] (1910) and *La guerra lontana* [The Faraway War] (1911), in addition to his other literary production, are particularly imbued with nationalist ideology and feeling. In a 1905 lecture on national life held in Rome, the patriotic affinities to Barrès and Maurras were striking. According to Corradini, "a nation is above all a common bond of generations following upon generations for the purpose of completing a mission across the centuries." Destroy the mission and you will destroy the nation's history, Corradini believed. For him, only nations are capable of making history (the action of individuals is "chronicle"), because history is a compendium of deeds of nations with respect to other nations' actions; national virility is the strength of will by which an entire people creates history.

In 1914 Corradini published a volume of his collected works summarizing his thought entitled *Il nazionalismo italiano* [Italian Nationalism]. He reiterated the antisocialist nature of nationalism and insisted on its social value. This merit flowed from nationalism's recognition that life had a collective value and that the nation is the major unit of collective life. Corradini then attributed to the nation the instincts of association and struggle; as a consequence, civilization without war is impossible. Therefore, the natural consequence of nationalism is imperialism, and morality is nothing more than another aspect of imperialism. Given these facts, the conditions of life for a nation are indissolubly linked to the circumstances of other nations. Likewise, Italy is a nation that depends economically and morally on other nations. It is therefore a "proletarian" nation that must redeem its independence. Just as socialism preaches that class consciousness will lead to redemption, so nationalism teaches that Italy must achieve a national consciousness to attain its just rights—economic prosperity, wealth, power, grandeur, and glory. While this struggle requires unity on the national plane, on the international front it imposes an alliance of the proletarian nations against the rich nations.

In Italy, Corradini charged, the liberals make policy; this role should shift to the nationalist movement, which would direct policy in opposition to both liberalism and socialism. Both socialism and liberalism are confusingly ambiguous—the first presents a liberal face and the second advocates social legislation. Nationalism, a "spiritual conception of human existence," avoids the ambiguity of both and moralizes public life in name of the sovereignty of the Italian people. Corradini denounced these movements as being capable of developing only governments lacking faith and idealism and corrupted by degenerate materialism. Nationalism's political program, on the other hand, aimed at the greatness of the fatherland through the national state. Corradini maintained that because the masses currently gave their votes to Catholics and Socialists, a national revolution was necessary to create a national state. This revolution must be made not for the individual (liberalism), or for the working class (socialism), but for Italy. Struggle, spirituality, and the national state were the watchwords with which nationalists hoped to reinvigorate politics, thought, and action.

Through Enrico Corradini, Italian nationalism succeeded in creating a new political language that remained in current use against liberalism and socialism for more than thirty years, as did its political program. Nationalist rhetoric dressed up its political conceptions so that they were extremely flexible and had broad appeal. On the one hand, nationalism was presented as a pseudoaristocratic doctrine, but on the other, it could be adapted to the tastes of the Italian petite bourgeoisie by claiming that it could complete the unfinished *Risorgimento* and attain the rights accruing to a "proletarian nation." In order to fulfill this mission, nationalists demanded a new ruling class worthy of setting the country's moral and social compass. For them, a national-social conception of the state must succeed the egoistic individualism of the corrupt, old, and impotent capitalistic bourgeoisie. The civil society longed for by nationalists inspired discipline, probity, patriotism, tradition, and obedience to the law. Some nationalists went further. Schooled in Nietzsche's ideas, they believed that this political renovation would be realized by an oligarchy of dominant persons. Before this time, Nietzsche had been considered a genius, but the implications of his thought were difficult to fathom; now his concepts such as the "superman" and "the will to power" were adapted by the nationalists for the purpose of rejuvenating the nation.

PART TWO

Age of the Masses

12

RUSSIAN COMMUNISM

The dominant tendencies on the right and left of the political spectrum outlined in the previous chapters played out during the twentieth century when mass politics came into their own. Within the socialist tradition, democrats hoped to wield the workers into an enormous electoral force capable of taking control of the parliamentary system and changing society through reforms. Emphasizing revolution rather than reforms or other aspects of the socialist tradition, revolutionary syndicalists called upon the workers to destroy the bourgeoisie's political power and destroy its authoritarian structures. The Russian Vladimir I. Lenin fought against both these tendencies, concentrating instead on the outlines of a communist society as advocated by Karl Marx.

VLADIMIR I. LENIN (1870–1924)

A convinced Marxist whose brother was executed for plotting to assassinate Tsar Alexander III, Lenin was arrested in 1895 and exiled to Siberia. Freed in 1900, he went to Switzerland and Germany, where in 1901, with other exiles, he founded a newspaper, *Iskra* [The Spark], with the goal of spreading Marxist doctrine in Russia and reorganizing and giving direction to the Russian social democratic workers' party founded at Minsk in 1898. Lenin had an intense intellectual and political life during the early years of the new century.

As a revolutionary he had put up with the personal defects of his comrades as persons persecuted for their political beliefs, but as a Marxist chieftain he criticized them for wasting their time splitting hairs rather than plotting the overthrow of tsarism and capitalism. His book *What Is to Be Done?* (1902) resulted from these ruminations. In this work Lenin asserted his faith in revolutionary and party action and expressed his intention to elaborate an organic plan to destroy capitalism and bourgeois society.

In Europe, Lenin acknowledged, a fierce battle raged between Bernstein's revisionist reformism and revolutionary socialism. In a series of writings, reformist thinkers and politicians had denied a host of fundamental Marxist precepts—increasing misery, the polarization of society, the class struggle, and the dictatorship of the proletariat. In most Western European countries, social democrats wanted the freedom to introduce bourgeois ideas and elements into socialism; Lenin accused them of opportunism. In France and Russia, for example, the political tendencies of reformism favored "economism," according to which workers must conduct an "economic," or "trade-unionist" struggle, which for Lenin was reducible to demands for small and insignificant reforms.

Lenin believed instead in the necessity of establishing a clear division line between bourgeois and proletarian ideology. Furthermore, there could be no mediation or third ideology, because in societies lacerated by the class struggle no ideology separate from classes existed. The more the proletariat did not understand this concept, the more bourgeois ideology was strengthened; thus supporters of the proletariat had to be intimately involved in creating a political consciousness among the workers and in denouncing the bourgeois "autocracy" in all its manifestations. How was this to be done?

Because of the greater complexity of the political struggle against capitalism—as compared to economic action—Lenin wrote that the working masses must be organized by professional revolutionaries. While the economic battle could be carried on through unions, the professionals had the difficult task of creating a powerful organization capable of overthrowing capitalism. Any worker capable of contributing to this task must not spend his time working in a factory but must devote his life to this paramount task at the party's expense. Lenin labeled as absurd the relegating of important questions to majority vote, as was done in unions. For a secret revolutionary group to entrust its future to this kind of primitive democracy would be simply naive. Puerile quibbling over democratic forms, characteristic of reformists, Lenin wrote, confused and split the workers, robbed scientific socialism of its revolutionary charge, and transformed parties from combative organizations into bureaucracies.

Lenin proposed several fundamental measures to restore Marxist militancy. First of all, eliminate trade unionism of the British type, founded on the absurd principles of voluntary association and elections, and create a new party organization guided by a small number of professional revolutionaries. Lenin suggested as a possible model the revolutionary organization of the Russian Zemlja i volja ("Land and Liberty" movement) of the 1870s, based on centralized conspiratorial methods. In short, the revolution could be brought about only by a proletariat directed by a highly structured party in an oligarchic manner. Lenin also took practical steps to implement his ideas. In London in 1903, at the Second Congress of the Russian Social Democratic Party, Lenin conducted his battle in favor of a strongly centralized party along the lines of *What Is to Be Done?* Leading the "Bolsheviks," he won the battle against the "Mensheviks," who opposed a centralized structure and advocated a gradual road to socialism. According to the thesis that came out of that conclave, the party would be the advance-guard and director of the great masses of the working classes.

Not comprehending the reasons for the dispute among revolutionary leaders, many Russians called for agreement in order to fight tsarism. The Menshevik leader I. O. Martov, however, accused Lenin of "Bonapartism," provoking a reply from Lenin on the party crisis. In this work, entitled *One Step Forward, Two Steps Back: The Crisis in Our Party* (1904), and in the Bolshevik newspaper, Lenin accused anyone who did not accept party discipline of being an anarchist and an ineffectual intellectual. It was the Russian Revolution of 1905, however, that stimulated Lenin to reflect not only on how to prepare a mass revolution but also, more important from a doctrinal viewpoint, how to structure a communist society.

According to Lenin, only armed insurrection could install the dictatorship of the proletariat. Only by means of this political instrument could the workers implement communism, the antithesis of bourgeois society. Marx had predicted that the dictatorship of the proletariat would not have been the dictatorship of a person but of an entire class; Lenin, however, accentuated the authoritarian aspects of this concept by emphasizing that in order to destroy the people's enemies, the dictatorship of the proletariat required unlimited power and had to be based on force and not law. In a work entitled *The State and Revolution* (1918), Lenin described the process of transformation of society from "bourgeois" to "proletarian." World War I had been raging for three years when he drafted the book, and a profound crisis gripped Russia. Tsar Nicholas II's abdication had not saved the monarchy and the Aleksandr Kerensky government had proved incapable of giving the country a "democratic" orientation after the March 1917 revolution (called the February Revolution, as Russia used the Old Style calendar at the time).

In *The State and Revolution* Lenin condemned the thesis propounded by reformists and bourgeois democrats that universal suffrage could express and implement the majority's will. No matter how much social democrats might argue against revolution, the substitution of the bourgeois state by the proletarian state could never be accomplished except through violent revolution. Whereas the proletarian state would eventually disappear on its own, the bourgeois state would not, and must be extinguished; state power was therefore necessary for the proletariat to eliminate bourgeois resistance. Lenin called upon the Bolsheviks to change their name to the "Communist Party"; through the dictatorship of the proletariat, this party would guide the passage from capitalism to "real socialism"—communism.

Lenin believed that only communism could produce true democracy, and he distinguished two phases on the march to communism: a first phase, when justice and equality could not yet be realized, and a second, "superior" phase, when the state would disappear as a consequence of the altered general economic conditions created by communism. Until the superior phase of communism had been achieved, socialists would impose the most rigorous discipline on labor and consumption by the state and society. This control would begin with the expropriation of capitalists and would be exercised not by state functionaries but by the armed workers. According to Lenin, the need to achieve democracy necessitated these measures, for the "democracy" praised by liberals and social democrats was merely a way station in the transformation of society from capitalism to communism. For these groups, democracy was just a formal construct; in order to achieve "real" equality, the bourgeois democratic system had to pass from bourgeois society to proletarian society—to communism.

On the doctrinal plane, therefore, Lenin broke completely with the social democrats who had dominated the Second International (1889–1914), rejecting Western-style parliamentary democracy and presenting communism as the only method for attaining a proletarian society.

THE BOLSHEVIK REVOLUTION

After the February Revolution of 1917, the Bolsheviks strengthened their position in the *soviets* (workers' councils). While the Mensheviks stumbled and debated whether the conditions for a socialist revolution existed, Lenin aimed to seize political power for the Bolsheviks and succeeded in the violent takeover in November 1917 (the October Revolution). At first the Bolsheviks had not opposed the Constituent Assembly, but elections for that body put them in a distinct minority. In January 1918 Lenin shut down the Assembly because, as the expression of bourgeois parliamentarism, it was incompatible with the dictatorship of the proletariat. The protest of Mensheviks and other socialist opponents of the Bolsheviks fizzled, and in February and March the Bolsheviks consolidated their position. At the Fourth Congress of the Soviets (March 1918), the Bolsheviks obtained an overwhelming majority. The Bolsheviks then proceeded to focus on their strategy, organization, and doctrinal position. The main documents outlining their decisions are the writings of Lenin, the Soviet constitutions of 1918 and 1923, and the 1925 party constitution.

In his writings of this period, Lenin consistently refers to Marxism interpreted primarily as "dialectical materialism"—the contradictions that exist in capitalist society are class conflicts between an exploiting bourgeoisie and an oppressed proletariat. With the Soviet revolution, the proletariat has assumed power and, according to Lenin, must impose its dictatorship. It is therefore necessary to reject any and all proposals of reformism and the doctrines of bourgeois social democracy, clarify the terms of Communist action and reinforce relationships between workers and peasants, prevent the formation within the new Soviet Union of opportunistic tendencies on the right and of extremist proclivities on the left, analyze proletarian tactics in the capitalist countries and in the colonial areas, and affirm the hegemony of the proletariat in theory and practice. According to Lenin, the adoption of the dialectical method could achieve all these aims. Based on history and social reality, this technique allowed activists to understand the process of historical transformation and to extract from concrete developments the solutions that would permit them to create the new Communist society.

Without doubt, the conflicts with opposing groups and the economic and political results of the civil war that followed the Communist seizure of power prompted Bolshevik leaders to intensify the process of political centralization, but Lenin's concept of all power to the party as a necessary instrument of the dictatorship of the proletariat was a primary stimulus. This view mandated that the party must first acquire state power for itself as the vanguard of the working class, and then win consensus in the country. By liquidating its opponents and through internal purges, the Bolshevik party concentrated power in an extreme manner. It removed all real authority from the soviets and rejected union requests to retain their independence. Since the Bolsheviks considered the separation of powers a bourgeois concept, the party created a centralized and hierarchical structure and affirmed itself as a supreme executive organ. In July 1918 the first revolutionary constitution, which disallowed the vote for the "exploiting classes," received approval; in this manner, an important part of the opposition was silenced.

In October 1919 Lenin wrote *The Proletarian Revolution and Kautsky the Renegade*, in which he claimed for the Bolshevik party the right to employ violence against the bourgeoisie and advocated Bolshevism as a tactical model that had validity in all countries. From late 1918 to May 1919 worker revolutions occurred in Germany, Austria, and Hungary, but their failure convinced Lenin that the Russian Bolshevik-Communist party must have a guiding function in the new Third International (Comintern), founded in March 1919.

Opposition developed to the excessive power concentrated in the party. Supporters of "democratic centralism" wished to avoid the increasing bureaucratization of the party apparatus and requested that constructive criticism be allowed. The "workers' opposition" group proposed union election of a coordinating body that would improve the economy and increase production; recalling Marx and Engels's *Manifesto*, Aleksandra Kollontai demanded autonomy for the working masses. This political opposition was liquidated, and in 1921 force was required to put down a mutiny of sailors at the Kronshtadt base. The rebels demanded freedom of expression and of the press, freedom of association for the soviets, and the secret ballot in the election of leaders.

Lenin justified his authoritarian line with the argument that permitting the formation of groups with their own political platforms signified creating factions that threatened party unity. Anarchists, socialist revolutionaries, petits bourgeois, and counterrevolutionaries stimulated the opposition. The Bolshevik party—the true Communist party—was the sole party of the working class and as such had the task of educating the advanced guard of the proletariat and of organizing the working masses. Unions no longer had their traditional function of defending workers from capitalist exploitation, but had to be the "transmission belt" between the party and the working masses.

In *"Left-Wing" Communism: An Infantile Disorder,* drafted in April 1920, Lenin attacked leftist revolutionaries who objected to a centralized party structure. Absolute centralization and the most severe discipline were essential conditions for the definitive victory of the proletariat. A truly revolutionary party delegated the leadership to a few authoritative persons. To distinguish between the dictatorship of the party and the dictatorship of the proletariat was absurd and ridiculous—the manifestation of ideological confusion and a petit-bourgeois revolutionary mentality. The crucial point was to make the Bolshevik party secure at the helm of the movement to destroy capitalism and to recognize the Soviet system as the revolutionary model for all countries, advanced or backward. For Lenin, Russian historical experience taught that working-class unity was essential for revolution; allowing the formation of political currents in the proletarian bosom meant to permit backward groups of workers to cave in to the wiles of so-called socialists, in reality petit-bourgeois forces, who nurtured counterrevolutionary projects.

EMERGENCE OF THE ONE-PARTY STATE

Once the external opposition of the capitalist powers had been defeated, the Bolshevik party had the task of building the socialist state. Only a single Communist party, which must become the organization of all the workers, could accomplish this assignment, not a majority organization. In the process, the Communist party of the workers had to destroy the old social order and create a new one. Thus whereas the democratic bourgeoisie talked about "liberty and equality," Communists would resort to an iron discipline and a rigorous regime to allow the proletariat to prevail (Ninth Congress of the Communist Party, March 29–April 5, 1920).

Engaged in the construction of the new socialist state, the Communist party could hardly tolerate anarchist or unionist deviations internally, because party unity must prevail (Tenth Congress of the Communist Party, March 8–16, 1921). This view justified the purge of the Communist party itself, which must remain the advanced guard of the working class and eliminate "Menshevik" opportunists ensconced in Bolshevik party ranks and who temporarily adapted to the Leninist line. Party policy could be discussed, but without sanctioning the creation of factions, which threatened the organization's unity. Criticism must not be allowed to develop into opposition and deviation. Ironically enough, after the end of World War I and the Civil War, disastrous economic conditions induced the Soviet government to make concessions on the land and also to small and medium industry. But this New Economic Policy (NEP) induced Lenin and other Bolshevik leaders to concentrate political power in their hands to an even greater degree precisely because the economic adjustments went counter to the Bolshevik program and had to be accepted out of necessity. This further concentration of political hegemony completely invested the party, resulting in the condemnation of all factions and the affirmation of the monolithic principle. Lenin declared that the party dictatorship was fully justified because the party was the advanced guard of the proletariat and represented the most progressive elements of society. In fact, the dictatorship of the proletariat could be exercised *only* through the Bolshevik Communist party.

The same principle imposed the idea that the Bolshevik party be the "hegemonic" party precisely because it must move the proletariat in new political, economic, and social directions. As a consequence, the Bolshevik party rapidly chose new political cadres, mobilized the masses, directed the economy, and assumed legislative power. This assumption of absolute power soon culminated in the destruction of all forms of pluralism and dissent. For the first time in the history of political systems, this event gave birth to a single party as a form of government—a development soon to be imitated for its originality in other European countries.

The idea of a single, unified party in which different viewpoints could be expressed in the executive organs without giving rise to factions, and in which divergent opinions could be overcome either by assimilation of the minority or through the application of party discipline in the name of the superior interest of the working class, had a great attraction that originated in the hypothesis of a new social harmony. This outlook guided the organization of the Communist party. The Executive Committee possessed the instruments and force to control central Soviet activities and public authorities. A political office (the Politburo) was established within the Executive Committee to direct political affairs, but the party's command center was the Secretariat, the true decisionmaking organ of the Executive Committee and Politburo. Local party organs took orders from the Executive Committee. With its vast organization, the party combined political, economic, and social functions. As the true helmsman of the state, the party imposed its authority over every institution, regulating the lives of all citizens. Its legitimacy derived from the need to construct a political domination powerful enough to create the dictatorship of the proletariat and to defeat counterrevolution. The serious internal and external threats to its existence eased the party's tendency toward centralization and its transformation from a dominant party within the political order as it remained in 1918 into a single party ruling that system.

The most powerful control organism, the Workers' and Peasants' Inspection Commission, established in 1919, was headed by Joseph Stalin. During the Eleventh Party Congress in March 1922, a participant, E. A. Preobazenskii, observed that Stalin had concentrated too much power in his hands, directing as well the Nationalities Commission, but Lenin replied that Stalin was the best man for both jobs. In April of the same year, Stalin was also nominated secretary-general of the Central Committee, but this time, Leon Trotsky leveled a series of criticisms at him. At that point, Lenin wrote directly to Stalin that Trotsky could not forget his old divergences with Bolshevism. Lenin thus acknowledged Stalin as a true Bolshevik and, quite consistently, entrusted him with the party's direction.

STALINISM AND ITS CRITICS

In 1923, sick and exhausted, Lenin modified his judgment and criticized Stalin, but by then Stalin had established an independent power base. Despite an aversion for the past, the autocratic tradition weighed heavily on the Bolshevik mentality—the affirmation of a leader who violently eliminates all internal opposition. Stalin combined in himself the single-party system and autocratic government. In his four years of power, Lenin had many theoretical and political disputes with party leaders, but he had always been respectful toward them and had recognized their good faith and their intellectual prowess; and even while aiming at party unity, Lenin had retained his dialectical mentality. On the other hand, Stalin wielded power autocratically. After Lenin died, a "troika" composed of Stalin, Lev Borisovich Kamenev, and Grigory Yevseyevich Zinoviev attacked Trotsky. Zinoviev, speaking in the name of the tried-and-true Bolsheviks, contrasted "Leninism" and "Trotskyism." According to Zinoviev, Leninist doctrine was the best means to combat the leftist "pseudo-Marxism" of both Trotskyists and Mensheviks. In *Leninism or Trotskyism* (1925), Zinoviev defined Lenin's ideology as the modern Marxism of the movements of national liberation and of proletarian revolution against the imperialism of monopoly capitalism. Later, however, when Zinoviev and Kamenev criticized Stalin's doctrine of building "socialism in one country," it was Stalin who presented himself as the loyal interpreter of Lenin's thought with his *Foundations of Leninism* (1924) and especially his *Problems of Leninism* (1926).

In his writings Stalin attempted to express his ideas in a clear and incisive manner. Rather than introduce many variables into his thought, Stalin made affirmations, returned to them, repeated them, developed his theses, and, finally, summarized his arguments in simple formulas appropriate to the ideological and cultural standing of the party apparatus. Stalin maintained that the party with its "hegemony" constituted a reference point because communism would be implemented by the Bolshevik party, understood as the party of the working class, to which the proletariat was profoundly devoted because of its intuitive qualities. In *Problems of Leninism,* Stalin justified the single party's power and rejected the idea of factions; he believed that while the dictatorship of the proletariat without doubt represented a concept much wider in scope and of an incomparably greater cultural richness than the directing function of the party, nonetheless, it was the party (and no other) that implemented the dictatorship of the proletariat. Of course there were accusations against the so-called "dictatorship of party leaders," but the very function of the party—oarsman of the proletariat—necessitated delegating to some party leaders the task of finding a way of destroying world capitalism. Given the supremacy of the single-party concept, the party leadership acted as an authentic government, its legitimacy deriving from the relationship between party and working class.

According to Stalin, Trotskyism, representative of bourgeois democratic nostalgia, endangered this intimate relationship between class and party that was the basis of Bolshevik Leninism. Not believing in the party's Bolshevik spirit, Trotskyism would allow the infiltration of opportunists into the party's monolithic structure. In order to fight this tendency, the Soviet Union must remain faithful to the Bolshevik-Leninist tradition, and all the world's Communist parties, in order to remain loyal to the same tradition, must adopt the Soviet organizational model.

Stalin's views provoked an inarticulate and ill-defined malaise within the Bolshevik party, prompting Stalin to resort to internal purges. He defined this cleansing as a law of development necessary for the prevention of deviations. In the 1930s Stalin decreed the infallibility of the party, which had brought about the revolution, but he claimed for himself the right to liquidate all opposition because it endangered the social gains achieved by the working class.

The literature of political science in the nineteenth century had distinguished between states as juridical entities and as governments. Contesting the bourgeoisie's monopoly of public affairs, Marxists had insisted—particularly after the Paris Commune of 1871—that the self-government of a society without classes would have produced the state's demise. This hypothesis became ever blander in Soviet doctrinal formulations, being postponed until the end of capitalist encirclement of the USSR. But with the establishment of a one-party political system and the affirmation of an indisputable guiding role for the party leader, the concept of the state took on a different significance. The state was no longer the center of economics, culture, or politics; the tasks associated with these activities now belonged to the party, which did not allow other institutions the right to engage in similar activities. The centralized and infallible party interpreted and represented the state, and it was no longer possible to distinguish between party and state apparatus: The power of the Communist party manifested itself as the power of the Soviet state. The idea that whereas Lenin had put the party at the center, Stalin put the centralized state there is a very debatable one; Stalin gave party policy the value of state decisions precisely because he needed to resolve the difficult problems created by Lenin's new order.

Given the autocratic position achieved by the party secretary in the Soviet system, the doctrinal opposition that appeared within Communism is easily understood. Leon Trotsky theorized internal democracy within the one-party state. His divergence with Stalin revolved around this central theme of "proletarian democracy," in which Trotsky criticized the bureaucratization of the party apparatus, the isolation from the masses, the lack of internal discussion, the inability to internationalize the revolution, and the snail's pace of industrialization. Against Stalin's theory of "socialism in only one country," imposed with an iron fist, Trotsky counterposed the "permanent revolution"; this concept viewed the revolution as beginning in one country but developing internationally and culminating worldwide.

Against "Trotskyism," Stalin and his supporters opposed what they called "Leninism," the supposed response of orthodox Communism to "bourgeois deviationism." The struggle culminated after 1927, with Trotsky's dismissal from the Third International's Executive Committee, his expulsion from the party, and in 1929 his banishment from the Soviet Union. In exile, a heretic, polemicizing with Stalin and his tyrannical form of government, Trotsky rethought Marxist doctrine and Soviet events. Three works emerged from this contemplation: *The Permanent Revolution* (1929–1930), *The History of the Russian Revolution* (1929–1932), and *The*

Revolution Betrayed: What Is the Soviet Union and Where Is It Going? (1937). Trotsky's fundamental theses in these works were that the road to communism imposed by Stalin on the Soviet Union did not lead to the construction of socialism; Soviet bureaucracy aimed only at becoming a dominant caste in order to ensure its wide privileges; and Stalin's repressive regime was transitory because it would be overthrown by the revolutionary proletariat, which would restore the true democracy of the soviets. In order to achieve these goals, Trotsky favored the establishment of a "fourth International," composed of revolutionary Communist parties, doing battle against the "Stalinized" Communist parties and the "bourgeois" social democratic organizations.

Opposition to Stalin's autocratic rule also stimulated communists to take their distance from official orthodox doctrine and sometimes to abandon Marxism completely. This was the case for Karl Korsch (1886–1961), author of a penetrating study entitled *Marxism and Philosophy* (1923). Expelled from the German Communist party and the Third International, Korsch continued to study Marx and to launch attacks on Kautsky's thought, but he eventually dissociated himself from Marxism. Other prominent communists accepted their condemnation by Communist officialdom but remained in the movement and hoped for a renewal of the Soviet regime. Typical of this group was the case of a Hungarian communist, György Lukács, author of *History and Class Consciousness: Studies in Marxist Dialectics* (1923). Despite the criticism leveled against him, Lukács agreed to work in Moscow, studying Lenin's Marxism and developing his own proposals for increased democracy.

The case of the Italian Antonio Gramsci (1891–1937) is completely atypical. From the beginning, Gramsci viewed the Bolshevik Revolution not so much as the work of a highly organized minority gathered into a party, but as a mass revolution made by the soviets. In the soviets—instruments of proletarian direct democracy—not only communists but also anarchists, reformists, and populists could participate in meetings and thus be represented; but the Bolshevik party, an organization devoted to action, could not renounce its hegemony, because it defended the general interests of the proletariat. Proletarian democracy, not bourgeois democracy, was true democracy, and proletarian democracy would be realized through new institutions such as the workers' councils in the factories. For Gramsci, the Soviet system aimed at implementing the active and permanent participation of workers in the life of their own institutions. But did Gramsci always remain faithful to these interpretations after 1926?

Born in Ales, near Cagliari (Sardinia), and living in the industrialized city of Turin, Gramsci was very familiar with the dual social aspect of his native Italy—the backward peasant countryside and the "industrial triangle" of the workers. He was profoundly influenced by Lenin and believed it possible to adapt Lenin's strategy to the Italian peninsula. After the foundation of the Italian Communist Party in 1921, Gramsci argued for its organization along the lines of the Bolshevik party, but after the advent of Fascism, he did not exclude the possibility of an alliance with Italian democratic forces, rejecting the Stalinist accusation that the Socialists were really "Social-fascists." In this view, which ultimately sought to conform communism to Italy, lay the seeds of a philosophy that differed from the prevailing Stalinism and had great attraction for Western communists after World War II.

Imbued with an antipositivist culture, Gramsci criticized the rigid materialism of the Bolsheviks, which derived from too heavy an emphasis on economic determinism. Gramsci believed that a revolution depended on ideas and will, expressed not by individuals but by a party that exercised its "hegemony" over the masses and coordinated all the political and social forces fighting against Fascism. His work, *La costruzione del partito comunista, 1923–1926* [The Building of the Communist Party, 1923–1926], contains his reflections in the years preceding his arrest in November 1926. Gramsci argued that the Communist parties had a directing function, but also an educational one. In order to fulfill these duties, the Communist parties needed the support of intellectuals who wished to construct a "new order."

The nature of the Communist party's primacy was what allowed Gramsci to believe in an understanding between Communists and Italian anti-Fascist forces and in a Western road to communism. Western industrial development and capitalistic institutions demanded a more prudent and complex strategy than that adopted in the Eastern world of 1917 Russia by the Bolsheviks. Because of its moral and idealistic force, the Italian Communist Party was capable of gathering around itself important allies in the anti-Fascist struggle and of assuming a directing role in preparation for the revolution; the party, in short, could be the guide in a "war of position" against capitalism. Furthermore, according to Gramsci, the Communist party was "the modern Prince," whose task was to assume its place in the consciousness of the people with the ultimate aim of destroying opposing organizations and of incorporating those with similar goals. Indeed, the thoughts contained in his *Prison Notebooks* (1948–1951, published after his death) are an amplification of these considerations—intense dialogues with the culture of Italian civil society, especially with Benedetto Croce's philosophy, in order to justify the Italian Communist Party's political line and to confirm the validity of his own reflections. The authority of the party must be linked with civil society in order to build a new form of social government different from the Soviet regime's bureaucratic orientation.

But while Gramsci dreamed in prison of a democratic socialism, Stalin tried and executed many old-guard Bolsheviks and Communists of all standings. The history of the Stalinist purges is well known; but the death sentences of members of the executive organs of the party such as Zinoviev, Kamenev, and Bukharin, for the purpose of eliminating all opposition to Stalin's power, demonstrated how the Bolshevik one-party system had evolved into a brutal and despotic government.

13

ITALIAN FASCISM

Whereas the Bolshevik party was born from a preexisting organization, the Fascist organization emerged from a movement, which was known as the Fasci di combattimento (Combat Groups) following World War I, in Milan, on March 23, 1919. This movement, led by Benito Mussolini, issued a polemical program against parties, representative democracy, and the system of parliamentary coalitions. Mussolini's newspaper, *Il Popolo d'Italia* [The People of Italy] conducted the movement's political propaganda. In the first postwar elections, held in 1919, the Fascists proved unable to elect any representatives to the Chamber of Deputies. Altering their electoral policy for the elections of May 1921, the Fascists joined an electoral alliance known as the "National Bloc," led by Giovanni Giolitti, the most prominent prewar politician. This list obtained 105 seats, which left the Fascists a distinct minority but well organized and anxious to maintain good relationships with deputies who had similar views on government.

THE ROAD TO POWER

At their Third Congress in November 1921, the Fascists—whose members had by now increased from some tens of thousands to over 200,000—transformed their "movement" into a party. Adopting the party model of their Socialist rivals, the Fascists established a central committee, composed of twenty-one members, flanked by a national council. The year 1921, therefore, witnessed in Italy the foundation of both the National Fascist Party (PNF) and the Italian Communist Party (PCI), both of which emerged from the troubled postwar climate.

Rather than elaborating its doctrine and defining its goals, the new Fascist party concentrated on organizing its members and coordinating its local organizations according to military principles dear to the veterans proud of their participation in the victorious war. Accordingly, the party received a hierarchical organization, with its members enrolled as members of combat squads. By 1922 the Fascists were already discussing how to organize the youth (Avanguardia giovanile fascista, from fifteen to eighteen years of age, Balilla, from ten to fifteen) and Fascist workers (Confederazione nazionale delle corporazioni).

At the head of this organization stood Benito Mussolini, called *Il Duce* (The Leader). On October 28, 1922, Mussolini guided the "March on Rome" and, as a result, received from King Victor Emmanuel III a mandate to form a government. Mussolini's government included not only Fascists but also Catholics, Liberals, Democratic Socialists, Nationalists, and two members who represented the armed forces. Although a majority of the Chamber of Deputies was composed of non-Fascists, the cabinet won a vote of confidence in Parliament.

Mussolini also obtained full powers, allowing him to claim a legal basis for all his government's actions. In this manner, the Italian Parliament exorcised the fear of communism created by the "Red Biennium" (1919–1921, when contemporaries believed that Italy was at risk for a communist revolution) and the power vacuum that resulted from political instability. Many non-Fascist deputies, convinced that Mussolini could restore stability and social harmony, voted for him, giving his government a majority despite the small number of Fascist deputies; indeed, many believed that they could vote him out of office whenever they pleased. Despite the violence perpetrated by the squads, Liberals, Radicals, and Catholics lent political legitimacy to the "March on Rome," defined by Fascists as a "revolution."

In this new political situation in which he headed the government, Mussolini felt the need to blunt the obvious illegality of the squads; hence they were transformed into the Voluntary Militia for National Security (MVSN), whose task was to defend the "political revolution" that had occurred on October 28. Il Duce assumed complete power over the party, and the organization's secretary-general was to be his closest collaborator.

This "revolution" did not alter Italy's institutional structure, but it did modify its parliamentary system, especially after March 1923, when the Nationalists entered the Fascist party. In January, Fascism's Duce, having become head of the government, had circulated a memo to the prefects, reminding them that the Fascist party had attained the position of a "dominant party." But this "dominant party" did not have command of a majority in the Chamber of Deputies. A new electoral law (the "Acerbo Law," for its author, Giacomo Acerbo) proposed giving two-thirds of the seats in the Chamber of Deputies to the electoral list that won the most votes (provided it received at least 25 percent of the total vote). After the elections of April 1924, the "Big List," prepared by the Fascist National

Council and including representatives of the moderate right, obtained an absolute majority; thus the Fascist party became the truly dominant party in a system that was still theoretically a multiparty system, and the political leadership passed from Parliament to the Fascists.

At the time, some constitutionalists remarked that the nation had gone from a multiparty democratic system to a parliamentary system of the British type—even if violence had been employed to accomplish the change. In a multiparty system of the kind that had existed in pre-Fascist Italy, the argument went, many parties agreed to form a government majority by means of ambiguous compromises that broke down when the first difficulties arose. In addition, because of the fluctuating nature of the majority, the executive power is conditioned by the decisions of political groupings. In a two-party system of the English type, in contrast, a party that has an absolute majority governs, while the opposition has the important function of checking on and criticizing government activity. This concept helps explain the support that Fascists received from non-Fascists, who argued that their support would actually help Italian parliamentary institutions to function more efficiently.

FROM DOMINANT TO SINGLE PARTY

But this "dominant party" worked to become a "single party." Fascists argued that if Fascism was a reaction against routine parliamentary politics and government by shifting combinations of parties and groups, the antiparliamentary "revolution" must continue. Since Mussolini was "party dictator," as the review *Critica Fascista* [Fascist Criticism] maintained, Fascism had both governmental and party functions. And, in fact, a series of decrees between December 1925 and November 1926 dissolved democratic parties and associations, liquidating the opposition and making the Fascist party the sole legal party. The next step was to give political direction to this organization. Mussolini stated that the Fascist party was "his" party and thus depended on the head of the government. The party's task was to create Fascists, but because Il Duce was both head of the government and head of the party, it also had to support Mussolini's cultural propaganda and his governmental action.

With regard to party doctrine, Mussolini had frequently affirmed that Fascism, stimulated by a need for action, had no specific doctrine. He maintained that Fascism was a movement of "combatants and producers"—two very generic terms. The condition of "combatant" was confusingly applied to everyone who had participated in the war and who hoped to achieve a better future; but the demands of ordinary soldiers and officers hardly coincided. Even the term "producer" was ambiguous because it was unclear whether it referred to the "producer" in an agricultural or industrial sense, or whether it meant the worker or the employer. In reality, with regard to his idea of "political action," Mussolini aimed more than anything at "popular consensus," that is, the consensus of "the people of Italy"—the title of his newspaper. He attempted to achieve this consensus by means of mass demonstrations, generous promises of government help, and appeals to national values. Mussolini also was skilled at exploiting the specter of disorder, civil war, and the Bolshevik peril. Most important, however, once he had created for himself the image of the leader who is above all devoted to the good of the nation, he employed his considerable capacity for communication along the lines spelled out by Gustave Le Bon in his *Psychologie des foules* [Psychology of the Crowd] (Paris, 1895).

The Fascist party pompously claimed a "Roman" heritage, adopting the trappings and symbols of ancient Rome. Mussolini was the *dux*, that is, the Roman general who led the militia and its legions; the fasces (a bundle of rods, the ancient symbol of authority) was Roman, as was the Fascist salute. A well-orchestrated rhetoric affirmed that Italy had been reborn in a new political and moral life inspired by the tradition of Roman civilization. The Fascist mission was supposedly a civilizing mission, as had been that of Rome; the Mediterranean was *"mare nostrum"* [our sea], and colonial pretensions were justified in memory of the conquests of the Roman Empire, which, after centuries, would rise once again on Rome's historic hills.

Fascism also considered itself a moral crusade. Since the Kingdom of Italy's constitution had not been modified, Fascism was nothing more than the political expression of a party that claimed to have made a revolution. Fascism fought socialism, democracy, and liberalism, but this battle must be fought not by the government but by the party that had custody of the nation's faith. According to the party, the "Fascist revolution" must penetrate in the spirit and consciousness of the people and, by transforming its way of conceiving life and the world, transform civilization. But what exactly was the doctrinal content of this party?

Leaving aside the negative aspects of the movement's ethics and politics, Fascism was a political system that possessed values, rules, and myths that were necessary to distinguish it from other movements. Historical analysis reveals the contradictory and unsystematic nature of Fascist ideology, but that does not mean that Fascism lacked its own thought system, distinct from other contemporary ideologies.

In its October 1926 constitution, the party affirmed that the Fascists comprised a militia in the nation's service that aimed at realizing the Italian people's greatness. The party had fundamental and indispensable functions: to educate the people, to direct the young in establishing the fatherland's greatness, and to indicate what were the moral tasks of good citizens. In order to achieve these aims, the party asked its members to believe, trust, and obey Il Duce's orders. As Fascist party head, Il Duce named the party secretary and approved the nomination of the hierarchs who constituted the party's National Council.

It has been observed that after 1926 a process ensued that reduced the party's role to a choreographic direction of the masses. In fact, however, Mussolini, uncontested party head, decided to transform the party secretary into his own personal secretary after he had expelled Roberto Farinacci from the office in March of that year. From then on, the secretary was prohibited from taking any command decisions, which power belonged exclusively to Mussolini. This "depoliticization" implemented by the new secretary, Augusto Turati, however, did not alter the party's political function within Italy's constitutional structure.

Historian Renzo De Felice, in his *Mussolini il fascista: Organizzazione dello Stato fascista, 1925–1929* [Mussolini the Fascist: Organizing the Fascist State, 1925–1929] (vol. 2, 1968), argued that, although for "classic" totalitarian regimes such as the Soviet Union and Nazi Germany the party was the foundation stone of the regime, for Mussolini the party had to be completely subordinated to the state and integrated into the regime with essentially secondary functions. In other words, not only did Mussolini nurture a personal distrust of the party, but he decided to strengthen the state and sacrifice the party to it. However, De Felice forgets that all the constitutional law manuals of the period emphasize that Mussolini was head of government and Victor Emmanuel III head of state. Everything was subordinated to the state, but a state conditioned by the Fascist party, the only legal party, and an organization headed by Mussolini. The novel aspect of the Fascist regime was its elimination of the multiparty system; the fact that different tendencies attempted to make the PNF into a modern mass movement within the state's framework is a different matter.

In order to bolster his thesis, De Felice cited a memo that Mussolini circulated to the prefects, dated January 5, 1927, in which he defined the duties of the "Fascist prefect" and his relationship with provincial PNF representatives. But this text called the prefect the "highest representative" of the Fascist regime who had the task of stimulating and harmonizing party activities. This meant that the prefect, because he was named by the Fascist government, must be considered a party member (even if he came from the bureaucracy) who embodied the central power; that is why local authorities must collaborate with him. In brief, Mussolini was worried that local Fascist party bosses might take decisions contrary to policies decided in Rome. The government's trust went to the prefect precisely because he was the highest local authority and directly represented the central government; the memo, therefore, serves as a monument to the centralizing and authoritarian nature of the Fascist government.

In January 1926 Mussolini received the power to issue laws; but the head of the government was also the head of the Fascist party, so, as Gaetano Mosca pointed out, his power no longer derived from Parliament but from his party's force. It should be recalled as well that, from that viewpoint, nonmembership in the Fascist party constituted a reason for possible exclusion from professional and administrative careers. This measure was implemented by Alfredo Rocco, a former Nationalist, who also drafted the public security law and a statute that made the Fascist Grand Council part of the constitutional structure; these steps concentrated all power in the executive and created a bureaucratic police state. Thanks to Rocco, Fascism built its own juridical structure and transformed the parliamentary system and the division of powers into an authoritarian government.

FASCISM AND IDEOLOGY

In contrast to action, the ambiguity of Fascist doctrine allowed the emergence of three diverse political theses; this fact gave Fascism a confusing outlook on the one hand, but a range of interesting interpretations of political and social reality on the other.

Nationalist jurists, especially Alfredo Rocco (1875–1935), contributed the first ideological design. Nationalist programmatic points were first spelled out in a manifesto published in the journal *Politica* [Politics], edited by Rocco and Francesco Coppola, on December 15, 1918. The document summarized the Nationalist program in the following points: negation of individualistic liberalism and egalitarian ideologies; reaffirmation of the state as a powerful force; the production by both liberalism and democracy of decadence, due to their dismantling the social hierarchy; and creation of a government of the elect to implement the great historical interests of the state. After they joined the Fascist party in 1923, the Nationalists injected these "juridical-constitutional" principles into the PNF's ideological structure.

Corradini's Nationalists had insisted on the importance of national unity, with the nation considered an ethical organism, and they had fought against parties—such as the Socialist—that, they claimed, negated national sentiment. Now Nationalists such as Coppola and Luigi Federzoni believed that the "Italy of the Future" could resolve the country's crisis through the "Fascist revolution." Nationalists agreed on the need to strengthen the state through "institutional reforms." Rocco, for example, believed that the liberal state was no longer capable of managing governmental power or the class conflicts that exploded after the end of World War I. From this idea issued the urgency of an authoritative leadership for the country.

In 1926 Rocco explained his doctrine of Fascism during a speech at Perugia that was approved by Mussolini and published in English by the American journal *International Conciliation*. Rocco rejected liberalism because individualism produced democracy, democracy popular sovereignty, popular sovereignty socialism, and socialism dictatorial bolshevism. For Rocco, therefore, democracy and socialism were political systems that derived from each other. The real antithesis to liberalism-democracy-socialism was Fascism, which refused to give power to the multitudes, in order to protect national interest and state authority. This reasoning left, as the only possible alternative, executive power concentrated in the hands of a powerful government leader capable of affirming state authority in all phases of national life.

Of equal importance was the ethical-cultural interpretation of Fascism as based on the national heredity of the *Risorgimento* and the liberal tradition of Cavour and his successors. This explanation was favored by philosophers, professors, and historians but is primarily linked with the name of Giovanni Gentile, an eminent pre-Fascist philosopher who attempted to give Fascism an idealistic foundation. In a March 8, 1925, lecture, Gentile discussed the reawakening of Italian national consciousness in the late eighteenth and the nineteenth centuries and talked about the "Fascist return" to the spirit of the *Risorgimento*. In his view, Fascism had "shaken the conscience" of Italians because it was a spiritual movement that corresponded to the deepest needs of the new Italy. The next day in Bologna, in a discussion of Neapolitan Hegelianism, Gentile stated that no other liberalism is conceivable but that of "liberty which organizes itself in the state." In this manner, true liberty, which is that held by people who feel the power of the ideal of the fatherland, replaces "egotistical liberty." Gentile returned frequently to this theme of a link between the Italian liberal tradition and Fascism. In his interpretation, Fascism had no need to define its doctrine and could not even be identified with the Fascist party, because Fascism was a life ideal. (*Che cosa è il fascismo? Discorsi e polemiche* [What Is Fascism? Speeches and Polemics], 1925).

Gentile proposed the thesis of a Fascist party that became ever more identified with the state in his publication of the Italian Encyclopedia (*Enciclopedia italiana*). This truly national work, born of Gentile's "strong Fascist faith," remained open to all Italians capable of making an important cultural contribution. The entry "Fascism," in volume 14 of the *Enciclopedia*, contains a strong doctrinal enunciation of Fascism as a spiritual movement animated by an ethical conception. According to this concept, Fascism gives great value to tradition and opposes "Jacobin" innovations; Fascism defends the concept of a nation, which is an "ethical reality." Fascism therefore not only rules the nation but also educates and promotes the life of the spirit.

A third interpretation of Fascism coexisted with those already discussed. Ever since Fascism's foundation, Mussolini had talked about corporativist unions that would allow the movement to supersede both socialism and liberalism. Those union leaders who sympathized with Fascism after 1922 were particularly attracted to corporativism, a major theme of Fascist ideology. (Corporativism may be defined as giving paramount attention to workers' economic interests and their organization according to economic sectors.) They envisioned a corporativist economy in which employers would leave aside their own egotistical concerns, consider workers as essential elements of production, and work in their interest. This antibourgeois sentiment, based on the principles of the revolutionary syndicalism of Georges Sorel, Filippo Corridoni, and others, wished to affirm not only the principle of state intervention in the economy but also an open governmental defense of worker interests.

This strand, known as "left Fascism"—represented by Edmondo Rossoni, Sergio Panunzio, Giuseppe Bottai, and Ugo Spirito—proposed an antibourgeois and anticapitalist Fascist government and sparked a debate on the themes of unemployment and a progressive role for Fascism. This doctrinal position was held only by a minority in the movement but was kept alive by intellectuals who observed with interest Soviet state planning and American attempts to combat the Great Depression. In 1933 Ugo Spirito published *Capitalismo e corporativismo* [Capitalism and Corporativism] (1933), a book that discussed the "crisis of capitalism" and praised corporativist economic planning. Spirito proposed to weld together the firm, the union, the Fascist corporation, and the state; according to him, capital should pass from shareholders to workers, who would then become proprietors of the "corporation" in proportion to their hierarchical position in the new entity. The important issue for him was to create worker unity through the mechanism of co-ownership of industrial concerns. The corporativists believed in a new state that would emphasize social issues, be original in substance and spirit, and defeat bureaucratic conservatism and capitalism.

Despite the existence of three major ideological themes, the PNF remained the only tool capable of coordinating national life. After 1929 the Fascist party had a recognized constitutional position in the state. According to Fascist jurists, the head of the party determined governmental policy, imparting unity to the country. But the overwhelming characteristic of the Fascist single-party state was the special relationship between the party itself and Il Duce, head of the Fascist party and of the government.

Fascism remained a political system characterized by a single party and by an authoritarian government, because preexisting centers of power that conditioned the dictatorship still functioned. In fact, Mussolini was forced to negotiate with numerous groups (e.g., industrialists, major landowners, etc.) within a constitutional context. Hannah Arendt noted in her famous study of totalitarianism that although Mussolini loved to use the term, he never attempted to install a full-fledged totalitarian regime. While he contented himself with a one-party authoritarian regime, it was Adolf Hitler who installed a real totalitarian government.

14

GERMAN NAZISM

It has been observed that with the fall of the German Empire the doctrine underpinning the German state disappeared because the kaiser represented the German "imperium." From its foundation in 1871, Germany had recognized in the Crown the concrete foundation of state authority. Paul Laband, in the first volume of his *Das Staatsrecht des deutschen Reiches* [The Public Law of the German Empire] (1876–1882), pointed to the imperial constitution as the legal basis of the Reich; the state as a juridical person had behind it the physical person of the emperor, who, in his turn, represented the German people. In this way state power operated through the kaiser and the state apparatus he directed. In the postwar political context, which legal authority was capable of restoring moral force to the state, in whose name Bismarck had given national unity to Germany?

Many observers believed that Parliament could become the concrete expression of the state's organic unity because it represented the people and expressed the two fundamental functions of political life—the legislative and the executive. If the old political doctrine had justified the kaiser's monarchical government, according to jurists such as Hugo Preuss and Hans Kelsen, the new republican state had to find its juridical reason for existing in Parliament.

THE FAILURE OF PARLIAMENT

Unfortunately for this theory, Parliament—with its shifting majorities, its unstable changes, the alterations caused by elections—did not appear able to lend authority to the state and constitute the foundation of its sovereignty. Moreover, the legal order lost at least part of its legitimacy because of its dependence on the legislative choices of an uncertain parliamentary majority. Criticisms such as these were voiced against Kelsen by thinkers such as Rudolf Smend in his *Verfassung und Verfassungsrecht* [Constitutions and Constitutional Law] (1928). State authority could be affirmed only by means of a powerful government because governments represent the idea of the state; government is not merely administration but also the capacity to decide. Politics is a complex reality that constantly presents new problems, and these problems must be faced by a government that must make policy and provide direction to state activity.

Developments in Russia and Italy illustrated that energetic governmental action could be undertaken only by a powerful political party. A strong party possesses political savvy, fights for a program, and knows how to handle political adversaries; a party with widespread support is a political unit capable of expressing determination at a governmental level and of giving concrete form to the state. In short, a national party with a political vision reflects popular unity. Some German thinkers believed that these qualities could be found in Italian Fascism and therefore attentively followed Italian developments after 1922. Carl Schmitt, for example, believed that neither Parliament, the expression of different social and economic groups, nor governmental coalitions, the result of transitory agreements, could produce stable juridical systems. In the Fascist regime, in contrast, the head of the party's decisionmaking capacity seemed able to restore state authority.

Germany's dramatic political and social situation after the war explained the doctrinal uncertainties—it had emerged from the conflict defeated, crushed by a grave economic crisis, shaken by strikes, agitation, and revolts, and lacking any clear political direction. In the January 19, 1919, elections for the Constituent Assembly, the German Social Democratic Party (SPD) received 38 percent of the vote, more than any other party. But this organization, marked by internal dissension, found it imperative to make deals of all kinds on serious issues. Even the new republic's constitution, approved on July 31, 1919, resulted from necessary compromises in an attempt to create a national consensus for the new political system. Furthermore, the new constitution was greatly influenced by U.S. president Woodrow Wilson's demands and was not rooted in German tradition.

In Germany after the political revolution that took place in 1918 creating the Weimar Republic, neither the Reichstag (elected by universal suffrage) nor the precarious coalition governments enjoyed great prestige, and the ideological disorientation was blamed on the SPD, the party most responsible for the revolution. The SPD faced paralysis because, since it feared communist competition, it could not openly reject the class-struggle concept, and, partly for that reason, it could not fulfill the demands of the petite bourgeoisie and of the war veterans.

In a climate of resentment and humiliation caused by the loss in the war, and of misunderstanding on the part of the victorious powers, internal dissensions deepened, and anxiousness alternated with the hope for a successful solution to the gloomy postwar crisis. It must be said, however, that between 1918 and 1928 Germany—with all its angst and delusions, its dreams of renovation, and its ambitions of greatness—enjoyed a fertile intellectual period that even today has a powerful attraction for European culture. The slow decline of the SPD and political factionalism aggravated the lack of confidence in Parliament and the entire political system, but it also produced, in addition to a discussion of politics, reflections on the condition of the individual in modern society.

In the 1928 elections the German National Socialist Workers' Party (NSDAP), or Nazis, received 2.8 percent of the vote. This organization, distrusted by both right and left, had always been distinguished by its patriotic fervor, its anti-Semitic spirit, and its aversion to Western capitalism. With Adolf Hitler as its *Führer* (leader), this party not only declared itself a national workers' party that put Germany's interests above everything, but also declared its absolute refusal to compromise with the parliamentary regime. In September 1930, during the first elections after the worldwide Great Depression began, the Nazis became Germany's second largest party, winning 6.5 million votes, 18.3 percent of the total, and receiving 107 seats in the Reichstag. The party also possessed an armed paramilitary force and a rigid hierarchical structure that allowed it to act in a unified manner and to attack its enemies. Thus began the Nazi rise to power.

From 1930 to 1932, the divisions widened between the head of the state, Parliament, and the governments. Because of the lack of a parliamentary majority and the inability to form a government, the power to name the chancellor was transferred to President Paul von Hindenburg, as the Weimar Republic's constitution mandated. New elections took place in June 1932; these elections gave the Nazis 37.2 percent of the vote, making them the country's largest party. Despite this development, Parliament still proved unable to put together a coalition government. After a series of political maneuvers, Hindenburg named Hitler chancellor on January 30, 1933.

THE NAZI ONE-PARTY STATE

Hitler's new government immediately restricted the scope of action open to opposition parties by limiting freedom of the press and association. In the elections of March 1933 the Nazis obtained over 17 million votes, 44 percent, and with the support of the Nationalists (8 percent), they

achieved a majority. Hitler now imposed his design for a single-party
regime. On March 24 the parliamentary majority voted him full powers,
and a law of July 14, 1933, established the Nazi party as the only legal
party. Thus also in Germany a political group had become a "dominant
party" within a brief span of time and had successively imposed itself as
a single party. In addition, this organization proclaimed the "total state"
(*Totalstaat*) and instituted a totalitarian government.

Over the next few months the new government abolished Germany's
federal structure and centralized the country's administration; dissolved
unions and jailed their leaders; liquidated the SPD on the grounds that it
had betrayed Germany; and declared the Nazi party a public agency protected by law. In August 1933, with the death of the elderly Hindenburg,
Hitler assumed the office of president while retaining his title as chancellor; from then on the army swore an oath to him personally. He was at the
same time guarantor of the law and chief magistrate. The Führer proclaimed his Germany the Third Reich, after the Holy Roman Empire and
the German Empire created by Bismarck. The Third Reich had a powerful
secret state police (the Gestapo) and security squads (the *Schutzstaffel*, or
SS) for the ideological defense of the new Nazi order.

Many writings that appeared in those years affirmed that the party
constituted a community of the elect, upheld moral values, and aimed to
regenerate political life. According to a law of December 1, 1933, the Nazi
party's constitution was fixed by the Führer, was the repository of the
German idea of the state, and, given its indissoluble link to the state, was
a public agency. The union of party and state was guaranteed by giving
high state functions to leaders holding high party office; as party head,
the Führer delegated party leadership to his representative, who in turn
was also a member of the government. The party's task was not only to
explicate the ideas of National Socialism, but also, through its educational
function, to create a unified public opinion so that the German people
could become a community. The most favorable conditions to permit the
development to the fullest of the moral and heroic Germanic man would
obtain in this setting. To fulfill this aim, student, youth, professional, and
bureaucratic associations of both sexes belonged to the party. Ordinary
citizens could also join the party, but citizenship was reserved exclusively
for members of the German race; therefore a Jew could not be a German
citizen nor a member of the party. As head of the party, the Führer controlled political power and all the powers of the state were concentrated
in his person.

Carl Schmitt elaborated the theory of the party's function. He affirmed in
Staat, Bewegung, Volk die Dreigliederung [State, Movement, People: Three
Structures] (1933) that the political and legal theories of liberalism and
democracy rested on an antagonistic dualism between state and people;

"state" signified authority, and "people" emphasized rights. It was possible to resolve this conflict by inserting between them a third, mediating, concept—the "party" as expression of a "movement." In this manner, National Socialism moved from a political structure balanced on two legs to one resting on three. According to Schmitt, in this new political construction, the "movement," that is, the party, supported both state and people.

This three-legged political structure could be found in the Nazi movement, in Fascism, and even in Bolshevism and was a typical twentieth-century development. Schmitt believed that this construction became visible not only where an attempt was made to emerge from the "blind alley" of liberalism and democracy but in order to create a new type of state. This new state conforms to the social and political reality of the twentieth century and to the doctrine of the German state described by Hegel. The "movement" thus supersedes both "state" and "people," while its organized political leadership, the party, supports the state apparatus and the social and economic order. Since political decisiveness is necessary for the structure of the state, the concept of leadership (*Führung*) is as well, making the party omnipresent. Furthermore, to maintain state unity and a solid juridical system, dictatorship is necessary in a modern political system (*Die Diktatur* [Dictatorship], 1921).

One of the political scientists who studied the structure and practice of National Socialism was Franz Neumann, who escaped Germany and went first to Great Britain and then to the United States. In his classic analysis, *Behemoth* (1942), Neumann disputes Schmitt's view. According to Neumann, despite Schmitt's theory of the three supports, the relationship between party and state remained vague in Nazi Germany—so much so that Hitler believed it necessary to issue an order declaring the party the repository of the German idea of the state and proclaiming the party indissolubly united to the state (March 9, 1935).

Beyond these theoretical considerations, the Nazi party claimed that it favored workers, and the Third Reich did achieve a patina of populism by imposing on German business social policies favorable to workers. The party established agents whose task was to help workers, requested guarantees against firings, improved social services, and organized leisure-time activities. Many social innovations, such as vacations, helped to increase worker sympathy for the new regime. In addition, the party claimed credit for having created the favorable social context necessary for the recovery of production and the decline of unemployment during the Great Depression.

Hitler's memoirs and doctrinal statement, *Mein Kampf* ["My Struggle," but translated into English with the original title] (1925, 1927), written while he was serving a prison sentence for a failed attempt to overthrow the government in 1923 (the "Beer Hall Putsch"), reveals a mediocre conceptual context and is replete with second-hand banalities. It contains violent attacks on social democracy, parliamentarism, communism, and Jews; and it expresses great faith in the one-party state, the leader who guides the masses, the racial unity of the German people, the mission of the new Reich. Hitler claimed not to believe in the national state but in the "people's state" *(Volksstaat)*, with "the people" understood as being an ethnic community; for that reason, the new Reich was to be composed exclusively of members of the German "race."

It was not the "theory" contained in *Mein Kampf* that publicized Nazi ideas, but rather criticism leveled at "inept" members of Parliament whose limited imagination could not conceive of a new lifestyle and who lacked all concept of greatness. Many intellectuals refused to accept the boring daily life of defeated Germany and hoped for a national revolution that would humble the current form of government and establish a powerful state.

There is ample literature on the historical and ideological origins of Hitler's ideas, but no agreement. Nineteenth-century Germans had hypothesized anti-Semitism and racial discrimination and had also argued that the Germans, as a purebred Aryan race, had as their mission to rule other peoples. Gottfried Feder had argued for expulsion of the Jews from Germany in *Der Deutsche Staat auf nationaler und sozialer Grundlage* [National and Social Foundations of the German State] (1923), and Alfred Rosenberg discovered a Jewish plot in *Die Protokolle der Weisen von Zion und die judische Weltpolitik* [The Protocols of Zion and Jewish World Politics] (1923). In *The Decline of the West* (1918–1922), Oswald Spengler described in catastrophic tones the end of Western civilization owing to the dissolution of traditional values. These kinds of arguments led to the exaltation of the "Prussian" spirit, the affirmation of the German race, and the need for a heroic destiny for Germany. The urgency of the creation of a third Reich was emphasized by Arthur Moeller van den Bruck in *Germany's Third Empire* (1923), because only German nationalism could rescue European values and construct a new order through the formation of a new party that differed radically from the traditional organizations. Moeller van den Bruck's book was typical of a German cultural milieu that combined philosophy, history, messianic visions, and romantic and irrational concepts. In these works criticism of the past aimed at stimulating a "real" German revolution that would drink from the mystical springs that had inspired the Holy Roman Empire—the First Reich.

NAZI RACISM

The historian George L. Mosse, in examining German ideas in his work *The Crisis of German Ideology: Intellectual Origins of the Third Reich* (1964),

indicated the fundamental points to consider in any analysis of Nazi doctrine: romanticism, the image of the "people" *(Volk)*, the rediscovery of
the ancient Germans, racism, and anti-Semitism. Mosse argued that all
these cultural elements were widespread among educated and well-off
people, especially students and professors. After 1918, however, nationalistic and patriotic ideology spread also among disillusioned conservatives, war veterans, and middle-class youth. This view maintains that the
Nazis did nothing more than emphasize traditional conservative ideals
because their leaders understood that they already shared many ideological presuppositions with other national and patriotic groups. The Nazis
exploited these principles in order to focus the political action of people
who believed in the values of German "civilization." They presented the
polemic against liberalism and democracy as German moral regeneration
and did not hesitate to make use of the entire German cultural arsenal,
from nineteenth-century romanticism to German conservative and reactionary ideology.

Along with exploitation of the German cultural heritage, mythical and
psychological factors also influenced Nazi action. Party members favored
a Hitler who spoke about German grandeur and moral and cultural superiority. This "myth" was based on a Germany that had always to fight
wars of liberation against Russia and France and justified the blind obedience of Nazis. Party members were profoundly moved by a fascination
with the charismatic leader, the Führer, who had a staunch faith in the
country's future, who governed with apostolic fervor, who knew how to
make decisions and how to impose himself.

Fichte had written his *Addresses to the German Nation* in 1807, when
French soldiers occupied Berlin. He had emphatically stated that for
Germans liberty meant remaining German and continuing to resolve
problems in harmony with the original spirit of the race. The Germans
possessed their own land, he wrote, their own language, their own way
of thinking—and the other races owed much to the Germans. Fichte's
statements were exploited by the Nazis to formulate the idea of a
Germanic Aryan race that had the duty to liberate itself from non-Aryan
influences.

Nazism sought to oppose its own world vision *(Weltanschauung)* to
Bolshevism, which founded its doctrine on the struggle of the proletariat
against the bourgeoisie. Nazi doctrine revolved around the struggle of
the German race to conquer its own "vital space" *(Lebensraum)*. From here
came the necessity of eliminating the Jews, incapable of creating their
own state but able to dominate the world through their international economic network; it was also necessary to fight the plutocratic, or rich capitalistic, states that imposed their traditional egotistical views upon others. In the end the superior Aryan race would prevail; in winning the

struggle, it would regenerate Europe and destroy democracy's atomizing ideas. The German people, authentic *Volk*, would determine the world's future because it was biologically, morally, and historically superior.

As in other one-party states, the German one-party system possessed a political ideology that it found necessary to impose through the instruments of mass communication, paramilitary organization, violence, a faithful bureaucratic apparatus, and a dense police network.

MULTIPARTY AND ONE-PARTY SYSTEMS

After World War I there were thus born in Europe, rather than mass parties, novel kinds of parties. These organizations demanded from their members exclusive loyalty and active participation. Allowed to translate into concrete practice their authoritarian concepts that emerged during the early years of the twentieth century, they would give rise to new forms of government that had nothing in common with the parliamentary system evolved by liberals. These parties could not avoid evolving into "single" parties, thus creating the one-party system as a counterpart to the multiparty system. This development set the stage for a struggle with the democratic states.

Despite agreement on the characteristics of one-party regimes, the differences between one-party authoritarian and one-party totalitarian governments should be understood. Even though both types of one-party regimes were openly undemocratic, there was a substantial difference in their executive modes of operation, and above all in their doctrinal rigidity and in their demand for ideological unanimity. Nazism, one example of a totalitarian government, not only aimed at ending the distinction between public and private spheres of activity, but also proposed drastic solutions in the name of a purifying and regenerating doctrine. In German Nazism, political ideology, consistently applied, ended by justifying all decisions taken by the head of government—no matter how dictatorial and despotic.

15

OPPOSING THE
ONE-PARTY STATE

As might be expected, after World War I, a tendency toward justification of authoritarian regimes appeared also among liberals and democrats. In all European countries the parliamentary system seemed to falter when confronted by the social and economic problems generated by the war and the peace settlement. Only partial and temporary solutions seemed forthcoming at a time when people expected dramatic solutions. This situation led to criticism from both right and left that parliaments were weak and inefficient.

LOSS OF FAITH

Many who wrote about the decline of parliament and the decadence of the multiparty system seemed more interested in developments within the new one-party systems rather than reforming the parliamentary system. This attitude helps to explain why the writings of some noted philosophers failed to have the expected impact.

This was the case of Max Weber's *Political Writings* (1921), published a year after his death, which were greeted with a profound silence. These essays lucidly defended parliamentary democracy. While acknowledging the well-known defects of the parliamentary system, Weber attributed to the multiparty order the task of preventing the establishment of an authoritarian state. He admitted that some sincere democrats hated parliamentary procedures and mechanisms but pointed out that democracies without parliaments produced authoritarian power without limits. Moreover, authoritarian systems are vulnerable to the fall of a charismatic leader, which leads to internal catastrophes. In contrast, the effective participation in power of strong representative institutions ensures political continuity, constitutional guarantees, and the civil order. While the chief

danger in a mass democracy is the possible injection of emotion into politics, Weber believed, a politically mature people has control of the
administration of its own affairs and determines the choice of its own
leaders through its elected representatives.

Many European intellectuals, however, had lost faith in political democracy that was based on debate and collaboration. According to the French
writer Julien Benda, this attitude was a true "betrayal of the intellectuals,"
the title of a work he published in 1927. Many of these cultural "priests,"
raised on rationalistic concepts and Enlightenment principles, joined the
bureaucratic apparatus of big parties with the hidden agenda of attaining
important positions and leading the masses. In short, they talked about
revolution and violence and preferred action to discussion and dialogue.

Some of these intellectuals replied that the old generation blinded itself
to the fact that in Russia and in Italy two new systems capable of resolving novel political, social, and economic problems had arisen. As time
went by, they argued, these one-party political systems would be imitated
by other European countries because "fascism" and "communism" really
constituted new governmental models: the capitalist and the proletarian.
Political scientists should study them because these two models provided
the real alternatives to liberalism and democracy.

Many socialists oriented themselves toward the "proletarian model" in
the name of working-class unity and hatred of the bourgeoisie. But some
"revolutionary socialists" interpreted fascism as the amalgamation of
communism and capitalism. Hendrick De Man published a work best
known in its French edition, *Au delà du marxisme* [Beyond Marxism]
(1927), which was very critical of communism. After 1930 many French
socialists were attracted by "national socialism," which appeared to be
related to fascism. They adopted the watchwords "order, authority,
nation" and founded organizations such as the French Socialist Party (to
be distinguished from the Section Française de l'Internationale Ouvrière
[SFIO], the traditional French socialist party) and the French Popular
Party. Pierre Drieu La Rochelle defined the antidemocratic orientation of
these groups in his *Socialisme fasciste* [Fascist Socialism] (1934).

If it is true that multiparty parliamentary institutions no longer corresponded to the desire of the masses, as even the British intellectuals H. G.
Wells and Harold J. Laski suggested, what was the reason for this profound change? One answer came from José Ortega y Gasset.

JOSÉ ORTEGA Y GASSET (1883–1945)

A well-known Spanish republican and founder of the journal *Revista de
Occidente* [Review of the West], Ortega y Gasset is best known for his
work *The Revolt of the Masses* (1930). According to Ortega, in the modern

world the masses have become the main protagonists of society. He defined the masses as being composed of generic individuals with unconscious appetites and demands. The result of this development was a great leveling of culture among the different classes and the sexes. The great question was: How has the coming of the masses altered politics? In liberal democracy, Ortega answered, there was always present the desire for tolerance, and the majority respected the rights of the minority. The masses do not follow the same line, and therefore, in those countries in which mass parties dominate, all opposition groups are wiped out.

The revolt of the masses can signify either a transition to a new form of human organization or disaster. Ortega admitted that fascism and communism represented two new kinds of political systems, but were they progressive or regressive? Ortega had no doubts—both were regressive in the context of liberalism. He agreed that the liberalism of the previous century should be updated by paying more attention to the social justice demanded by the masses, but "statism" should be criticized because state interference in all aspects of life threatened civilization. "Statism," Ortega believed, spells violence and direct action under a higher form, raised to the level of law.

Thus trust should be placed not in the state but in parliament, an institution capable of resolving political and social problems if it were modernized and brought up to date. Even serious criticism of parliamentary action does not lead to the conclusion that parliaments should be suppressed, Ortega argued, but instead that they should be reformed. The problem Ortega described was the inability of Europeans to employ parliamentary institutions correctly, which he attributed to the lack of clear goals. He blamed European countries for having narrow outlooks, for emphasizing their own race and language, and for seeking to control other countries. Because of the revolt of the masses and the consequent demoralization, Europeans forgot that they had created an important civilization; in order to solve their problems, they should not resort to one-party systems but seek to live together in peace and work toward European union through their national parliaments.

Ortega argued against the "mass regimes" of fascism and communism because he believed in the dignity of the individual and in the necessity of defending the rights of man. Even though he was elected to the Constituent Assembly of the Spanish Republic on a Socialist list, he never identified with the ideals and hopes of leftist intellectuals; he instead remained a philosopher and sociologist of European stature faithful to the idea of Fascist-free Spanish modernization. Ortega was profoundly dismayed to observe the masses support totalitarian regimes and choose to be governed by ambitious and despotic leaders just when they were beginning to enjoy wealth of the kind once reserved for the privileged classes.

This view is a major reason for Ortega's importance—he stressed the close link between mass societies and fascism and saw fascism as a European, not an Italian, evil. Mussolini had come to power with a parliamentary majority because the masses believed that through Fascism they could participate in the great decisions of the day and reap important social benefits from the new regime; but in his attack on democracy and liberalism, the Fascist Duce disguised his goal of suppressing all debate and opposition. Above all, then, *The Revolt of the Masses* was an attack on fascism, which Ortega considered a violent petit-bourgeois movement dragging Europe into a disastrous conflict of nationalities.

HANS KELSEN (1881–1973)

Another stout defender of parliamentary institutions was the German thinker Hans Kelsen. Though Kelsen was known for a series of works, his major ideas may be found synthesized in his *General Theory of Law and State* (1945). According to Kelsen, social revolution, a consequence of World War I, rendered the prewar contrast between liberalism and socialism irrelevant; this debate was replaced by the struggle between forms of government that reflected two different ideologies—democracy and autocracy. The dictatorship of the proletariat, implemented by the Russian Bolsheviks, was at odds with democratic ideals; but out of fear of the proletariat, the European bourgeois reaction also assumed an antidemocratic form, such as in Italian Fascism.

According to Kelsen, parties and parliamentary institutions are crucial in the fight against one-party states. Political parties permit political groups to organize, to scrutinize the management of public affairs, to block the dictatorship of a single party, and to allow the realization of modern democracy. In a multiparty state, the majority of citizens, through their parties, universal suffrage, and parliament, also reach a consensus known as the general will. Despite the criticism of parliamentary institutions, he continued, parliament remains a collegial organ, freely elected by the people, representing the community. If its purposes and procedures are respected, it is fully capable of resolving the social problems of modern times. Unlike dictatorships, parliamentary systems reflect the general will, which in practice means the rule of a majority elected by direct universal suffrage.

Against the one-party state, Kelsen proposed the principle of majority rule, according to which the government implements decisions made by a majority of representatives freely elected to Parliament. The government expressed by this majority safeguards civil order but does not prevent the minority from expressing its opinion or from eventually becoming transformed into a majority as the result of free elections. People have the right to give their opinions, and if a government utilizes the delegation of power given to it by a party in order to impose its will, that government becomes authoritarian. Parliamentary democracy—with its majority-minority dialogue—permits the resolution of differences between government and opposition, and even of class conflicts. In brief, Kelsen believed that tolerance led to social peace and liberty.

With the spread of dictatorship on the European continent, England stood forth as a bastion of parliamentary democracy, despite the economic ravages of the Great Depression and the emergence of a fascist movement led by Sir Oswald Mosley. Some members of the Labour party took a public stand against the dictatorships in Soviet Russia and Fascist Italy. The moderate wing headed by Ramsey MacDonald argued that the danger of authoritarian dictatorship could be avoided by a sense of respect for parliamentary institutions. An alliance with the Liberal party loomed in order to achieve a parliamentary majority against the Conservative party. Very important in this context was the thought of the illustrious economist John Maynard Keynes.

JOHN MAYNARD KEYNES (1883–1946)

Keynes achieved fame from his warning that the demand of the Allies for enormous reparations from Germany after World War I would disrupt the European economy (*The Economic Consequences of the Peace*, 1919). With the beginning of the Great Depression in 1929, Liberal and democratic circles focused greater attention on Keynes's criticism of the rigidity of classical economics and monopolistic state theories. This development signaled the political success of Keynesian economics—and the recognition that inflation, unemployment, and credit were political as well as economic issues. For example, the expansion of credit would decrease unemployment. Unlike classical liberals, Keynes advocated state intervention in the economy, but in a manner that would not bring about the socialization of the economy.

Keynes made his political outlook clear in his *Essays in Persuasion* (1931). This work advocated "social liberty" that would be brought about through an understanding between liberalism and labor; the alliance would also make the coming of a one-party system less probable. Rather than the elimination of parties, then, Keynes championed understandings among large parties that together could shape the future society.

After Labour's 1931 electoral defeat, Keynes's theories came under greater scrutiny. The New Fabian Research Group was constituted to study how to implement Liberalism and satisfy collective needs, according to Keynes's ideas.

Keynes's 1936 work, *The General Theory of Employment, Interest, and Money*, appeared to provide an answer to both the planned and the corporativist economies of the Soviet and the Italian Fascist types. Rather than an economy based on exchange, Keynes envisioned one founded on monetarism; goods are not exchanged for other goods, but for money, which, being the basis of production, conditions investments and transactions. It is thus entrepreneurial initiative that precedes production and anticipates demand. From the behavior of individuals is derived the contradictory dynamism that finds the automatic equilibrium described by classic liberal economics. But a monetarist economy must deal with large industrial units, union demands, and state action that puts money into circulation.

Classical economics dictated salary cuts during recessions. By trimming labor costs, the theory went, a budgetary balance would be achieved. But if consumption is a function of national income and the way in which it is divided, Keynes argued, then it is necessary more than anything to increase consumption and increase demand. The tendency toward consumption if income rises is a psychological law that conditions production, he pointed out. While the entrepreneur anticipates demand, cost, and benefits, unions also must play an important role in the economy by favoring contracts according to economic sector and by allowing employers to anticipate labor costs. Finally, Keynes maintained, the state also had a crucial role; it must accept an active part in an economy that would be regulated to some extent—by supporting income redistribution and by aiding the economically weak. The state's other crucial role consisted in its ability to lower the cost of credit; this ability meant that it influenced investment, which depended on the interest rates set by central banks.

To summarize, in Keynes's economic thought may be found implicit criticisms of both the corporativist economic system of Fascist Italy and the planned Soviet economy. Beyond that, however, Keynes's reinterpretation of liberal economics underpinned much of the governmental economic policy of the Western world following World War II.

CATHOLIC OPPOSITION TO THE AUTHORITARIAN REGIMES

Although the official churches in Italy and Germany cannot be said to have vigorously and openly opposed the dictatorships established in those countries, both European democratic Catholic and Protestant circles observed the formation of one-party systems with unease. Fascist anti-communist declarations seemed reassuring at first, but Mussolini's attitude toward the Italian Popular (Catholic) party was disquieting (Mussolini succeeded in getting the Vatican to drive its liberal leader, Don Luigi Sturzo, into exile and to abandon the party itself). Many democratic Catholics remained faithful to the principles of pluralism and parliamentary democracy. In France, for example, democratic Catholics formed a parliamentary group in 1924 whose program included reforms, decentralization, pluralism, and representation of all interest groups.

Democratic Catholics criticized the Concordat signed between the Vatican and the Fascist government in February 1929. Then the Spanish Civil War (1936–1939) threw them into profound crisis. In Spain, Nazis and Fascists supported with arms the imposition of General Francisco Franco's paternalistic dictatorship. Franco and his supporters depended on the army for support and foreshadowed a one-party state created with the agreement of the Catholic clergy.

French Catholics such as François Mauriac and Georges Bernanos objected to such a regime, while Emmanuel Mounier and his supporters, gathered around the review *Esprit* [Spirit], defended democratic institutions. In *Révolution personnaliste et communautaire* [Personal and Communitary Revolution] (1935), Mounier admitted that new representative institutions and economic democracy were necessary, but since all societies were pluralistic, many groups deserved representation and respect. His argument was that the individual must have primacy over collective organisms. Mounier's ideas greatly influenced other European Catholics.

JACQUES MARITAIN (1882–1973)

Jacques Maritain's philosophical and religious conceptions, designed to combat atheism, were grounded in spirituality, as illustrated in his *Primauté du spirituel* [The Primacy of the Spiritual] (1927). Inspired by Saint Thomas Aquinas, Maritain argued that if spiritual good must have precedence over temporal good, then the common good of the citizenry must be put above the personal good of individuals. This view could not help but to lead him to exalt the state, which he believed capable of assuring the common good to all its citizens.

Hitler's rise to power and the subsequent outbreak of the Spanish Civil War, however, caused Maritain to undergo a profound examination of conscience, which ended in his identification of a Christian element in democracy and in his rejection of the conformity imposed by a dictatorship. As he explained in *Integral Humanism* (1936), the Christian must understand, spontaneously, how to act as a Christian. This book criticizes bourgeois liberalism, which, Maritain believed, defends abstract individualism and democracy understood as parliamentary deals, but it also exhorts Christians to become engaged in the renovation of society according to an evangelical spirit and to the precepts of a democratic community. According to Maritain, a new Christianity is necessary, one open to the rights won by the contemporary world, such as freedom of thought and respect for the rights of man. A new humanism must also emphasize human dignity and not statist absolutism. From here, Maritain's proposal—a criticism of the German jurist Carl Schmitt—advocated a new democratic order, with the legislative and executive powers clearly distinct and separated, and with representative assemblies capable of defining the general rules of common life. In this way, universal suffrage is not simply a symbol; it becomes the preamble for all social institutions, from associations to local agencies.

Maritain's work reveals a modern religious conception that, unlike Catholic conservative views, looks forward to a lay Christian state and defends a pluralistic political system. Maritain acknowledged the expansion of secularism and Marxism and in response proposed as an alternative a political conception that is intrinsically Christian. He did not recommend a return to medieval forms but rather the renovation of existing political and social systems. A subtle thinker, Maritain exercised considerable influence on other European democratic Catholics.

THE ITALIAN LIBERAL OPPOSITION

As might be expected, Italian liberals attempted to oppose Il Duce. Since Italian Fascism was unprecedented, liberals in that country had been slow to recognize the danger. Real liberal opposition arose only after 1924, after Fascists had killed Socialist deputy Giacomo Matteotti, touching off a severe crisis that the regime only barely managed to survive.

In 1924 Liberal leader Giovanni Amendola published *La democrazia* [Democracy], in which he accused the Fascist party of impeding the normal functioning of the Chamber of Deputies, transforming a majority into an instrument of anticonstitutional repression. The PNF had fused state, party, and nation and had usurped the executive power. Amendola and his collaborators expounded these ideas in their review, *Il Mondo* [The World], while it was still possible for opposition publications to exist.

At the same time, an influential book advocating British liberalism and the parliamentary system it had created appeared and was quickly translated into other languages. Guido De Ruggiero's *History of European Liberalism* (1924) expounded liberalism as a way of life founded on the rights of the individual, which could not be denied by an authoritarian party. De Ruggiero believed that sooner or later liberal values would emerge victorious.

BENEDETTO CROCE (1866–1952)

A world-famous philosopher, Benedetto Croce profoundly rethought liberalism in response to the Fascist takeover. After some wavering regarding the meaning of Fascism, Croce reacted drastically in January 1925 after the publication of the "Manifesto of Fascist Intellectuals" under the aegis of his former friend Giovanni Gentile. He drafted an opposing statement (*Il Mondo*, May 1, 1925) in which he proclaimed his belief in the historical conception of free competition and of the alternation of parties in power, which together gradually produce progress. This statement touched off a long period during which Croce served as the moral conscience of anti-Fascism, not so much as the champion of the philosophical school of idealism that he had previously represented but as the "philosopher of liberty."

Before 1925 Croce had analyzed political activity as economic activity, with its own essence and laws. With the rise of Fascism, however, his liberal thought became transformed into a theory according to which liberalism represented the history of liberty. Croce's most important works in fleshing out this theory are *The History of Italy from 1871 to 1915* (1928), *History of Europe in the Nineteenth Century* (1932), and *History as Thought and Action* (1938). In these works Croce disputed Gentile's assertions that Fascism continued the liberalism of the *Risorgimento* and that the mistaken conception of the so-called ethical state could be derived from Italian Hegelianism. According to Croce, liberalism propounded a global vision of history and was "the religion of liberty."

Croce did not formulate future hypotheses or political formulas about what would replace Fascism after its fall, because he considered it a negative "parenthesis" in Italian history. Whereas De Ruggiero's *History of European Liberalism* emphasized nineteenth-century British liberalism, Croce's *History of Europe in the Nineteenth Century* praised the French Doctrinaires, who understood and magnificently expressed the moral and political value of liberty after Napoleon's fall. According to Croce, the French Doctrinaires constituted the first example of a cultural movement that had fought courageously against political absolutism, and their example could inspire those who struggled against Fascism. Beyond this case, Croce also cited antecedents of the July Revolution in France (1830), when liberal parliamentarians had formed two parties, the "Party of Resistance" and the "Party of Movement." Croce thus praised the French model of a liberal party of movement, which would govern in order to acquire greater liberty and to bring liberal reforms into all parts of society.

LIBERAL SOCIALISTS:
CARLO ROSSELLI (1899–1937)

Along with the liberals, radicals and reformist socialists, too, looked to Britain, though not for the principle of the alternation of power but with attention to the Labour party. In 1922, at Edinburgh, the Labour party had explicitly renounced violence and had accepted the representative system. On the continent, Carlo Rosselli tried to erect British Labour concepts into a doctrine.

Rosselli, who had traveled to Britain, emphasized British Labour ideas in several Italian journals from 1922 to 1924, interpreting them as a melding of liberal and socialist ideas. In the meantime, Fascism affirmed itself in Italy, and Rosselli was arrested for his opposition to it. In 1928 and 1929, while in "internal exile" on the island of Lipari, Rosselli wrote *Liberal Socialism*, first published in French in 1930. In this work Rosselli argued that the battle against Fascism was above all a fight for the reconquest of lost liberties and that it would be up to the next generation to rescue the workers' movement from its defeat by Fascism and to restore civil rights. Unlike Croce, Rosselli did not believe that Fascism was merely a "parenthesis" after which everything would return to the way it had been. Rosselli called for the creation of a new political formation that, no longer linked to the past, could elaborate a new program for Italy's regeneration.

Rosselli founded a fighting organization called Justice and Liberty, which he hoped could unite anti-Fascists and overthrow Fascism, after which the organization would be transformed into a large political party. His murder, along with that of his brother, by the Fascist secret police in 1937 deprived his political organization of his leadership, but the combination of socialism and liberalism has continued to attract European intellectuals.

MARXIST RESPONSES

Dominated by the Soviet Union, Marxists after World War I viewed fascism as the last stand of capitalism and social democratic party members as "socialfascists." As a result, the Kremlin imposed a policy of noncooperation between Socialist and Communist parties. With the rise of Hitler, however, the USSR recognized Nazi Germany as a real threat to its security. After Hitler came to power in 1933, the USSR was anxious to emerge from its diplomatic isolation and reach agreements with powers that might ally with it in case of war with Germany. As a counterpart to this effort, the Comintern (the Communist International) imposed a new policy of rapprochement between European Communist and Socialist parties known as the Popular Front.

At the Seventh Congress of the Comintern in August 1935, the Popular Front policy received its justification in a report presented by Georgi Dimitrov. Dimitrov opposed the workers' unified front to the "capitalist-fascist" unified front. According to Dimitrov's reasoning, the Communists defended bourgeois democratic liberties in capitalist countries because the interests of the proletariat dictated it. From here the necessity was clear of reaching agreement on common action with social democratic parties, with reformist-dominated unions, and with working-class organizations in general, against fascism.

In France, as early as March 1934, a group of writers and scientists formed a vigilance committee of antifascist intellectuals, followed in July by a unity-of-action pact between the SFIO and the French Communist Party (PCF); this pact was the forerunner of the Popular Front electoral alliance. The French model was followed by the Italian Socialist and Italian Communist parties (PSI and PCI) in exile and influenced the future of both movements after World War II. In late 1935 a Spanish Popular Front was formed with the participation of Radicals, Republicans, Anarchists, Socialists, and Communists.

The Spanish and French Popular Fronts achieved significant electoral successes. In February 1936 the Spanish "Frente Popular" won and came to power with Manuel Azaña as prime minister. In France the "Front Populaire" won in April, giving France a Socialist prime minister, Léon Blum, for the first time. During the same year, the Soviet Union ratified a new constitution in which universal suffrage was guaranteed to all citizens.

These developments gave rise to a discussion on the possibility of establishing "popular democracies" in countries with traditional parliamentary systems; these constructions, to be achieved in collaboration with other antifascist political forces, were to progress to Soviet-type governments because the USSR represented Communist orthodoxy and was the only regime in which the revolution had succeeded.

Many Western Communists, however, had doubts about the Soviet autocratic government, and Moscow reacted by expelling those who expressed them. Moreover, stories circulated about the harsh penalties inflicted in the USSR—not on the vilified bourgeoisie but on old comrades. These condemnations were justified by citing Marxist dogma, but it was clear that they emanated from Stalin, who tolerated no dissension. Western Communists reacted by perceiving a different kind of communism. If Marxism was a method of analyzing social reality, this method could not help taking into serious consideration the diverse historical and cultural conditions of different countries. Particular actions that had been necessary in tsarist Russia were perhaps not necessary in other European countries. The October Revolution was a great historical event, and the Soviet model was a valid one, but not everything could be resolved by orders coming from Moscow or by internal purges. In cultivated European circles a critical revision was initiated of the Soviet Central Committee's action after Lenin's death, and the idea of a European democratic communism slowly began taking shape.

CONTINUING INFLUENCE

The opposition to the authoritarianism of a one-party state and to the dictatorship of a charismatic leader was alive in all European countries—from the literary to the legal camp, and from the economic to the religious sector. The people whose ideas have been illustrated in this chapter provide only a sampling of significant personalities in an ideological resistance to the single-party system in different countries and areas of cultural activity.

It is in part the legacy of these opponents that new forms of government emerged in Western Europe after the fall of the Fascist and Nazi regimes. These were governments characterized by the existence of many political parties and free institutions and associations. Through the influence of these democratic thinkers, new constitutions inspired by the values of justice and liberty were written, values generally subscribed to by both governmental and opposition organizations. Their ideas also produced the highly charged ideological debates that both stimulated a new generation and defined postwar politics.

16

THE WEST: MARXISM VERSUS CAPITALISM

Ironically, during the period following World War II, strong criticism of the Western European parliamentary democracies originated not from fascistic ideologies or rightist political tendencies but from a leftist culture imbued with Marxist doctrine. After 1948, beyond the contrast between "Americanism" and the Soviet system, which provided the theoretical basis of the Cold War, constant opposition to Western representative regimes marked European thought. This criticism had its origin in anti-bourgeois sentiment and Marxist theory.

Marxism is notably a social and economic doctrine, but it is also a philosophical doctrine that analyzes the dialectical processes of society and supports what it considers the dynamic forces that propose new human relationships. With the beginning of the Cold War between the United States and the Soviet Union, Moscow hoped to coordinate the ideological opposition of the different Communist parties against Western European governments allied with "American imperialism." However, it is important to distinguish between Soviet policy and Marxist movements in the different European countries. Western European Marxist thought has been grounded in ethical considerations, sociological outlooks, and political ideals.

Despite the links between Western Marxists and the various Communist parties of their countries, Marxists in the West did not break with the idealistic and positivistic strands that characterized their cultural and philosophical traditions; indeed, reference to these themes and problems has enriched the quality of their Marxism. In fact, the Soviet government frequently castigated the theoretical autonomy of the European communists, considering them "eclectic" or "humanistic." At the same time, by contrasting themselves with Soviet Communism, considered static and bureaucratic, Western European Marxists were able to propose alternatives that integrated Western culture and corresponded to the needs of the diverse Western European countries. For that reason, it is possible to distinguish between Soviet political thought and "Euromarxism." Despite its political links to the USSR, Euromarxism expressed itself in an autonomous manner when it criticized Western society. Moreover, several different orientations existed within the movement. The three major schools within Euromarxism were the French, German, and Italian.

FRENCH MARXISM

A pessimistic view of the relationship between individual and society historically tormented French thought, but after World War II, French philosophers profoundly addressed the problem of "being." Existentialist philosophy presented itself in many varieties and tendencies, but Marxist existentialism came forcefully to the attention of European culture primarily through the work of Jean-Paul Sartre (1905–1980).

After 1948 Sartre became the very model of the intellectual engaged in a heroic struggle to improve the human condition, and he employed a Marxist dialectic in the battle. Marxist dialectics, however, did not prevent him from criticizing Eastern European Communism with a critical eye in his essay "Les communistes et la paix" [The Communists and Peace], published in the review *Les temps modernes* [Modern Times] (1952–1954). Previously considered a "critical fellow traveler," Sartre broke with the French Communist Party while embracing Marxism. He continued to accept the doctrine of historical materialism, even though he did not go along with its more mechanistic aspects. Criticism of political economy and the complex analysis of class structure were, according to Sartre, secondary scientific elements with respect to the core of Marxist doctrine. Sartre believed that Marxism was essentially a philosophy of man operating in a determined situation but attempting to overcome it.

In 1960 Sartre published the *Critique of Dialectical Reason* with the goal of "correcting" official Marxism, but in his analysis of the human condition he remained opposed to the American spirit, arguing that a society such as the American could never have "clean hands." It should be remembered that the majority of Sartre's audience and his followers were avowed Marxists and active Communist party members. Nonetheless, Sartre's Marxism, characterized by a powerful criticism of the bourgeois condition, gave French Marxism great intellectual vitality.

Another French Marxist, Maurice Merleau-Ponty (1908–1961), the political editor of *Les temps modernes,* interpreted Marxism as reflection and research, not as a static theory, rejecting the premise that any law governs the course of history. He fervently believed in the revolution and stoutly defended the cause of the proletariat. In rejecting the capitalist system, he was always inspired by a Marxist logic, according to which Western representative institutions were controlled by "American imperialism." However, he condemned the Stalinist purge trials, the Russian gulags, the bureaucratic nature of the Communist Party of the Soviet Union (CPSU), and Soviet doctrinal immobility.

Frequently a distinction is made between French existentialism and structuralism, but in a Marxist perspective it is possible to consider structuralism as a corrective of existentialism. The dilemma of existential loneliness in bourgeois society is the dilemma of the human consciousness within a bourgeois structure. This construction is the sum total of the laws and relationships that are imposed on people and that condition their behavior. This philosophical conception assumed political significance in the thought of Louis Althusser (1918–1992) and Michel Foucault (1926–1984).

Althusser was concerned with cultural affairs in the French Communist Party for twenty years; out of this experience came two books: *For Marx* (1966) and *Reading "Capital"* (1966). In criticizing a Marxism that itself had become bureaucratic and bourgeois, Althusser discussed the "break" between Marx's thought and the bourgeois world. According to Althusser, "humanistic" philosophy had distorted Marx's thought because it presupposed a doctrinal continuity between the two; instead, Marx must be read as the founder of a modern scientific school.

Althusser never rejected the concept of class, which was so integral to Marxism, but this aspect of his ideology did not stop him from denouncing Soviet ideology in two works, *Lenin and Philosophy* (1969) and *Humanisme et stalinisme* [Humanism and Stalinism] (1973). Instead he directed this criticism toward what he considered degenerate Russian politics and did not defend the bourgeois social structure.

Michel Foucault placed his antibourgeois arguments in a prevalently historical context and criticized the bourgeois conception of history. His work on the relationship between power and knowledge, *The Order of Things* (1966), is a rejection of the rational Western vision. His intention of "returning" to Marx is made explicit in almost all his works. Foucault's research on the relationship between means of production and means of information, like his analysis of the structure of power, is based on Marxist premises. In this connection, his *Histoire de la vérité* [The History of Truth] (1955) condemned bourgeois society, which, under the guise of rationality, imprisons humanity by entrapping it in a net of laws and powers.

The political goal of French Marxism with respect to a specific form of government was frequently unclear, but its aversion to parliamentary institutions was always profound. French leftist intellectuals have always been marked by a lively sense of liberty and have regarded institutions as ties that limit individual existence. Because of these common sentiments, many intellectuals, including Sartre, supported the student revolts that erupted in France during the spring of 1968 with the occupation of the Sorbonne.

Was the student movement an "elusive revolution," political thinker Raymond Aron wondered, or anarchy with a Marxist background? Without doubt, at the origin of the student movement was the disequilibrium between the widespread diffusion of culture and the slow acceptance of social changes on the part of the academic world. In a rush of renovation, the student movement brought scholastic structures before the docket, but ended up by criticizing traditional representative institutions and by proposing new forms of democracy. In the student movement's terms, "consensual" democracy's goal must be the consensus of the working masses; "substantive" democracy must aim at extracting social gains from the political system; "participatory" democracy must adopt plebiscitary forms of interrogating the people along with the technique of holding assemblies.

The proposals of the student movement proved to be its Achilles' heel, but the romantic desire for social renovation and moral regeneration was sincere. The industrial condition of advanced societies was regulated by utilitarian laws, but the party system permitted frequent abuses by managers.

The hope of overcoming the daily compromises imposed by parties through the creation of new moral values attracted many young people intent on doing battle with capitalism. The revolts, which had had a first phase in American universities such as the Berkeley campus of the University of California, spread to Germany, Italy, and other European countries, and the pseudorevolutionary rhetoric was quickly absorbed in many academic circles. In those years academics confused Marxism and structuralism, Lenin and Freud. They claimed to interpret present reality according to new criteria and liquidated the past by talking about concepts such as the "liberalization of man" or the "emancipation of women."

When the flow of proposals was exhausted, however, and the hope of a new culture slackened, the weakness of an alternative politics became readily apparent. Looking forward to applying the structures of backward societies to advanced ones and implementing ideas that did not have a strong backing in society proved impossible.

GERMAN MARXISM

German Marxists have always savagely criticized Western civilization. In an attempt to underline the contradictions of capitalist society, German

Marxism had the merit of imposing and developing important themes and problems of contemporary society. In its theoretical constructs, postwar German Marxism has been inspired by the German Frankfurt school, which was smitten by the connection between Hegelianism and romantic philosophy. Thus, the sociologists who revived the Frankfurt Institute after 1950 deserve particular attention.

Theodor W. Adorno (1901–1969), longtime director of the Frankfurt Institute, questioned all philosophical and political givens. In his *Negative Dialectic* (1966) he attacked the West's "authoritarian" technological system and its "positivistic" philosophy. According to Adorno, positivist theory corresponded to capitalist society, which subjected its members to its economic structure and weakened all dissenting forces. The origins of the bourgeoisie's social and philosophical system, he maintained, were rooted in the Enlightenment mentality, concerned only with the proper functioning of social mechanisms rather than the values that underpinned them. In this manner society had become "massified" and alienated. Adorno enriched his work not only by his studies of Marx and Hegel but also through his knowledge of Weber, Nietzsche, and Freud. As a result, his criticism of capitalism and its social system has had widespread influence, having been utilized by European Marxist currents and by more generic "dissent" currents as well.

Adorno's "negative" discourse agreed with the criticism of "rationalization" voiced by Max Horkheimer (1895–1973). Adorno and Horkheimer, in their *Dialectic of Enlightenment* (1947), had not limited themselves to contesting the Enlightenment only as a means of reasoning but had also put industrial society on trial. In this way, they remained in the Marxist ambit, even if they did not believe in Soviet society as a constructive alternative to Western society.

For Horkheimer, the workers' movement, and especially the German proletariat, no longer served as society's conscience, or even as a revolutionary subject. He assigned these roles to philosophy, and more generally to culture, as the only entities capable of shaping society. These precepts apparently put Horkheimer far from dogmatic Marxism, even if he recalled Marx's cultural role in molding the proletariat. Horkheimer began from an interesting premise: Though Bolshevism was a degeneration of the communist revolution, Marxism could nevertheless give life to a better society. Horkheimer criticized bourgeois society and "individualistic" interests and, while propounding a just society, insisted that Western civilization was in full crisis.

The same points could be made about Jürgen Habermas, who may be considered as perpetuating the German Frankfurt school. Using sociological methods, he "delegitimized" the modern state, criticized public opinion, put technological society on trial, rejected liberalism, and devalued the concept of political participation. After his profound criticism of Western society, he mulled over a "reconstruction" of historical materialism but proved unable to identify the type of society that could provide a valid form of government.

The negative views of bourgeois society held by German thinkers were shared by other European political philosophers, even on the right. The reasons for this influence are, on the one hand, that German opinions allowed a critical analysis of Western society, intimately linked to American capitalism, and on the other, that West German Marxism did not impose acceptance of the forms of government that existed in Eastern Europe.

Ironically, German Marxist thought produced a sharp dissonance between the positive economic realities of West Germany, in full productive development, and the doctrinal negation of this reality by German Marxists and their sympathizers. In the German Democratic Republic (the former East Germany), that part of the Frankfurt school's philosophy that condemned Western society was fully accepted while criticism of the Soviet authoritarian order was rejected.

ITALIAN MARXISM

The close of World War II marked the end of the philosophical debate between Benedetto Croce and Giovanni Gentile that had dominated Italian thought for twenty years. At that point, Antonio Gramsci's thoughts and "notes," written in prison, were published and quickly became famous. These included especially the *Prison Notebooks*, which consisted of six volumes: *Il materialismo storico e la filosofia di Benedetto Croce* [Historical Materialism and the Philosophy of Benedetto Croce] (1948); *Gli intelletuali e l'organizzazione della cultura* [Intellectuals and the Organization of Culture] (1949); *Il Risorgimento* [The Risorgimento] (1949); *Note sul Machiavelli, la politica e lo Stato moderno* [Notes on Machiavelli, Politics, and the Modern State] (1949); *Letteratura e vita nazionale* [Literature and National Life] (1950); and *Passato e presente* [Past and Present] (1951).

The publication of the *Notebooks* seemed to open a new cultural dialectic founded on the communist-liberal contrast and set the cultural tone for the Italian Communist Party. In the essays in the *Notebooks*, secretly shorn of their references to Trotsky, Amedeo Bordiga (an early Italian Communist exponent condemned for his orthodox views), their criticism of the Stalinist line, and any allusions considered inconvenient to the policy of then party secretary Palmiro Togliatti, Gramsci provided the cultural and doctrinal continuity of the PCI. Communist intellectuals presented Italian neo-Marxism as a critical examination of the relationship between party organization and proletarian revolution.

Books on Gramsci published by Italian Marxists exhibit a pro-Western sensibility. According to this literature, Gramsci confronted the "historical" problem of democracy, and in fact Gramsci did not ignore the Italian cultural tradition. He presented an important reconstruction of historical events during the struggle for Italian unity, a reconstruction in which he utilized the thought of important political writers of his time, including Croce and Gentile. This ability to count on and use the cultural tradition of his own country allowed Gramsci to avoid a bland universalism and to propose a method of fighting Fascism in concert with other Italian democratic forces. Thus Gramsci could be introduced by Italian Marxists as the theoretician of the democratic road to power that would be followed by the Italian Communist Party.

A mass organization supported by flanking associations and the Italian Socialist Party, the PCI aimed at outpolling Italy's largest party, the Christian Democrats, and at replacing it as the country's largest governing party. Following Gramsci's teachings, the PCI did not abandon the "revolutionary myth" but constantly revised and reformulated it according to changing historical and political circumstances.

The paramount position of Gramsci's thought allowed many Communist intellectuals to affirm that electoral methods had been respected by the Italian Communist Party and that with its victory Italy's parliamentary democracy would be modified only by giving the PCI new significance as the "Modern Prince." Because it aimed at implementing idealistic values such as social justice, and because its support rested on both northern workers and southern peasants, "Gramscism" has been interpreted as the challenge of idealism to the capitalist order. In 1971, at the meeting of the Twenty-fourth Congress of the Communist Party of the Soviet Union in Moscow, Enrico Berlinguer claimed the right of all Communist parties to follow their own policy, distinct from that of the CPSU. Nominated PCI secretary in March 1972, Berlinguer launched the following year the idea of a "Historic Compromise" between leftist, secular, and Catholic forces. In *La proposta comunista* [The Communist Proposal] (1975), he defended his proposal in the context of Italian parliamentary democracy, but his ideas also agreed with the Gramscian orientation of Italian Marxism.

On the cultural plane, there exists today in Italy the problem of the political significance to be attributed to Gramsci's thought while he was in prison. In the first edition of the *Prison Notebooks*, published between 1948 and 1951, the essays were organized, according to Togliatti's directives, thematically rather than chronologically. The goal was to bolster the thesis that from the French Revolution to Weber, to Croce, and to Gramsci himself, democracy had moved forward in Europe. In 1975, after Togliatti's death, a critical edition of the *Notebooks* with the essays in chronological order appeared. At that point it also became obvious that the previous edition had eliminated references to Bordiga, Trotsky, and Stalin. Since then Togliatti's hypothesis of an autonomous Italian communist tradition has continually been called into question. The PCI, however, responded to this argument with the contention that Gramsci favored the widening of the state's sphere in its relationship to civil society because that idea furthered his political agenda. With the end of the Italian Communist Party a certain disorientation in interpreting Gramsci's political thought has developed. Some scholars believe that during the decade of his imprisonment (1927–1937), Gramsci's reflections evolved. In the dramatic solitude of a small cell, Gramsci followed as best he could the problems of Italy, the Soviet Union, and the United States but never had the opportunity to reelaborate his notes in any organic synthesis before his death. Thus the reflections in his notebooks should be considered as Gramsci's "incomplete" political legacy that favored a new, "social" method of governing.

Whatever the final judgment of Euromarxism may be, in the forty years following the end of World War II the political opposition in Western Europe, inspired by Marxism, has fulfilled an important political and cultural role and has strengthened parliamentary democracy in those countries.

The Western multiparty system has overcome political conflicts without seeking to eliminate opposition forces through repressive means. Political groups have requested greater equality, and individual governments have attempted to respond to the requests so as not to lose the support of the electorate. Western civil society has frequently been defined as "bourgeois" and accused of neglecting the "proletariat," but the transformation of social classes in the West has forced a revision of Marxist schemes because that ideology had not foreseen the growth of the middle class—and especially the economy's service sector—as a result of increasing wealth. At the same time, however, bourgeois democracy has not been able to shake off scandal, and by the 1990s this issue raised fundamental constitutional questions.

17

Eastern Europe Versus
the Soviet System

In the Eastern European countries, each Communist party prevented opponents from organizing themselves politically, but opposition manifested itself against the "model" that each single Communist party had to follow. This opposition slowly grew in importance and achieved doctrinal significance. Combined with Soviet errors, inflexibility, and the Communist world's inability to reform itself, it eventually contributed mightily to the demise of Communism itself.

The Soviet Model

In the Soviet model, the state owned the means of production, collectivized the land, centralized economic production, and prevented all forms of political association independent of the Communist party. The party wielded power in the name of the workers and had the task of implementing the dictatorship of the proletariat. Theoretically, party members meeting in periodic congresses were sovereign and determined policy by electing the Central Committee; from this body, authority flowed to the executive organs—the Politburo, the Secretariat, and the secretary. In reality, however, this "democratic centralism" favored a highly rigid, hierarchical structure in which decisions were made at the top and ratified by party members, instead of vice versa. The legislative, executive, and judicial branches of government took orders from the party, despite the formal state structure that gave the appearance of political power to the voters. In addition, although the Soviet Union was organized as a multinational federation of "independent" republics, ethnic Russians actually ran the entire Soviet state. This state, moreover, claimed as its raison d'être the right to serve as a "guide" in the struggle for emancipation of all people under bourgeois domination and for the prevention of counterrevolution.

The Soviet model was not imposed immediately in Eastern Europe after the end of World War II, and it seemed briefly that the states of this region might adopt a mixed economic and political system somewhere between Western and Eastern models. This hope, however, ended with the beginning of the Cold War in 1948, when the Soviet Union felt the need for self-defense and to consolidate its control over the "socialist" countries. All alternatives to the Soviet model were therefore dropped; following the Soviet example, private economic activity was suppressed, agriculture was collectivized (except in Poland), and the multiparty system disappeared completely even where more than one party remained in existence. Western political institutions, Western capitalism, and Western culture were condemned.

Despite Russian power, however, opposition to the Soviet model assumed a clear ideological character after the signing of the Eastern European Mutual Assistance Treaty on May 14, 1955. This agreement, known as the Warsaw Pact, was not merely a military response to the North Atlantic Treaty Organization (NATO) but a legal act of military subordination on the part of Eastern Europe's peoples' democracies to Soviet hegemony. The provision of the alliance that best illustrated this fact was the obligation of the Red Army to intervene by force of arms to render "mutual fraternal aid" to its allies. The Warsaw Pact not only justified the presence in Hungary and Romania of Soviet troops but also ratified the political subordination of Eastern Europe to Moscow and the submission of the pact members to a principle of intervention that recalled the nineteenth-century Holy Alliance.

Ideological opposition to the Soviet regime, however, should be seen in its doctrinal evolution as "dissent," rather than as simply opposition to Marxism. More often than not, opposition movements presented themselves as defending their religious faith or their nationality. While frequently confused, dissent in the East was generally advanced as the demand for rights that in fact justified opposition to Soviet oppression.

Discussion revolved around the "constructive revision" of Communism, of popular intellectual revolt, of a "Charter" of rights regarding Communism's "Christian" values, of the practical application of "democracy." Moreover, a cultural fervor that rapidly turned into opposition to the Soviet political model swept Eastern Europe after Soviet leader Nikita Khrushchev's report to the Twentieth Congress of the CPSU (February 13, 1956) denouncing Stalin's crimes. To monolithic Soviet Communism, the various oppositions proposed their own alternative unifying myths, also monolithic. Thus the Polish opposition emphasized its traditional

Catholicism, and the Hungarians appealed to national sentiment. In both cases, solidarity was concretely rooted in the historical and ideological past and present and left no room for competing myths—including Soviet Communism.

THE RELIGIOUS OPPOSITION IN POLAND

An exact picture of the religious opposition in all of its manifestations, of the different churches, especially the Catholic Church, in the countries of Eastern Europe is still difficult to apprehend in all its details. Without doubt, Vatican Council II called by Pope John XXIII to renovate the Church's evangelical spirit had important repercussions in the countries politically subordinated to the USSR. Not only did Vatican II support "the Silent Church," but it also allowed militant Catholics to contest Soviet cultural predominance.

The most spectacular case of religious opposition was that of Poland. Anxious to differentiate themselves from other Slavs, especially the Russians, the Poles made the Catholic religion the basis of their cultural identity.

Indeed, the Catholic religion had characterized Polish history, literature, and art. Moreover, Catholicism represented a profound link to Latin culture. Rome was at the center of a vibrant culture that for centuries had looked beyond political frontiers. Thus, with the coming to power of the atheistic Marxist ideology, Catholicism as a popular tradition justified opposition to a doctrine that was alien to the Polish religious and cultural heritage. Unable to criticize openly the political order imposed by Moscow, a large part of the Polish intelligentsia adopted a pro-Catholic attitude.

"Mobile" universities were organized that provided courses to teach the history of Polish Catholicism. The sixtieth anniversary of modern Polish independence (1978) was not only a historical event but also became a happy occasion of acknowledging the Church's patriotic function of defending Polish nationality. In order to avoid open contrasts with the political authorities, the organizers of the celebration emphasized the medieval Church in expressing this theme. The Middle Ages, however, was the period in which a common Catholic religion had strongly contributed to the birth of Poland—Poles readily understood the connection with modern times.

Indeed, medieval studies flowered in Poland in the period from 1948 to 1989. During the Middle Ages Catholicism had been preached; the first Catholic churches had been built; Polish literature, in Latin and Polish, had been born; and the Polish state had had its origins. During the same

age the first corporations (institutions in which groups with similar economic interests gathered) had arisen; the foundation of these corporations
had been stimulated by material interests and the necessities of production, but the relationships among members had been based on Christian
morality, which signified individual obligations and social goals.

From these modest and apologetic historical beginnings, a gradual pro-
gression toward a negative interpretation of the Communist order
emerged and gained an irresistible momentum. In contrast with those
institutions, with the passage of time Communist institutions had lost
their communal character and degenerated into nothing more than the
Communist party's political network for the purpose of controlling the
activities of workers.

Animated by a desire to see their traditional faith treated with respect,
the Polish anti-Communist opposition manifested itself in the demand
for union organizations that were not Communist but Catholic. In July
1980 Lech Wałesa, an electrician at the Lenin shipyards in Gdansk (the
former German city of Danzig), led a new union inspired by Catholic
principles but advised by councillors who were cultured medievalists
and priests. The new primate of Poland, Joseph Glemp, urged moderation and compromise between Communist governmental authorities and
the new union, Solidarity *(Solidarnosc)*. This new workers' union courageously presented a social democratic program in opposition to the official Communist party (POUP), and in the name of the workers solemnly
affirmed its doctrinal autonomy.

Undoubtedly, the election of a Polish pope, John Paul II, in December
1978 conferred courage and prestige on the Polish religious opposition.
But the anti-Communist opposition had the support of cultural circles
that identified Polish Communist leaders as the arm of Soviet hegemony.
In 1981 the Polish Historical Society established a series of publications
dedicated to historical research on Poland in English. This series, "The
Polish Nation," included the major Polish historians on its editorial
board. Thus when Solidarity was outlawed in 1981 the political opposition could count on the country's support on the basis of popular religious ideals. This force eventually became overwhelming and overthrew
the Communist system and Soviet hegemony.

It is important to note, however, that Solidarity did not argue against
the validity of some important reforms that had been given in the past,
and its action went beyond purely union concerns. In fact, Poles focused
their opposition primarily against Soviet control while at the same time
insisting on respect for an ancient Catholic cultural tradition. The Poles
wished to conserve the social aspects of Marxism such as guaranteed
employment, medical care, and other benefits.

THE HUNGARIAN NATIONAL OPPOSITION

Theoretically, Marxism is an international doctrine, but in Eastern Europe Soviet Marxism imposed directives dictated by Russian military might. The different national Communist parties were considered "delegates" of the Kremlin to put into operation the political and social methods of Soviet Marxism. In this difficult situation of dominance and dependence, some countries appealed to their national traditions as a means of resisting Russian encroachment. This was especially true of Hungary, which is neither Slavic nor as religiously conditioned as Poland.

In 1945 the Hungarian government, composed of antifascist parties, included only two Communist ministers. By 1948 the Communists, led by Mátyás Rákosi, had become the largest party in the country. They imposed "fusion" on the social democrats of the workers' party and took over all the most important command posts in the government. The Hungarian Communists, however, were subordinated to Moscow, which forced them to crack down on any and all dissenters. Even László Rajk, minister of the interior, received a death sentence in 1949. In fact, the degree of subordination to the Soviet Union demonstrated by the government became particularly humiliating because of the haughty attitude displayed by the emissaries sent by Moscow to exercise political control over the country.

Slowly, however, vindication of Hungarian national dignity developed within the Communist party itself and had as a cultural reference point class consciousness. György Lukács (1885–1971) had written in his *History and Class Consciousness* (1923) that workers had to reverse their cultural subordination to capitalism by achieving a clear consciousness of their role. Since Hungarian popular consciousness originated from Hungarian (Magyar) ethnic distinctiveness from Germans and Slavs, Hungarian Marxists argued that the consciousness of the Hungarian working class could not be separated from Hungarian nationality. This identification between Hungarian class consciousness and national consciousness allowed the Hungarian Communist party to impart a Magyar tone to Hungarian Communism, but cultural autonomy was also necessary. Beginning in 1953, in fact, Hungarian intellectuals such as István Bibó and Tibor Déry manifested opposition to Soviet cultural and political hegemony, giving rise to this autonomy.

The Hungarian Revolution of October 1956 was touched off by students of the Petöfi club. The revolt was supported by many intellectuals as well as by workers who set up workers' councils. An immediate political change followed, and Communist leader Imre Nagy formed a government of national unity. Nagy revived the "democratic cooperation" among different parties not to please the Americans so much as to return to the situation preceding the period of Soviet hegemony.

As is well known, on November 4 the Red Army intervened against the rebels, but Magyar resistance clearly appealed to patriotism. After the Soviet repression, János Kádár officially spoke of a "Hungarian counter-revolution," but the participation of the people in the Budapest insurrection gave the Magyar opposition a significance that can only be defined as nationalist.

The Moscow government rejected the pretension of Magyar Marxists to cultural autonomy because it recognized that national Communism implied disintegration of the Soviet-dominated political system in Eastern Europe. Moscow, however, did not comprehend that the ideological opposition that already existed within each Eastern European regime was assuming a greater "social" character. Yet, beginning in the mid-1960s, there was discussion in Eastern Europe of the "crisis" of Marxism and the end of the Communist "myth" (Leszek Kolakowski), and proposals emerged for alternative policies that would emphasize personal liberty (Adam Schaff). In Poland writers such as Jacek Kuron and Karol Modzelewski denied that their country was a "socialist" state, since it was the party bureaucracy that controlled the state. These two writers believed that the bureaucracy prevented the return of power into the hands of the working class, for whom the revolution had been made, and therefore they had no faith in the capacity of Communist regimes to reform themselves. Both were expelled from the Polish Communist party and jailed for their efforts.

YUGOSLAV DISSENT

To speak about a "social" opposition within political systems that touted "equality" as their official goal was almost impossible. The key here, however, was that the structure of the different Communist parties had become static after their coming to power; as a result, they had created a strong social disparity between party leadership and the masses, and party leaders worked to preserve their privileges.

In theory, this phenomenon had already been discussed by Robert Michels in his work on oligarchies in political parties, but the development in Communist countries had been denounced by the Yugoslav writer Milovan Djilas. A participant in the Resistance, Djilas had long been a loyal member of the Yugoslav Communist party and a loyal supporter of its leader Josip Broz (known as Tito). In 1953 he began analyzing the problems of democracy within Communist parties in the newspaper *Borba*. His examination of internal recruiting mechanisms and the standard of living enjoyed by party managers led him to conclude that with the bureaucratic crystallization of Communist party cadres had come formation of a "new class" in a system that advocated the end of classes. Djilas's book, *The New Class: An Analysis of the Communist System* (1957), was published in New York and got him condemned to a seven-year jail term. But the sociological research into the "new class" illuminated the social split between the ruling class and the governed masses. The Communist system had generated a party bureaucracy that had become "a privileged social stratum." This "new class" expanded its powers by using the party as a base; it proclaimed itself the "champion of the working class" but searched for new ways to consolidate its position and authority. The functionaries who controlled the bureaucratic apparatus assured privileges for themselves and their followers. It was possible for this mechanism to exist because only one party existed. The Communist party, Djilas concluded, had become "the party state."

In 1969, Djilas published *The Unperfect Society: Beyond the New Class*, again in the United States. He denounced the new political class created by Communism as having assumed the monopoly of power and of employing the "brute force of spiritual domination," in conjunction with an army and secret police, to bolster the "centralistic monolithic" structure that the party had become. However, Djilas wrote, after more than ten years an opposition that criticized the political privileges of the "new class" had arisen.

Lively discussions of the problems of "actually existing" socialism took place also in the Croatian Yugoslav review *Praxis*. Founded in the mid-1950s, this journal published the articles of foreign writers and had an international editorial board that included Herbert Marcuse and György Lukács. The review discussed the problem of alienation in socialist societies and the origins and current role of the bureaucracy. In discussing these issues, writers took into consideration the ideas of Western thinkers and criticized the decentralization that they observed taking place in Yugoslavia. Recalling Marx, who wrote that the elimination of alienation was crucial for the elimination of bureaucracy, the authors argued that Yugoslav administrative decentralization merely substituted multiple layers of local bureaucracy for a centralized one. Industrial self-government was a long way off because, as in capitalist countries, labor in socialist societies remained just another commodity.

Thus the influence of the Frankfurt school on the collaborators of *Praxis* appeared strong, as did that of French existentialism, because the review dealt with current reality, including socialist reality. The journal seemed especially influenced by Sartre and his thesis that Marxism had caused Marx's thought to become ossified, an idea spread by numerous articles and seminars that *Praxis* sponsored. The criticism of the Eastern European socialist system that this discussion engendered brought about a reaction that caused the review to cease publication in the 1970s.

THE "PRAGUE SPRING"

In Czechoslovakia criticism of the socialist system began with the criticisms of Communist party economists in the early 1960s. They held nationalization and centralized planning responsible for the crisis of the Czechoslovak economy. At the same time, Czechoslovak intellectuals of all kinds blamed the country's current problems on the Communist party. Political scientists suggested that the party discuss the relationship between socialism and democracy and make the party more responsible to the people.

This was the origin of the "Prague Spring," the participants of which, believing in socialism's capacity to reform itself, did not question the system itself. The writers of this period hoped to make politics more democratic and to establish a "mixed" economy in which public and private enterprise could coexist and where socialism could progress in harmony with the free market. The reformers examined all the different aspects of how democracy and economic efficiency could be combined—including the characteristics of business, worker self-government, salaries, and the role of shareholders. Perhaps naively, they hoped to match the economic success of the West through reform of the socialist system, but they realized that they had to reach a compromise with the Communist party. Identified with the state, the party controlled both politics and the economy, and so the reform efforts were doomed to failure.

On August 21, 1968, Warsaw Pact troops ended the fertile "Prague Spring" period. In the succeeding months the reformers lost all illusion that the Communist parties of Eastern Europe could conduct any substantial revision of the socialist system. Those parties could only manage the power that the Soviet Union delegated to them—and their thinking indeed hardened into old and outworn Marxist categories according to Soviet ideas.

This realization made it clear that the Soviet model could not be renewed but only overthrown, along with Soviet hegemony, when the opportunity came. Interestingly enough, however, the model of the Italian Communist Party was followed with increasing attention by Eastern European intellectuals. Here was a party that could criticize Soviet policy and follow a democratic road to power in the West, while operating in a capitalist system and seemingly accepting the free market. The PCI did not reject Gramsci's ideas, and Italian Communists also advocated policies opposing those of liberal political forces in a free Parliament.

Thus, while Western Europeans discussed the British and French political models, Eastern Europeans looked to the PCI as an organization that
had freed itself from Soviet domination and intended to come to power
by achieving voter consensus, to govern in a democratic manner, and to
permit a free opposition to criticize its policies. After 1989 and the fall of
the Berlin Wall, the PCI and its successor (the Democratic Party of the
Left, PDS), continued to have influence.

RESTRUCTURING SOVIET COMMUNISM

Given the Soviet Union's inability to deal with the ferment in the
Communist world, except through force, Communism's days would be
numbered if the USSR itself faltered. Beginning in the mid-1970s, this is
exactly what occurred when the health of the long-reigning Soviet leader
Leonid Brezhnev declined drastically and the Soviet Union's political system proved unable to replace him with an effective leader. The situation
was compounded after Brezhnev's death, when two old and sick longtime party leaders followed him, each quickly dying soon after assuming
office. At the height of this political crisis, a younger leader, Mikhail
Gorbachev, took the helm. By the early 1980s, however, the USSR was in
full economic and moral decline, with Gorbachev forced to recognize the
need for a thoroughgoing, drastic, and complete reform if the Communist
system was to survive. He instituted a new policy called perestroika
(restructuring) and in 1987 published a book in English explaining his
ideas.

Perestroika: New Thinking for Our Country and the World paints a remark-
able picture of the last attempt to reform the Communist system from top
to bottom. In this book Gorbachev gave an honest assessment of the problems that Communism faced in the 1980s, but he did not repudiate
Socialism (which is the term Gorbachev used, but which here will be
employed interchangeably with Communism). Gorbachev gave a brief
history of the USSR since the 1917 revolution, claiming great progress for
Russia as a result of that event, especially considering the historical context of early Communism. Gorbachev attributed the errors made after the
revolution in part to the international capitalist opposition to the revolution, the urgency of building a new society, Russia's backwardness, its
need to make up the technological gap in a hurry because of the Nazi
threat, and its isolation. This context cannot fully explain the mistakes,
Gorbachev conceded: "There were mistaken premises and subjective
decisions." Over the decades the errors compounded the problems, causing them to accumulate; despite the enormous progress brought about by
Communism, those problems had produced the current inertia, conservatism, and stagnation.

How would the USSR's great problems—economic stagnation, declining economic growth, the paradox between high technological achievements and ordinary, everyday failures—be overcome? Perestroika and glasnost (openness).

According to Gorbachev, perestroika had already been initiated and was producing excellent results but still needed to permeate the USSR's entire political, social, and economic system and to rejuvenate both the Communist party and the state. He explained that this policy meant that individuals must become intimately involved with and support the policy. In the past, he admitted, individuals and the media had been struck down for criticizing government policy and debate had not been tolerated; now, however, criticism, self-criticism, discussion, and debate were essential if perestroika were to succeed and resolve the problems of Socialism. In brief, perestroika imposed greater democratization of Soviet life, "of all aspects of Soviet society," which Gorbachev fully supported. This was the glasnost policy that had already brought about so many positive results and was an integral part of perestroika—the two principles went hand in hand.

Gorbachev recognized that both policies ran counter to the long-term experiences of the Soviet citizen, who in the past would have been punished for implementing the ideas he now advocated as essential. For this reason, the Soviet leader attempted to put them into context and to provide both perestroika and glasnost with an ideological pedigree.

Past repression had resulted from party errors, not from the nature of Socialism, he argued. Indeed, Gorbachev objected, it was precisely the lack of democracy that had been most responsible for Communism's problems. Gorbachev then established Lenin as an ideological source and a father of perestroika, especially citing his late works. Gorbachev strenuously denied that Lenin was authoritarian, as claimed in the West, and considered this thesis a sign of ignorance or deliberate distortion. On the contrary, he wrote: "In effect, according to Lenin, socialism and democracy are indivisible." Gorbachev argued that Lenin believed not only that democracy was necessary if workers were to gain power but also that expanding democracy alone could consolidate that power. Further, Gorbachev attributed to Lenin the principle that the wider the sweep of the work to be done and the deeper the reforms, the greater the number of people whose interest must be aroused to participate in it: "This means that if we have set out for a radical and all-round restructuring, we must also unfold the entire potential of democracy."

Thus radical reform of Soviet society and its economy amounted to an internal revolution, but Communism as a doctrine and Soviet Communism as practice were intimately interwoven with the international dimension. In addition, by the late twentieth century, it was impossible for superpower politics not to have a global aspect. Gorbachev's book addressed the crucial issue of the USSR's relationship with the outside world.

While *Perestroika* discussed the USSR's world interests, the book focused on two main areas: the troubled people's democracies and Western Europe. Gorbachev took pride in the spread of Communism and what he considered its accomplishments in other countries. He admitted, however, that there had been and continued to be serious problems, which, again, he blamed not on Socialism but on "miscalculations" by the ruling parties in those countries. In line with his general theme, Gorbachev argued that—despite what he considers their undeniable achievements in transforming their societies—the Communist nations were also in need of restructuring and openness. Furthermore, he promised a new relationship with those countries based on the "absolute independence of each party and country."

At the same time, Gorbachev wrote, the Communist countries constituted a community, and therefore they should cooperate in economics and develop a common foreign policy consistent with the independence he advocated. In order to further Socialism's economic dynamism, Gorbachev set out a program of international meetings between the organs of the "fraternal" countries to increase economic integration. He also stressed Socialism's "humane" face by pointing out that the Communist parties and states respected each other, were concerned with both their own interests and those of others, and honored "the experience of others."

With reference to Western Europe, Gorbachev provided a rapid survey of relations between East and West illustrating why the region had a preeminent position for the USSR. He ended with the engaging concept of what he called the "common European home." In effect, this phrase indicated that all of Europe—East and West and including the USSR—should intensify its cooperation, leading eventually to a great "unified" entity.

Finally, Gorbachev enunciated a general principle for the relationship between Third World countries and the developed world—that each nation is entitled to make its own choices in the way it wishes to develop, and that these choices should not provide the occasion for international conflicts. In this section, and in his discussion of relations with the United States, Gorbachev criticized capitalism and its American champion. Despite these criticisms, however, Gorbachev called for disarmament, an end to ideological conflicts, and friendly relations between the Cold War rivals.

In his book Gorbachev presented a grand design for the reformation of the Communist world. Had these reform principles been enunciated and implemented earlier, the entire nature of "actually existing Socialism" might have been different, encouraging an entirely new relationship between the people's democracies and in their domestic affairs; if successful, his suggestions might even have affected relationships with the West. Gorbachev intended his perestroika and glasnost policies to save Soviet Communism—but historical events overtook the Soviet leader and the USSR.

18

MODELS IN
WESTERN EUROPEAN
POLITICAL THOUGHT

At the end of World War II the destruction wrought by the conflict appeared so vast that it forged a common experience. In addition to the outlandish cost of the war in the loss of property and human lives, it had uprooted millions of people and constrained them to move from the areas where their ancestors had lived for centuries. Despite all the suffering and injustices, however, and despite old problems that remained and new ones that loomed, the hope for an era of peace spread in Europe. There was a vivid desire for reconstruction and, among the young, a yearning for dialogue. Some values seemed to have lost their significance, and new principles would have to underpin the postwar political order.

"AMERICANISM" AND "SOVIETISM"

Despite the optimistic outlook, the spring of 1948 witnessed instead a drying up of many illusions and hopes as the "Iron Curtain" fell upon Europe. The separation was painful especially for those who had looked beyond their own political boundaries for inspiration and had firmly believed in solidarity and collaboration with other Europeans. A "cold" war had replaced the "hot" one. This situation meant that intellectual neutrality was impossible, as ideological deviations were not welcome in either camp. "Bipolarism" replaced ideological compromise, and there was little choice for intellectuals and politicians but to follow the directives of either the United States or the Soviet Union.

The stunning diplomatic events that followed World War II such as the Berlin blockade dramatically influenced European political thinkers.

Germany had been divided into four occupation zones, but in May 1949 the Western Allies allowed the American, British, and French zones to join together to constitute the German Federal Republic; then in the Soviet zone, the rival German Democratic Republic materialized, with its capital in East Berlin. The problem of East and West Berlin sanctioned the division between the American and Soviet superpowers, each of which sought to justify its political position on the cultural plane.

Thus the United States and the USSR gave birth to two opposing doctrines: "Americanism" and "Sovietism." To choose one of these dogmas meant to criticize and condemn the other, for these views soon became polarized into opposing visions of prosperity and revolutionary agitation. As an instrument of cultural propaganda, the prospect of wealth was no match for the myth of revolution, because, while the first held out the hope of material improvement, the second promised new idealistic values and deep social transformations. But would the revolutionary myth improve the standard of living and leave individuals free?

For supporters of "Americanism," the East European bloc embodied totalitarianism, dictatorship, and autocracy. For Soviet supporters, Western Europe remained the land of monopoly capitalism, salary dependence, and bourgeois exploitation of workers. Thus writers who defended liberalism were frequently condemned with the term "Americanism," and a policy of cultural "alignment" aimed at the ideological lumping together of all thinkers who rejected Marxist doctrine. Moreover, writers who believed in the value of social justice were craftily drawn by sympathizers of the Soviet system into popular protest demonstrations and were designated as theoreticians of the anticapitalist renovation of society.

It is important to indicate how this debate evolved in Europe. The polemics against collectivism seemed based on the opposed nature of liberalism and communism, both of which grew from economic presuppositions. Proponents of the American model employed the doctrines of economists such as Friedrich A. Hayek and Milton Friedman, both at the University of Chicago. According to Hayek, it was individualism that would enable a society to avoid "the road to serfdom"—the title of his well-known 1944 book. The disciples of Hayek and Friedman based their argument on the interdependency of political and economic liberty. Political liberty is possible only if a free market exists; where economic liberty does not exist, neither does political liberty. Hayek's *The Constitution of Liberty* (1960) and Friedman's *Capitalism and Freedom* (1962) best represented the terms of the argument.

Responding to the philosophy of liberalism, which claimed to renovate faith in the dignity of man, the Soviets countered with the standard dualism—working class versus capitalist imperialism. In this manner, the Soviets succeeded in extending the terms of the struggle beyond the domestic arena, from the fight against the bourgeois to the struggle against imperialism.

From the climate of passionate polemics that resulted, a sense of a humanistic European culture—with its origins in antiquity and which had diffused itself during the Middle Ages, the Renaissance, and the Enlightenment—reemerged. This European culture had mixed with local elements and had adapted itself to the necessities of the different countries. Despite the political dualism, therefore, Europeans attempted to give concrete expression to the concepts of liberation and renovation, which had been so important at the close of the war.

In order to understand the historical reasons for the contrast between communism and capitalism, Western European culture delved into a study of past political thinkers. Some scholars discovered the continuing relevance of Jean-Jacques Rousseau, whereas others preferred Montesquieu; some emphasized the political value of Filippo Buonarroti's ideas, and others drew inspiration from Giuseppe Mazzini; some searched for political solutions in Marx, and others looked for answers in Max Weber's sociological observations. This return to theorists of the past allowed European intellectuals to examine the reasons for different outlooks and to avoid becoming overly conditioned by the politics of the opposing political blocs. This historical perspective also stimulated the circulation of ideas, leaving the terms of the cultural debate open.

In a political and cultural context of such complexity, it is not easy to follow all the different lines of European political thought because proposals, hypotheses, judgments, and theories frequently overlapped. Much has been written about idealistic revolts, silent revolutions, change of values, social transformations, and doctrinal dogmatism, but the ideological history of Europe between 1948 and 1989, with all its twists and turns, concluded with the end of the Eastern political bloc and the victory of cultural pluralism.

In light of the end of the Cold War, it is easy to ignore the importance of doctrinal tendencies that dominated these forty years. In this sense, it is prudent to examine the governmental forms established in Europe during this period.

After 1948 Western European governmental forms were defined as "parliamentary democracies" to distinguish them from the "people's democracies" set up in Eastern Europe. French critic Raymond Aron argued in his work *Democracy and Totalitarianism: A Theory of Political Systems* (1965) that the difference between the two forms of government depended on party characteristics. In the parliamentary democracies the governing party accepted the coexistence of other parties and received endorsement of its policies through debates and votes; in the people's democracies, the governing party monopolized political activity and imposed its will on society as state policy. It may be added that in the parliamentary democracies the fundamental presupposition was the presence in parliament of an opposition party or parties—in other words, a multiparty system—whereas in the peoples' democracies the Communist party ruled alone and imposed its decisions on the country (a one-party state).

This is the crucial distinction between "democracy" and "monocracy." The latter term, however, cannot be reduced to the single-party regime; as a political doctrine, "monocracy" means a system that assigns an exclusive and totalizing function to some cultural units such as "class," "work," and "proletariat." "Democracy," on the other hand, does not signify solely political liberty of action conceded to two or more parties but is polyvalent, with many centers of power; this means to distinguish between the head of the state and the head of the government, between parliament and public opinion, between entrepreneurs and unions, between governmental and opposition forces.

Though judgments on the types of governments adopted in Western Europe may diverge, it is important to indicate what forms of governments in the postwar era have achieved the status of political models. Two Western European states provide such models because of the political function they have assigned either to their parliament or to their chief of state. These countries are Britain and France.

THE BRITISH MODEL

How did "liberated" Europe view England? For continental Europe, Great Britain was not only the country that had successfully fought Nazism but also the country that had found national unity in its Parliament. Government and opposition had loyally collaborated in the House of Commons to fight against the enemy; as effective representatives of the real political forces in the country, both developed their action within the parliamentary context. The prime minister chose the members of the cabinet, but the opposition leader set up a shadow cabinet in order to prepare for the orderly transition of power. The parties had an electoral function, but Parliament guided the country.

Amazingly enough, the military victory that the Conservative government achieved over Nazi Germany did not condition the elections, and in 1945, the British people elected a Labour government. But in England electoral change hardly signaled a reduction of the faith that the people had in Parliament. A government that had won the elections enjoyed electoral stability for five years, but the majority in the House of Commons was obliged to protect the rights of the minority. The government proposed laws but by tradition was ready to accept amendments and modifications in the course of parliamentary debate. People who had lived under totalitarian regimes could not but be impressed by a system of government that gave Parliament a central role in legislating and governing.

Under the spur of the Labour party, the British parliamentary system also sought to implement the welfare state; this meant a political order capable of assuring all citizens health, housing, education, and a minimum wage. This project of a welfare state, formulated in the name of civil solidarity, found a wide consensus in Parliament, for it seemed to be a response to the social system propounded by the communists. The concept of the welfare state had a powerful influence on European reformism and found concrete application in harmony with British doctrinal considerations in Sweden.

These are the major reasons that explain why the British political system achieved the status of a model in Europe. Three thinkers have been particularly important in this development.

In 1949 Isaiah Berlin, born in Riga, Latvia, in 1909, published an article entitled "Political Ideas in the Twentieth Century" that aimed to clarify the "sense of continuity of European intellectual tradition." In his opinion, humanitarian individualism and romantic nationalism were the two great political movements of the nineteenth century, and the adherents of both had been misled into believing that social and national problems could be resolved by intelligence and virtue. The exaggerated forms of these currents were communism and fascism.

Neither communism nor fascism had found fertile ground in England, and, turning to the British intellectual milieu, Berlin looked forward to a new concept of society, one in which values would not be analyzed in terms of desires but—while taking account of individual and social interests—in terms of behavior. Taking his distance from both "American materialism" and "Communist fanaticism," Berlin proposed a general rethinking of political theory in order to defeat "the enemies of reason and individual freedom." Certainly, evils were less acute in societies traditionally opposed to extremism, such as the British, but precisely for this reason, British political philosophy must reconsider with tolerance individual and collective interests.

In his inaugural lecture at Oxford University on May 31, 1958, Berlin linked political theory and moral philosophy and lauded negative liberties "from" things. He cited a liberal tradition that, from Hobbes, Locke, and Adam Smith to John Stuart Mill, had defended civil liberties and individual rights against "coercion," "exploitation," and "humiliation." Now, according to Berlin, the stress should be placed on positive liberties, and intellectuals should emphasize, rather than "liberty from," "liberty to."

This meant that as members of society individuals must have the liberty to make rational choices and to be able to possess and dispose of whatever permitted them self-realization. Berlin believed that if positive liberty must be safeguarded, limits must be placed on the sovereignty of others in such a way as to ensure the inviolability of individual liberty. In order to achieve this end, a plurality of values must always be recognized and respected.

Berlin was aware that the British political system was founded on this principle, but it was still necessary to insist on the difference between the two liberties, positive and negative, in order to avoid the twin dangers of excessive nationalism and Marxism.

Like Berlin, Karl Popper was also born abroad and was called to teach at an English university (in this case, the London School of Economics). Popper's first work in English, *The Poverty of Historicism* (1944), was an accusation against German historicism, which Popper argued had furnished the doctrinal basis of both Fascism and Nazism. He followed this book in 1945 with *The Open Society and Its Enemies*, in which he contrasted the "closed" to the "open" society. The "closed" society is a totalitarian social system, whereas the "open" one is based on the critical use of reason, which serves to defend the liberty of individuals and groups by means of democratic institutions. Only an open society, Popper wrote in his introduction, "provides an institutional framework that permits reforms without violence" and as a consequence the use of reason in political matters. Parliamentary democracies allow criticism of politicians and their replacement through elections. Democracy is a parliamentary order that allows substitution of the political class and social changes without revolution. Popper argued that a democratic state may be distinguished from a dictatorial one by asking whether its institutions allow the replacement of governments without either violence or the physical elimination of the opposition. In parliamentary democracies the constant use of reason prevails; reason rejects violence and imposes itself through the logic of its arguments.

Popper discovered enemies of the open society even in antiquity, but for him the two great enemies of democracy in the modern world are Hegel and Marx. Popper acknowledged the merits of each but noted that Hegel was the apologist of the Prussian state and elaborated the premises for totalitarian movements from Fascism to Nazism, and Marx, though he saw clearly the evils of capitalism, launched with his economic determinism the myth of an egalitarian society and broke the ground for the totalitarian excesses of Communist society. Against these enemies, he concluded, it is necessary to strengthen and defend "those democratic institutions upon which freedom, and with it progress depends."

In this ideological apposing of the "closed" and the "open" society, there is praise neither for "Americanism" nor for capitalist society, but only recognition of the rational role played by the British Parliament, which, ever since the Glorious Revolution of 1688, has followed a rational line in examining political problems.

Popper's successor as head of the London School of Economics was Ralf Dahrendorf, born in Hamburg. Although familiar with Marx and cognizant of the importance of social conflict, Dahrendorf believed in a new liberalism (*The New Liberty: Survival and Justice in a Changing World*, 1975). Dahrendorf kept his distance from the American model, favoring an English-type liberalism founded on the "alliance" between liberalism and democracy. In his writings, Dahrendorf had argued that there are social forces too powerful to be stopped, and the struggle for the rights of citizens is one of these. But the major function of the "new liberalism" is to shape the future rather than fixating on abstract principles. The proponents of equality have altered modern society, Dahrendorf argued, but now it is time to emphasize that individual rights are not an aim in themselves but tools to increase opportunities, such as the opportunity to develop one's capacities to the fullest. Dahrendorf's political model for a free society is England.

In his book *On Britain* (1982), Dahrendorf told the story of his "love" for England and justified his defense of British "institutions and attitudes." In Britain "there is a fundamental liberty about life which is not easily found elsewhere." Dahrendorf praised the House of Commons, where government and its opposition sit opposite each other. The prime minister and the head of the opposition sit closely together but carry on a continual polemic with one another. In England governments have an apparently unbeatable position, but they can easily lose the next elections and lose power. For Dahrendorf, the British Parliament reflects the nation as no other, and its political system is "democracy at work."

THE FRENCH MODEL

The problem of the role of the head of state has frequently been at the center of French political debate, which is particularly sensitive to the question of Bonapartism. Ever since the French Revolution of 1789, the issue of how much power the head of state should have was a constant one, and was apparently resolved with the crisis of May 16, 1877, which shook the Third Republic and greatly reduced the power of the presidency for the next several decades.

The problem returned to the fore, however, after the liberation of Paris in 1944. Once the proposal to resurrect the Third Republic met defeat, a Constituent Assembly was elected to prepare a constitution with a unicameral legislature. This plan met defeat in May 1946 because of the opposition of General Charles de Gaulle and the Christian Democrats

(MRP). A new Constituent Assembly was elected, and in October 1946 the bicameral Fourth Republic with a weak presidency was established. De Gaulle and his movement (RPF) opposed this construction and favored a political system with a strong executive power. The political crisis that weakened the Fourth Republic as a result of the Algerian War allowed de Gaulle, recalled to power in 1958, to propose a new constitution with a strong presidency. The French approved this document in October of the same year, and the Fifth Republic was inaugurated.

De Gaulle remained in power from 1959 to 1969, after which the system he founded continued through the election of several presidents. In spite of predictions to the contrary, the system remained intact, even with the appointment of prime ministers from parties other than the president's.

With the passage of time the Fifth Republic has become a political model of representative government for other European countries. It is a parliamentary order with a strong executive, not an imitation of the United States. The head of state, who is elected by universal suffrage, is the guardian of the constitution, the guarantor of governmental continuity, and defender of the will of the citizens and of state interests. The salient characteristics of the French system have been analyzed in different ways by René Capitant and Maurice Duverger.

Capitant, a professor and minister after the war, identified four fundamental principles of democracy: autonomy, equality, secularism, and authority. These principles were necessary for a democratic revision of the parliamentary regime established by the Fourth Republic; he believed that the republic was illegitimate because it concentrated political sovereignty in Parliament's hands, violating the principle of popular sovereignty.

Capitant's judgment on the Fifth Republic, however, was a positive one. The formal distinction between head of state and head of government was very important for the separation of powers, and with the constitution of the Fifth Republic, Parliament ceased to be sovereign. Sovereignty was returned to the head of state, the origin of governmental power, as recognized by the president's power to name the head of government. From this fact derived the prime minister's subordination to the president of the republic.

According to Capitant, with the 1958 constitution, universal suffrage underpinned the authority of the president of the republic and the National Assembly. In this manner, the significance of the political participation of citizens changed in a profound manner, since it was no longer the political parties that nominated the president by cutting deals; now it was the people who elected the president and the National Assembly, and it was the people who reserved the right to confirm or withdraw their confidence in both.

Unlike Capitant, Maurice Duverger took a negative view of the Fifth Republic at its establishment. He had criticized the Fourth Republic because of the excessive power of the parties, and he had called for a strong executive power. With the advent of the Fifth Republic, he underlined the conservative aspects of the new construction. He agreed that the political tendency had been toward a stronger executive but argued that the structure of de Gaulle's republic blocked the alternation in power of great coalitions and that the political system prevented the affirmation of presidential politics. Duverger feared that under the new constitutional order France might become a "republican monarchy," with the monarch elected by the center parties (*La monarchie républicaine* [The Republican Monarchy], 1974).

Though this development did not come about, Duverger did anticipate the "political cohabitation" (the president and the prime minister from different parties) that materialized after the 1988 elections. Altering his previous views, Duverger became the theoretician of "presidentialism," arguing that the presidential system allows for efficient, stable government that remains in contact with the nation—qualities essential for complex modern societies. He also believes that the presidential system can resolve crises that endanger democracy—which parliaments lack the instruments to do. Duverger also emphasized the differences of the French and the American presidential systems. In the United States, unlike in France, the president governs without any formal link to the legislature.

In his book *The French Political System* (1985), Duverger synthesized the characteristics of the French constitutional order, which he considers radically different from the British parliamentary and the American presidential models. The French system, he believes, has its origins in the French Revolution of 1789 and is a "historical formation." Because of its structure, the French constitution of 1958 is open to different governmental possibilities. There are three governmental institutions, the president of the republic, the government, and the Parliament, all of which operate in a party system. This system can function well because it rests on a solid national consensus and on several electoral mechanisms—a majoritarian system and a runoff for parliamentary elections, and universal suffrage to elect the president. The two political alternatives are either the hegemony of the president, if he has a majority in parliament, or a president opposed by a parliamentary majority. This system, according to Duverger, allows for a reformist policy and permits progress toward equality.

The French system has become a political model for European constitutionalists and political theorists, particularly when discussing the theme of a presidential republic. The French order's great strength is that it has combined political stability with flexibility.

In brief, the British and French parliamentary democratic models, though dissimilar, feature a common characteristic: pluralism—of ideas, parties, and labor and business organizations. For this reason they have frequently been contrasted with the governments set up in Eastern Europe after 1945 that followed the Soviet model—all marked by one-party social systems, monolithic thought systems, and monopolistic economies.

Interestingly enough, there is another system that combines aspects of the French and the British models—Germany's. The German system provides for strong parliamentary government. It allows broad representation but excludes from parliament parties that fail to achieve at least 5 percent of the vote. This feature has prevented very small splinter organizations from creating governmental instability of the kind that characterized Italy. German postwar stability and the country's cultural and economic influence may make Germany a political model, especially to Eastern Europeans after the fall of Communism.

DEMOCRACY

In the second half of the twentieth century in Western Europe, reflections on the concepts of liberty and equality have been widespread, and there has been lively discussion of forms of representation and political participation. But the dominant theme has been democracy. It would be difficult to find examples of political scientists or philosophers who have not confronted this theme in some way: "real" democracy versus "false" democracy; "participatory" democracy contrasted to "representative" democracy; "superior" democracy preferred to "decadent" democracy.

The same applies to the analysis of parties; the problem of democracy has been the common denominator. When proposals for electoral reforms are made, they are made in the name of democracy. Critical considerations on the practical functioning of parliaments have had as their common goal respect for democracy.

This concern with democracy has stimulated reinterpretations of writers such as Rousseau, Tocqueville, Marx, and Mill. The long debates on European unification have always involved intensive discussion of the democratic themes. When decisions are made by common European institutions, representatives of one country or another invariably make reference to democracy. Ethnic minorities and champions of the rights of different regions base their claims for autonomy on democratic rights. The defense of human rights has been presented as the defense of the rights of citizens. Even great domestic and international political compromises are interpreted as acts of democratic tolerance. In Italy—the country that brought the Socialists into government in the 1960s and the Communists as major participants in the political system—Liberals,

Socialists, and Communists all defined themselves as democrats. It is often difficult to distinguish between liberal democracy and social democracy in European political literature because the exponents of both have used the language of democracy.

Democracy has also played a crucial role in the debate over the most urgent theme in Europe—political unification. As a result, political scientists have carefully examined the nexus of democracy and European federalism. In the past, federalism had been utilized in the struggle against fascism and its nationalistic pretensions, but after 1948 in Western Europe it was repeatedly proposed as an alternative to the American and Soviet blocs. In conformity with these ideas, the European Parliament, elected for the first time in 1979 and meeting in Strasbourg (France), immediately demanded that the institutions of the European Community be made more democratic. The theoretical elaboration of European unification has deemphasized the national state, the role of political parties, and the powers of individual governments and has emphasized popular consensus.

Which criteria have guided these discussions? A "utilitarian" approach has been consistently adopted and followed by political scientists, jurists, and historians. This methodology has found its primary exponent in the noted Italian political scientist and philosopher Norberto Bobbio. He has argued that the future of democracy in a polyvalent society cannot be separated from the utility it represents for ordinary citizens. Bobbio has emphasized rationalism of the kind propagated by Enlightenment thinkers. He has cited the examples of individual liberty and civil equality, two ideals that should not be pursued as absolute categories but by implementing reforms and renouncing appeals to revolution. For Bobbio, civil society can be defended by respecting constitutional norms and by checking on public officials. In a like manner, international understandings should rest on reciprocal tolerance and on a common desire for peace.

The collapse of the "monocratic" regimes of Eastern Europe in 1989 marked a turning point for European political thought because any opposition to Communism meant implicit ideological support for Western political structures. The "political order of a free people" theorized by Hayek in 1979 was the antithesis of the "political order of an oppressed people" characteristic of Communist countries. The existence of a "monocracy" not only disguised the possible defects of representative systems but also conferred a philosophical value on the defense of constituted interests. That "implicit" defense has now disappeared, and European intellectuals—East and West—will have to refine not only the concept of democracy but also its practical mechanisms if parliamentary democracies are to flourish in a modern society.

BIBLIOGRAPHICAL
ESSAY

A word about the works mentioned in the text: They are not cited here, nor are the primary writings of the authors, which can be found easily under the author's name in the library. A note at the beginning of the book explains the use of translated titles in the text itself.

In this bibliographical essay we make no attempt to be exhaustive, but we hope that it will serve as a useful guide to further reading. Only English-language books are cited here, and—with rare exceptions when there are no other convenient sources—articles and theses have been omitted. The reader should also keep in mind that for intellectuals of more recent periods audiovisual sources are also available, although they are not cited here. These as well as printed sources may be found by using the electronic tools at the disposal of modern researchers and readers. Finally, it is worth noting that the English-language literature on some of the authors discussed in this book presents surprising gaps. Also, lest we become too dependent on electronic research facilities, readers would be well served by taking advantage of bibliographies and footnote citations in the works mentioned here. Biographies are listed only when they may be particularly useful for an analysis of the political thought of the person under consideration.

INTRODUCTION

Aside from works that discuss political theory in the abstract, there are no recent books comparable to the present text. The closest general work is George H. Sabine, *A History of Political Theory*, 3rd edition (New York, 1961), the scope of which begins in ancient times and reaches fascism and socialism. Another book, even older but still useful for the context of European political thought, is a collection of essays, J. P. Mayer, et al., *Political Thought: The European Tradition* (London, 1942). A full development of the themes treated in our Introduction is Salvo Mastellone, *A History of Democracy in Europe: From Montesquieu to 1989* (Florence, 1995). On the twentieth century, there are Karl Dietrich Bracher's *The Age of Ideology* (London, 1984) and Norberto Bobbio, *Ideological Profile of the Twentieth Century* (Princeton, 1995).

CHAPTER 1: RESTORATION MODELS
AND UTOPIAN CONSTRUCTIONS, 1815–1830

Helen B. Posgate's *Madame de Staël* (New York, 1968) gives a good, brief overview of this important woman's life and influence, but the classic biography remains J. Christopher Herold, *Mistress to an Age: A Life of Madame de Staël* (Westport, CT, 1975). For the entire range of Johann Gottlieb Fichte's ideas, see Daniel Breazeale and Tom Rockmore, eds., *New Perspectives on Fichte* (Atlantic Highlands, NJ, 1966). W. O. Henderson's *Friedrich List: Economist and Visionary* (London, 1983) is a good discussion of List's all-important economic ideas.

There is ample literature on Saint-Simon. Frank E. Manuel, *The New World of Henri Saint-Simon* (Cambridge, MA, 1956), is a clear exposition of Saint-Simon's thought within the context of the times by a well-known scholar. Arthur John Booth, *Saint-Simon and Saint-Simonianism* (London, 1871), is old but provides a clear illustration of Saint-Simon's thought and its connection to socialism. Ghiţa Ionescu, *The Political Thought of Saint-Simon* (London, 1976), is a collection of texts but is valuable for a long introduction that discusses Saint-Simon's political thought.

Jeremy Bentham's ideas should be considered within the context of English utilitarianism, which included not only Bentham but other important thinkers as well, such as John Stuart Mill. General works that might be profitably consulted on this school include Elie Helévy, *The Growth of Philosophical Radicalism* (London, 1928), a general examination of the ideas of Bentham and the English utilitarians by a famous French historian of England. The book includes a discussion of William Godwin, also mentioned in this chapter; Godwin's political and social theories are examined at length in John P. Clarke, *The Philosophical Anarchism of William Godwin* (Princeton, 1977), and D. H. Munro, *Godwin's Moral Philosophy* (London, 1953), is a good, brief, introduction to his thought. John Plamenatz, *The English Utilitarians* (Oxford, 1966), also provides a general view of the utilitarians, including Bentham, Mill, and others. Leslie Stephen, *The English Utilitarians*, vol. 1 (New York, 1950), deals with Bentham's philosophy. F. R. Leavis, ed., *John Stuart Mill on Bentham and Coleridge* (New York, 1950), includes a classic essay by Mill on Bentham. John Dinwiddy has written a brief introduction to Bentham's thought, *Bentham* (Oxford, 1989). D. J. Manning's *The Mind of Jeremy Bentham* (New York, 1968) also discusses his ideas in general. For more specialized analyses, see David Lyons, *In the Interest of the Governed* (Oxford, 1973), for Bentham's ideas on utility and the law; on his impact on nationalism, see Elmer Louis Kayser, *The Grand Social Enterprise* (New York, 1932).

Analyses of Robert Owen's beliefs can also be readily found, but they are best understood in a general context. This is done particularly well by J.F.C. Harrison, *Quest for the New Moral World* (New York, 1969). R. G. Garnett, *Co-operation and the Owenite Socialist Communities in Britain* (Manchester, 1972), provides an analysis and evaluation of communitarian thought during the period. Charles Fourier's thought receives a brief but clear treatment in Nicholas V. Riasanovsky, *The Teaching of Charles Fourier* (Berkeley, 1969), and Jonathan Beecher, *Charles Fourier: The Visionary and His World* (Berkeley, 1986), is good on both the theory and its relationship to society.

Chapter 2:
Early Liberalism

The most thorough biography of Humboldt in English, with ample consideration of his ideas, is Paul R. Sweet, *Wilhelm von Humboldt: A Biography*, 2 vols. (Columbus, OH, 1978–1980).

Of the thinkers examined in this chapter, Benjamin Constant seems to have drawn the most attention from English-speaking scholars. Among the books that discuss his ideas, William H. Holdheim's *Benjamin Constant* (London, 1961) is a good, brief introduction, including a chapter on political theory. Elizabeth W. Schermerhorn, *Benjamin Constant* (Boston, 1924), is a biography that emphasizes Constant's influence on liberal government in France. On Constant's more general impact on modern Liberalism, consult Stephen Holmes, *Benjamin Constant and the Making of Modern Liberalism* (New Haven, 1984).

In general, the practical action of Thiers and Guizot, rather than their thought, seems to have more fascination for scholars, but books that consider both together are the most valuable. René Albrecht-Carrié, *Adolphe Thiers* (Boston, 1977), is a good, short general introduction to Thiers's life and action by a noted scholar of Europe. J.P.T. Bury and R. P. Tombs, *Thiers, 1797–1877: A Political Life* (London, 1986), is probably the best biography in English. John M.S. Allison, *Thiers and the French Monarchy* (London, 1968), originally published in 1926, addresses the nature of Thiers's liberalism. An introduction to Guizot's political thought and action is Douglas Johnson, *Guizot: Aspects of French History, 1787–1874* (London, 1973). Elizabeth Parnham Brush's older work (original publication date, 1929), *Guizot in the Early Years of the Orleanist Monarchy* (New York, 1979), is a good examination of a complex period. Finally, E. L. Woodward, *Three Studies in European Conservatism* (London, 1963), analyzes Guizot's thought and place in European history and includes sections on Metternich and the Catholic Church during this period.

Chapter 3:
Hegel: From Civil Society to State

As might be expected, the literature on Hegel is vast. What follows is a sampling.

Frederick C. Beiser, ed., *The Cambridge Companion to Hegel* (Cambridge, 1993), is a useful introduction to Hegel's thought and collects a series of essays on various aspects of his philosophy. Raymond Plant, *Hegel: An Introduction* (London, 1983), is a brief introduction that includes a chapter on civil society. J. N. Findlay, *Hegel: A Re-examination* (London, 1970), is a larger but still manageable treatment of Hegel's thought.

On the more strictly political implications of Hegel's thought, see Shlomo Avineri, *Hegel's Theory of the Modern State* (Cambridge, 1972), Charles Taylor, *Hegel and Modern Society* (Cambridge, 1979), and Judith N. Shklar, *Freedom and Independence: A Study of the Political Ideas of Hegel's "Phenomenology of Mind"* (Cambridge, 1976). A collection of Hegel's works on politics, notable for a long introductory essay by Z. A. Pelczynaski, has been published under the title *Hegel's*

Political Writings. On some of the issues raised in the discussion of his political thought, consult Michael O. Hardimon, *Hegel's Social Philosophy* (Cambridge, 1994), and Laurence Dickey, *Hegel: Religion, Economics, and the Politics of Spirit* (Cambridge, 1987). On the question of the French Revolution, see Joachim Ritter, *Hegel and the French Revolution: Essays on the Philosophy of Right* (Cambridge, MA, 1982).

It is important to put Hegel also in the context of general philosophy. William Desmond, ed., *Hegel and His Critics* (Albany, 1989), is a collection of essays that view aspects of Hegel's thought in light of other philosophers and includes several essays on the relationship with Marx's thought. Lucio Colletti has written a book dedicated entirely to the relationship between Hegelianism and Marxism, *Marxism and Hegel* (London, 1973). On Hegel's influence during his period, William J. Brazill's *The Young Hegelians* (New Haven, 1970) is a good source. Finally, it is also interesting to see how Hegel was considered by two contemporary philosophers who are mentioned in later chapters—Theodor W. Adorno, *Hegel: Three Studies* (Cambridge, MA, 1993), and Georg Lukács, *The Young Hegel* (Cambridge, MA, 1975).

CHAPTER 4:
JACOBIN EQUALITY AND NATIONAL LIBERATION

Aside from the volume by Talmon cited in the text, there is very little in English on Buonarroti, who certainly merits greater study by English-speaking scholars. Elizabeth L. Eisenstein, *The First Professional Revolutionist: Filippo Michele Buonarroti* (Cambridge, MA, 1959), argues cogently that Buonarroti was the first person to practice a new vocation, that of a "professional" revolutionary. The book also has a good bibliographical essay. On other aspects of Buonarroti, see two articles by Arthur Lehning, "Buonarroti's Ideas on Communism and Dictatorship," *International Review of Social History* 2 (1957): 266–287, and "Buonarroti and His Secret Societies," *International Review of Social History* 1 (1956): 112–140.

Mazzini was more fortunate for a period, but the scholarly output has not kept pace with his continuing importance. Roland Sorti's *Mazzini: A Life for the Religion of Politics* emphasizes that Mazzini's concept of revolution included all classes and nationalities. Denis Mack Smith, *Mazzini* (New Haven, 1994) does not pay a great deal of attention to political theory. Mazzini's thought is examined briefly and succinctly by the great historian and exile from Fascism, Gaetano Salvemini, in his classic *Mazzini* (Stanford, 1957, but originally published in Italy some twenty-five years earlier). Spencer M. Di Scala provides more information on Mazzini's thought in *Italy: From Revolution to Republic, 1700 to the Present* (Boulder, 1995). Frank Coppa has published an article relating Mazzini's religious to his political thought: "The Religious Basis of Giuseppe Mazzini's Political Thought," *Journal of Church and State* 12:2 (Spring 1970): 237–253. Mazzini's political action may be followed in a series of older but still useful books, including Gwilm O. Griffith, *Mazzini: Prophet of Modern Europe* (New York, 1970); E.E.Y. Hales, *Mazzini and the Secret Societies* (London, 1956); and the still-useful Bolton King, *Mazzini* (London, 1903).

An idea of Babeuf's communism may be gleaned from R. B. Rose, *Gracchus Babeuf: The First Revolutionary Communist* (Stanford, 1978), and David Thompson tells the story of the attempted revolution in his brief *The Babeuf Plot: The Making of a Republican Legend* (Westport, CT, 1975). For the sources and development of Etienne Cabet's thought, see Christopher H. Johnson, *Utopian Communism in France: Cabet and the Icarians, 1839–1851* (Ithaca, 1974).

CHAPTER 5:
DEMOCRACY, SOCIETY, AND LIBERALISM

The literature on Alexis de Tocqueville is extensive. Saguiv A. Hadari has published a brief analysis of his work, *Theory in Practice: Tocqueville's New Science of Politics* (Stanford, 1989), and Larry Siedentrop, *Tocqueville* (Oxford, 1994), is a general introduction to Tocqueville's thought. Roger Voesche, *The Strange Liberalism of Alexis de Tocqueville* (Ithaca, 1987), puts Tocqueville in the context of his age, and Seymour Drescher, *Tocqueville and England* (Cambridge, MA, 1964), discusses his relationship with England.

A number of scholars have examined the "problems" raised in Tocqueville's writings. These include Pierre Manent, *Tocqueville and the Nature of Democracy* (London, 1996), Marvin Zetterbaum, *Tocqueville and the Problem of Democracy* (Stanford, 1967), Seymour Drescher, *Dilemmas of Democracy: Tocqueville and Modernization* (Pittsburgh, 1968), and, finally, the brief but cogent Irving M. Zeitlin, *Liberty, Equality, and Revolution in Alexis de Tocqueville* (Boston, 1971). Alan S. Kahan's *Aristocratic Liberalism* (New York, 1992) discusses both Tocqueville and John Stuart Mill.

The literature on Mill is vast, and readers should have no trouble finding books on him. A good idea of Mill and his world can be obtained from Gertrude Himmelfarb, *On Liberty and Liberalism* (New York, 1974). Commentaries on Mill's theories include Maurice Cowling, *Mill and Liberalism* (Cambridge, 1963), a brief but convincing treatment; Charles Douglas, *John Stuart Mill: A Study of His Philosophy* (Edinburgh, 1895), an older but still useful work; H. J. McCloskey, *John Stuart Mill: A Critical Study* (London, 1971), a more strictly philosophical study; and Alan Ryan, *J. S. Mill* (London, 1974), a thorough treatment of his work and influence. A study of Mill's impact in France is Iris Wessel Mueller, *John Stuart Mill and French Thought* (Urbana, IL, 1956). A specialized collection of essays on different aspects of Mill's thought has been published by Wesley E. Cooper, Kai Nielsen, and Steven C. Patten, eds., *New Essays on John Stuart Mill and Utilitarianism* (Guelph, Ontario, 1979).

On some of the other writers mentioned in this chapter, the life and theories of Louis Blanc are presented in Leo A. Loubère, *Louis Blanc* (Chicago, 1961), and Alastair Buchan wrote *The Spare Chancellor: The Life of Walter Bagehot* (East Lansing, MI, 1960).

CHAPTER 6: LIBERAL DEMOCRACY

The biography by Ann R. Cacoullos, *Thomas Hill Green: Philosopher of Rights* (New York, 1974), is a good introduction to Green's life and thought. Melvin Richter, *The Politics of Conscience: T. H. Green and His Age* (Cambridge, MA, 1964), studies the person and the impact of his thought. I. M. Greengarten, *Thomas Hill Green and the*

Development of Liberal-Democratic Thought (Toronto, 1981), is an analysis of Green's thought, with an appendix comparing Green and Mill.

A good introduction to Acton's life and philosophy is Gertrude Himmelfarb, *Lord Acton: A Study in Conscience and Politics* (Chicago, 1961), and G. E. Fasnacht, *Acton's Political Philosophy* (London, 1952), is a valuable summary of his political beliefs. Lionel Kochan, *Acton on History* (London, 1954), is a short introduction to Acton's historical ideas. Damian McElrath et al., *Lord Acton: The Decisive Decade, 1864–1874* (Louvin, 1970), is a collection of essays and supporting documents on Acton's liberal and religious development; the work has a good bibliography.

On Joseph Chamberlain, see Richard Jay, *Joseph Chamberlain: A Political Study* (Oxford, 1981), for his political thought, and Elsie E. Gulley, *Joseph Chamberlain and English Social Politics* (New York, 1974), for a thorough analysis of his political action. William L. Strauss, *Joseph Chamberlain and the Theory of Imperialism* (New York, 1971), examines his view of imperialism.

Hobhouse can be viewed through John E. Owen, *L. T. Hobhouse: Sociologist* (Columbus, 1974), which analyzes his theories and their impact. Hugh Carter, *The Social Theories of L. T. Hobhouse* (Port Washington, NY, 1968), presents a short emphasis on Hobhouse's theories, and Stefan Collini, *Liberalism and Sociology: L. T. Hobhouse and Political Argument in England, 1880–1914* (Cambridge, 1914), examines the connection of liberalism and sociology in Hobhouse's thought.

CHAPTER 7: THE CLASS STRUGGLE: SOCIALISM, COMMUNISM, AND SOCIAL DEMOCRACY

The Chartist movement has been well studied. Henry Weisser, *British Working-Class Movements and Europe, 1815–1848* (Manchester, 1975), is an excellent and well-documented history of Chartism in all its aspects. Dorothy Thompson, *The Chartists: Popular Politics in the Industrial Revolution* (New York, 1984), studies the social groups supporting Chartism, and G.D.H. Cole, *Chartist Portraits* (London, 1941), provides portraits of Chartist leaders and their action. Asa Briggs, *Chartist Studies* (London, 1959), presents Chartism in different locations and Chartist policies on particular issues. John Saville, *1848: The British State and the Chartist Movement* (Cambridge, 1987), tells the story of Chartism during its waning days.

Full-length political biographies of Chartist leaders include Alfred Plummer, *Bronterre: A Political Biography of Bronterre O'Brian, 1804–1864* (London, 1971); Graham Wallas, *The Life of Francis Place* (London, 1951); Donald Read and Eric Glasgow, *Feargus O'Connor: Irishman and Chartist* (London, 1961).

Finally, J.F.C. Harrison and Dorothy Thompson, *Bibliography of the Chartist Movement, 1837–1976* (Atlantic Highlands, NJ, 1978), includes manuscripts, contemporary printed sources, and secondary sources.

The literature on Marx and Marxism is vast, and the reader will have no trouble finding books. The list below is restricted to introductions to Marx's thought and to the movement, and to particular areas of interest.

Fritz J. Raddatz, *Karl Marx: A Political Biography* (Boston, 1978), emphasizes Marx's political action. Oscar J. Hammen, *The Red '48ers: Karl Marx and Friedrich Engels* (New York, 1969), focuses on a critical period. W. O. Henderson, *The Life of*

Friedrich Engels, 2 vols. (London, 1976), is a detailed life of Marx's partner and an account of his impact on European Socialism.

G.D.H. Cole, *What Marx Really Meant* (Westport, CT, 1970), is an attempt by a well-known scholar of Marxist movements to explain Marx's ideas. George Lichtheim, *Marxism: An Historical and Critical Study* (New York, 1963), a particularly clear work, remains a valuable study of the development of Marxism. Louis B. Boudin, *The Theoretical System of Karl Marx* (New York, 1967), is a good general view; Richard Smith, *Introduction to Marx and Engels* (Boulder, 1987), is a clear explanation of the theory. Dirk J. Struik, ed., *Economic and Philosophic Manuscripts of 1844 by Karl Marx* (New York, 1964), has a long introduction. Bertram D. Wolfe, *Marxism: One Hundred Years in the Life of a Doctrine* (New York, 1965), is a retrospective look at Marxist ideology. Iring Fetscher, *Marx and Marxism* (New York, 1971), analyzes the development of Marxism.

Jean L. Cohen has taken a critical look at important Marxist concepts in *Class and Civil Society* (Amherst, 1982). Hal Draper, *Karl Marx's Theory of Revolution* (New York, 1978), attempts to clarify one of Marx's major ideas. Richard N. Hunt, *The Political Ideas of Marx and Engels*, 2 vols. (Pittsburgh, 1984), looks at the entire thought of the two in detail. Marshall Cohen, Thomas Nagel, Thomas Scanlon, eds., *Marx, Justice, and History* (Princeton, 1980), is a collection of essays on different aspects of Marxism. Henri Lefebvre, *The Sociology of Marx* (New York, 1968), views Marx's sociological concepts, and a complex book on Marx's economic ideas is James F. Becker, *Marxian Political Economy* (Cambridge, 1977). C. Wright Mills, *The Marxists* (New York, 1963), is a classic work on different Marxists by an eminent sociologist.

Ferdinand Lassalle was analyzed by Eduard Bernstein, *Ferdinand Lassalle* (London, 1970), in which the revisionist philosopher viewed Lassalle as a social reformer; in addition, there is a short biography of Lassalle by David Footman, *Ferdinand Lassalle: Romantic Revolutionary* (New Haven, 1947). Helmut Trotnow, *Karl Liebknecht* (Hamden, CT, 1984), is a political biography of the revolutionary. There is also a biography of August Bebel that emphasizes his political action—William Harvey Maehl, *August Bebel: Shadow Emperor of the German Workers* (Philadelphia, 1980).

Eduard Bernstein has received classic treatment by Peter Gay, *The Dilemma of Democratic Socialism: Eduard Bernstein's Challenge to Marx* (New York, 1962), in which the author emphasizes the political paradoxes of democratic socialism. Guenther Roth, *The Social Democrats in Imperial Germany* (Totowa, NJ, 1963), views the social democratic–influenced German working class in the context of national politics. There is an extensive literature on the British Socialist movement and the British Fabians especially. Consult Margaret Cole, *The Story of Fabian Socialism* (Stanford, 1961), for a history of the movement and A. M. McBrian, *Fabian Socialism and English Politics, 1884–1916* (Cambridge, 1966), for its theories and action. Unfortunately, Antonio Labriola has not received the attention he deserves in English, but see the brief essay by the Russian Marxist thinker Georgii V. Plekhanov, *The Materialist Conception of History* (New York, 1940). Karl Kautsky has been more fortunate and is the subject of Massimo Salvadori's wide-ranging *Karl Kautsky and the Socialist Revolution* (London, 1979).

The interest in Rosa Luxemburg has generally been strong. Stephen Eric Bronner's *Rosa Luxemburg: A Revolutionary for Our Times* (New York, 1987), is a short biography; Paul Frolich's *Rosa Luxemburg: Her Life and Work* (New York, 1969), is a longer treatment; the most thorough work is J. P. Nettl, *Rosa Luxemburg*, 2 vols. (London, 1966). In addition, Lelio Basso, *Rosa Luxemburg: A Reappraisal* (New York, 1975), is an analysis of her thought by an eminent Italian Marxist.

Tom Bottomore and Patrick Goode, *Austro-Marxism* (Oxford, 1978), is a collection of texts notable as well for a long introduction. The reader might be interested also in an account of practical socialist action in the Austrian capital between 1919 and 1934, Helmut Gruber, *Red Vienna* (New York, 1991).

CHAPTER 8:

ANARCHISM

Good general accounts of anarchism in different countries include Paul Avrich, *The Russian Anarchists* (Princeton, 1967); Nunzio Pernicone, *Italian Anarchism, 1864–1892* (Princeton, 1993); and Andrew R. Carlson, *Anarchism in Germany* (Metuchen, NJ, 1972).

Edward Hyams, *Pierre-Joseph Proudhon* (New York, 1979), explores Proudhon's life and ideas. K. Steven Vincent, *Pierre-Joseph Proudhon and the Rise of Republican Socialism* (New York, 1984), examines his ideas and their political impact. Constance Margaret Hall, *The Sociology of Pierre Joseph Proudhon, 1809–1865* (New York, 1971), analyzes Proudhon as a sociologist. Aleksandr Herzen has received classic treatment in Edward Hallet Carr, *The Romantic Exiles* (Boston, 1961), and Martin Malia's *Alexander Herzen and the Birth of Russian Socialism* (Cambridge, MA, 1961) is a thorough treatment of Herzen's influence in his native land.

Books on the Commune are plentiful, but Jean T. Joughin, *The Paris Commune in French Politics* (New York, 1973), should be mentioned because it discusses the idea of the Commune in French political life up to 1880. Mikhail Bakunin has received spotty scholarly attention; editions of his work should be consulted for interesting introductions. E. H. Carr has written an excellent biography, *Michael Bakunin* (New York, 1937). Arthur P. Mendel, *Michael Bakunin: Roots of Apocalypse* (New York, 1981), focuses on the more dramatic parts of his theories. Anthony Masters, *Bakunin: The Father of Anarchy* (London, 1974), sees Bakunin's ideas as having relevance for the modern world. Aileen Kelly, *Mikhail Bakunin* (Oxford, 1982), takes a psychological approach to her subject. T. R. Ravindranathan, *Bakunin and the Italians* (Montreal, 1988), is a specialized work on a country in which Bakunin had great impact.

On another revolutionary, Samuel Bernstein's *Auguste Blanqui and the Art of Insurrection* (London, 1971) scrutinizes Blanqui's thought and action, and Patrick H. Hutton, *The Cult of Revolutionary Tradition* (Berkeley, 1981), investigates Blanquist thought and action in French politics up to 1893. Peter Kropotkin has been the object of a number of scholarly studies. Stephen Osofsky, *Peter Kropotkin* (Boston, 1979), is a short biography, and Martin A. Miller's *Kropotkin* (Chicago, 1976) is a longer, primarily intellectual, biography. An older work, George Woodcock and Ivan Avakumović, *The Anarchist Prince* (London, 1950), bills itself as a "biographical study." Finally, tracing Kropotkin's theory, its development, and its impact is Caroline Cahn, *Kropotkin and the Rise of Revolutionary Anarchism* (Cambridge, 1989).

William Morris has attracted considerable attention. The noted scholar E. P. Thompson, *William Morris: Romantic to Revolutionary* (New York, 1977), evaluates his ideas and practical action, and Fiona MacCarthy, *William Morris: A Life for Our Time* (New York, 1995), is a detailed account of his life.

On syndicalism, see James Charles Butler's *Fernand Pelloutier and the Emergence of the French Syndicalist Movement* (Ann Arbor, 1960). The most important syndicalist thinker's political ideas may be found examined in Richard Humphrey, *Georges Sorel: Prophet Without Honor* (Cambridge, MA, 1951); Jack J. Roth's *The Cult of Violence: Sorel and the Sorelians* (Berkeley, 1980) remains the standard work on Sorel and the impact of his ideas.

CHAPTER 9:
SOCIAL SCIENCE AND POLITICS

Auguste Comte and his philosophy were commented upon by John Stuart Mill, *Auguste Comte and Positivism* (Ann Arbor, 1968). L. Levy-Bruhl published a work translated into English in 1903 that remains useful for understanding Comte's system: *The Philosophy of Auguste Comte* (Clifton, NJ, 1973). Mary Pickering, *Auguste Comte: An Intellectual Biography*, vol. 1 (Cambridge, 1993), is a detailed dissection of his life and thought. Edward Caird, *The Social Philosophy and Religion of Auguste Comte* (New York, 1968), is a series of articles on various aspects of Comte. Christopher Kent, *Brains and Numbers* (Toronto, 1968), traces Comte's influence in Victorian England.

James G. Kennedy, *Herbert Spencer* (Boston, 1978), is a short work that focuses on Spencer's thought. Jonathan H. Turner, *Herbert Spencer: A Renewed Appreciation* (London, 1985), discusses his continuing relevance. J.D.Y. Peel, *Herbert Spencer: The Evolution of a Sociologist* (London, 1971), stresses the evolution of Spencer's thought. Jay Rumney, *Herbert Spencer's Sociology* (New York, 1966), is a clear explanation of his ideas.

Benjamin Evans Lippincott, *Victorian Critics of Democracy* (New York, 1964), includes a good chapter on Henry Maine.

Emile Durkheim is considered in the following works: Robert Nisbet, *The Sociology of Emile Durkheim* (New York, 1974), a general work; Robert A. Nisbet, *Emile Durkheim* (Englewood Cliffs, NJ, 1965), selected essays on particular problems; Keith Thomas, *Durkheim* (Oxford, 1992), a brief introduction to his thought; and Ernest Wallwork, *Durkheim* (Cambridge, MA, 1972), analyzes Durkheim's view of morality.

There is a good chapter on Tönnies in Arthur Mitzman's *Sociology and Estrangement* (New York, 1973). Werner J. Cahnman, *Weber and Toennies: Comparative Sociology in Historical Perspective* (New Brunswick, NJ, 1995), is an excellent treatment of both thinkers. Max Weber is the thinker in this chapter on whom probably most has been written; aside from the classic biography by his wife, Marianne Weber, *Max Weber: A Biography* (New York, 1975), we will mention only works on his political thought. Ilse Dronberger, *The Political Thought of Max Weber* (New York, 1971), is a thorough analysis of his political ideas and their context. Peter Bremer, *Max Weber and Democratic Politics* (Ithaca, 1996), is an abstract treatment of the theme. Wolfgang J. Mommsen, *The Political and Social Theory of Max Weber* (Chicago, 1989), had its origins in a series of lectures—later amplified—on particular aspects of Weber's thought and their implications. Ronald M. Glassman and Vatro Murvar, *Max Weber's Political Sociology* (Westport, CT, 1984), is a collection of essays on Weber's ideas. Karl Loewenstein, *Max Weber's Political Ideas in the Perspective of Our Time* (Amherst, 1966), looks at the continuing impact of his thought. Edward Bryan Portis, *Max Weber and Political Commitment* (Philadelphia, 1986), discusses Weber as a social scientist. Wolfgang Mommsen, *Max Weber and German Politics* (Chicago, 1984), portrays Weber in the context of German national politics. Arthur Mitzman, *The Iron Cage: An Historical Interpretation of Max Weber* (New York, 1970), is a standard work.

CHAPTER 10: THE AUTHORITARIAN STATE AND ANTIPARLIAMENTARISM

Theodore Zeldin, *The Political System of Napoleon III* (London, 1958), based on an imposing array of original sources, seeks to discover what the regime was rather than what it said it was. Richard M. Chadbourne, *Ernest Renan* (New York, 1968), is a short introduction to Renan's life and thought. H. W. Wardman, *Ernest Renan: A Critical Biography* (London, 1964), set in the context of his times, is good for the general reader. Sir Mountstuart E. Grant Duff, *Ernest Renan: In Memoriam* (London, 1893), is old but was written by a person who knew Renan and who put his impressions of him and his ideas in a book.

Leo Weinstein, *Hippolyte Taine* (New York, 1972), is a manageable introduction to Taine's thought. Andreas Dorpalen, *Heinrich von Treitschke* (New Haven, 1957), is a well-documented biography. Two older works are still useful: H. W. Davis, *The Political Thought of Heinrich von Treitschke* (New York, 1915), and Antoine Guilland, *Modern Germany and Her Historians* (New York, 1915).

Robert W. Lougee, *Paul de Lagarde, 1827–1891* (Cambridge, MA, 1962), argues that Lagarde was influential for the "conservative" revolution that began after 1890. Fritz Stern's *The Politics of Cultural Despair* (Berkeley, 1963) has a long chapter on Lagarde. Michael D. Biddiss, *Father of Racist Ideology* (London, 1970), is an evaluation of Gobineau's social and political thought and its context and evolution. An exploration of the development of racist ideas and their impact in Europe is George L. Mosse, *Toward the Final Solution: A History of European Racism* (Madison, 1985). Engels wrote a famous analysis of Dühring's thought; see Frederick Engels, *Herr Eugen Dühring's Revolution in Science (Anti-Dühring)* (New York, 1970).

Ettore A. Alberoni, *Mosca and the Theory of Elitism* (Oxford, 1987), is a clear commentary on Mosca's beliefs, set against the context of their time and including a section on their influence up to 1985. James H. Meisel, *The Myth of the Ruling Class* (Ann Arbor, 1962), also has a translation of one of Mosca's most important works.

Joseph Lopreato, *Vilfredo Pareto* (New York, 1965), is a critical essay on Pareto's thought followed by short excerpts from his work. Warren J. Samuels, *Pareto on*

Policy (Amsterdam, 1974), is an interpretation of Pareto's *Treatise on General Sociology*. Charles H. Powers, *Vilfredo Pareto* (Newbury Park, CA, 1987), is a brief and clear introduction to Pareto's life and work. S. E. Finer, *Vilfredo Pareto: Sociological Writings* (New York, 1966), is notable for a detailed introduction. Raymond Aron has written a study of Pareto, *Social Structure and the Ruling Class* (Indianapolis, 1969). Arthur Mitzman, *Sociology and Estrangement* (New York, 1973), includes a good chapter on Michels. Michels's theories have also been analyzed in Seymour Martin Lipset, *Michels' Theory of Political Parties* (Berkeley, 1962). The work of Mosca, Pareto, and Michels is frequently discussed together, such as in Robert A. Nye, *The Anti-democratic Sources of Elite Theory: Pareto, Mosca, Michels* (London, 1977), and Ettore Alberoni, ed., *Elitism and Democracy: Mosca, Pareto, and Michels* (Milan, 1992). James H. Meisel, ed., *Pareto and Mosca* (Englewood Cliffs, NJ, 1965), is a collection of essays by distinguished scholars on aspects of the political thought of both thinkers. The distinguished Italian political philosopher Norberto Bobbio has written *On Mosca and Pareto* (Geneva, 1972). Armand Patrucco's *The Critics of the Italian Parliamentary System, 1860–1915* (New York and London, 1992) is an excellent study of Mosca and Pareto. There is also the brief Sadi Dal-Rosso, *Autocracy in the Works of Gaetano Mosca and Robert Michels* (n.p., 1976).

CHAPTER 11:
POPULAR NATIONALISM

Texts on the political thought of the authors mentioned in this chapter are scarce in English, but readers might wish to consult books on their literary activities not cited in this bibliography.

C. Stewart Doty, *From Cultural Rebellion to Counterrevolution: The Politics of Maurice Barrès* (Athens, OH, 1976), emphasizes the influence of social and political issues on Barrès as well as Barrès's political action. Robert Soucy, *Fascism in France: The Case of Maurice Barrès* (Berkeley, 1972), is an intellectual biography that draws attention to parallels between Barrès's thought and fascism. William Curt Buthaman, *The Rise of Integral Nationalism in France* (New York, 1970), is a general treatment emphasizing Maurras. Michael Sutton, *Nationalism, Positivism, and Catholicism: The Politics of Charles Maurras and French Catholics, 1890–1914* (Cambridge, 1982), offers more than the subtitle promises. On the Italian nationalists, Alexander De Grand's fine study, *The Italian Nationalist Association* (Lincoln, NE, 1978), discusses some of the personalities mentioned in this chapter and in Chapter 13. The best work in English on Corradini is Ronald S. Cunsolo's Ph.D. dissertation, "Enrico Corradini and Italian Nationalism, 1896–1923" (New York University, 1963).

The following more general treatments are also useful: Samuel M. Osgood, *French Royalism Under the Third and Fourth Republics* (The Hague, 1960) and *The French Right* (New York, 1971). Michael Curtis, *Three Against the Third Republic* (Westport, CT, 1976), is an examination of Barrès's and Maurras's criticisms of the Third Republic (in addition to those of Georges Sorel).

CHAPTER 12:
RUSSIAN COMMUNISM

As might be expected, the literature on this subject is vast and the reader will have no trouble finding sources in addition to the sampling of useful texts provided here.

John Plamenatz has written a helpful book, *German Marxism and Russian Communism* (New York, 1965), describing the relationship between the two movements.

On Lenin, consult the following detailed and well-documented biographies: Robert Service, *Lenin: A Political Life*, 2 vols. (Bloomington, IN, 1985–1991), and Louis Fischer, *The Life of Lenin* (New York, 1964). Leon Trotsky, *Lenin: Notes for a Biographer* (New York, 1971), was written after Lenin's death by his former collaborator and is more in the nature of an interpretation. Bertram D. Wolfe, *Three Who Made a Revolution* (New York, 1983), is a famous account of Lenin, Trotsky, and Stalin.

A long work entirely devoted to Lenin's political ideology is Neil Harding, *Lenin's Political Thought*, 2 vols. (New York, 1977–1981). The French postwar Marxist Louis Althusser published a series of essays on Lenin, *Lenin and Philosophy and Other Essays* (London, 1971). Christopher Hill wrote on Lenin's politics and the Bolshevik Revolution in *Lenin and the Russian Revolution* (London, 1967). Finally, Nina Tumarkin traced Lenin's continuing influence in Russia up to the publication of her book in *Lenin Lives!* (Cambridge, MA, 1983).

As in Lenin's case, the reader will find a surfeit of books on Stalin. Isaac Deutscher, *Stalin* (New York, 1967), is a standard work. A more recent book by Robert Conquest, *Stalin* (New York, 1991), may serve as a good introduction to Stalin. Robert C. Tucker, *Stalin as Revolutionary, 1879–1929* (New York, 1973), argues for the force of personality; the same author's *Stalin in Power* (New York, 1990) treats the general theme of Stalin's "reign" and claims that a revolution was attempted "from above." As for the issue of the Soviet terror discussed in this chapter, Robert Conquest's *The Great Terror: A Reassessment* (New York, 1990) traces the phenomenon to the Communist Party's past. Finally, with regard to the great number of works "produced" by Stalin, the reader may find the following useful: Robert H. McNeal, *Revolution and Peace: Stalin's Works: An Annotated Bibliography* (Stanford, 1967).

As in the previous two cases, there is an abundance of works on Trotsky. The standard biography remains Isaac Deutscher, *The Prophet Armed: Trotsky, 1879–1921* (New York, 1955), and *The Prophet Unarmed: Trotsky, 1921–1929* (London, 1959). A brief biography is Robert D. Warth, *Leon Trotsky* (Boston, 1977). A good analysis of Trotsky's political thought is Baruch Knei-Paz, *The Social and Political Thought of Leon Trotsky* (Oxford, 1978), and a brief introduction to the same subject is Irving Howe's *Leon Trotsky* (New York, 1978).

On Karl Korsch, see Patrick Goode, *Karl Korsch: A Study in Western Marxism* (London, 1979).

CHAPTER 13: ITALIAN FASCISM

Unlike Russian Communism, Italian Fascism has frequently been treated as having no political ideology, as a mindless movement of the right, or as a pale reflection of Nazism. Consequently many of the more interesting ideologists of Italian Fascism mentioned in this chapter have been ignored by English-speaking scholars. For some time, however, an interesting debate has been under way over whether Fascism had a coherent political ideology or not and whether it had "leftist" roots. This debate was touched off by the multivolume biography of Renzo De Felice, which has not been translated; an idea of his argument, however, may be found in his brief interview with Michael A. Ledeen, *Fascism: An Informal Introduction to Its Theory and Practice* (New Brunswick, NJ, 1976). Borden Painter Jr. has published an overview of this debate, "Renzo De Felice and the Historiography of Italian Fascism," *The American Historical Review* 95:2 (April 1990): 391–405. Most recently the debate was given renewed life by the translation into English of Zeev Sternhell's *The Birth of Fascist Ideology: From Cultural Rebellion to Political Revolution* (Princeton, 1994), which argues that Fascism issued from revolutionary syndicalism and was a coherent ideological opponent of both Marxism and liberalism.

David D. Roberts also traces the influence of revolutionary syndicalism on Fascism in *The Syndicalist Tradition and Italian Fascism* (Chapel Hill, NC, 1979). A. James Gregor has argued that Fascism was a "modernizing" movement; see *The Ideology of Fascism* (New York, 1969) and *Italian Fascism and Developmental Dictatorship* (Princeton, 1979). The Marxist viewpoint on Fascism was expressed by Palmiro Togliatti, *Lectures on Fascism* (New York, 1976). Alexander De Grand's *Italian Fascism* (Lincoln, NE, 1989) has an interesting discussion of ideology. Renzo De Felice's *Interpretations of Fascism* (Cambridge, MA, 1977) provides a synopsis of the interpretations of Fascism. Michael A. Ledeen, *Universal Fascism* (New York, 1972), tells the story of the attempt to "internationalize" Italian Fascism and its ideology.

Of the personalities mentioned in this chapter, only Giovanni Gentile has received some coverage in English-language books. H. S. Harris investigated his thought in *The Social Philosophy of Giovanni Gentile* (Urbana, IL, 1966). Other works, such as V. M. Evans, *The Philosophy of Giovanni Gentile* (Aberystwyth, Wales, 1926), and the Ph.D. dissertation of Matthew C. Cavell, "Giovanni Gentile's Reform of Education in Italy" (New York University, 1931), are old.

On Edmondo Rossoni, see John J. Tinghino, *Edmondo Rossoni: From Revolutionary Syndicalism to Fascism* (New York, 1991).

CHAPTER 14:
GERMAN NAZISM

As might be expected, there is a vast literature on Nazism, and the reader will have no trouble finding it; only a small number of the relevant works can be mentioned here.

Of the people named in this chapter, Carl Schmitt has received much serious attention. See Joseph W. Bendersky, *Carl Schmitt: Theorist for the Reich* (Princeton, 1983). Paul Gottfried has examined Schmitt's political thought in his *Carl Schmitt: Politics and Theory* (New York, 1990). The distinguished Italian political scientist Giovanni Sartori has written "The Essence of the Political in Carl Schmitt," *Journal of Theoretical Politics* 1:1 (January 1989): 63–75. Gershon Weiler has published *From Absolutism to Totalitarianism: Carl Schmitt on Thomas Hobbes* (Durango, CO, 1994). Daniel Lerner's *The Nazi Elite* (New York, 1993) includes a chapter on Gottfried Feder and other Nazis. Alfred Rosenberg has received more attention in English. See Albert Richard Chandler, *Rosenberg's Nazi Myth* (New York, 1968), and James B. Whisker, *The Philosophy of Alfred Rosenberg* (Costa Mesa, CA, 1990). Whisker has also published *The Social, Political, and Religious Thought of Alfred Rosenberg: An Interpretive Essay* (Washington, DC, 1982). Further reading on Rosenberg's ideas include Robert Cecil, *The Myth of the Master Race: Alfred Rosenberg and Nazi Ideology* (New York, 1972). On the direct relationship of Rosenberg with the Holocaust, see Fritz Nova, *Alfred Rosenberg: Nazi Theorist of the Holocaust* (New York, 1986).

On Arthur Moeller van den Bruck there is a long chapter in Fritz Stern's *The Politics of Cultural Despair* (Berkeley, 1963), and the brief text by Paul Harrison Silfen, *The Volkisch Ideology and the Roots of Nazism: The Early Writings of Arthur Moeller van den Bruck* (New York, 1973).

More general works on aspects of national socialism and its impact worth mentioning here are the influential Martin Broszat, *The Hitler State: The Foundation and Development of the Internal Structure of the Third Reich* (London, 1982), which maintains that the government of the Reich shared power with the old conservatives; see also the same author's *German National Socialism, 1919–1945* (Santa Barbara, 1966). On the "scientific" underpinnings of the Holocaust, see Daniel Gasman, *The Scientific Origins of National Socialism: Social Darwinianism in Ernst Haeckell and the German Monist League* (London, 1971). See also the considerations of a famous German intellectual on the Nazi phenomenon and its meaning: Friedrich Meinecke, *The German Catastrophe: Reflections and Recollections* (Boston, 1950). On Oswald Spengler, consult the short work by the well-regarded H. Stuart Hughes, *Oswald Spengler: A Critical Estimate* (New York, 1962).

CHAPTER 15:
OPPOSING THE ONE-PARTY STATE

On Julien Benda, see Ray L. Nichols, *Treason, Tradition, and the Intellectual: Julien Benda and Political Discourse* (Lawrence, KS, 1978). On Pierre Drieu La Rochelle, there is Robert Soucy, *Fascist Intellectual: Drieu La Rochelle* (Berkeley, 1979), a detailed political and intellectual biography.

Most aspects of Ortega y Gasset's thought are well represented in the secondary literature. See the concise treatment by Andrew Dobson, *An Introduction to the Politics and Philosophy of José Ortega y Gasset* (Cambridge, 1989). There is also Rockwell Gray, *The Imperative of Modernity* (Berkeley, 1989), a well-informed intellectual biography, and Franz Niedermayer, *José Ortega y Gasset* (New York, 1973), a brief introduction to the philosopher. Julián Marías, *The Structure of Society* (Tuscaloosa, AL, 1987), is a clear account of his thought. On particular angles, there are Robert McClintock, *Man and His Circumstances* (New York, 1971), a study of Ortega's ideas on education; Oliver W. Holmes, *Human Reality and the Social*

World (Amherst, 1975), a discussion of his philosophy of history; José Sánchez Villaseñior, SJ, *Ortega y Gasset: Existentialist* (Chicago, 1949), a critical examination of his thought; and Harold C. Raley, *José Ortega y Gasset: Philosophy of European Unity* (Tuscaloosa, AL, 1971).

Hans Kelsen's pure theory of law is investigated by Ronald Moore, *Legal Norms and Legal Sciences: A Critical Study of Kelsen's Pure Theory of Law* (Honolulu, 1978), and William Ebenstein, *The Pure Theory of Law* (South Hackensack, NJ, 1969). There are also short essays on Kelsen's thought that are valuable: *Essays in Honor of Hans Kelsen, Celebrating the Ninetieth Anniversary of His Birth* (South Hackensack, NJ, 1971) and *Essays on Kelsen* (Oxford, 1986). The general work edited by W. J. Stankiewicz, *Political Thought Since World War II* (New York, 1964), which includes critical and interpretive essays, also deals with Kelsen.

As might be expected, much has been written on Keynes's economics, but the following might aid in measuring his political impact as well. Robert Skidelsky has written a massive biography: *John Maynard Keynes*, vol. 1, *Hopes Betrayed, 1883–1920* (New York, 1986); and *John Maynard Keynes*, vol. 2, *The Economist as Savior, 1920–1937* (London, 1992). Athol Fitzgibbons focuses on Keynes's ideas regarding political economy in *Keynes's Vision: A New Political Economy* (Oxford, 1988). Seymour E. Harris, *The New Economics: Keynes' Influence on Theory and Public Policy* (New York, 1965), is a comprehensive account of his subject. John B. Davis, *Keynes's Philosophical Development* (Cambridge, 1994), discusses the changes and development of Keynes's thought. Milo Keynes, *Essays on John Maynard Keynes* (Cambridge, 1975), is a collection of essays that give breadth to the subject.

Emmanuel Mounier has received more coverage in English than might be expected. See the brief introduction by Eileen Cantin, *Mounier* (New York, 1973). Michael Kelly, *Pioneer of the Catholic Revival* (London, 1979), is an examination of Mounier's ideas and influence. R. William Rauch Jr., *Politics and Belief in Contemporary France* (The Hague, 1972), is a study on Mounier and Christian Democracy between 1932 and 1950. John Hellman has also discussed his influence in *Emmanuel Mounier and the New Catholic Left, 1930–1950* (Toronto, 1981). Joseph Amato attempts an explanation of the French Catholic understanding of the world in his *Mounier and Maritain* (Tuscaloosa, AL, 1975).

Much has been written on Jacques Maritain, but his political significance is not always easy to nail down. For this influence, consult Susan M. Power, *Jacques Maritain (1882–1973), Christian Democrat, and the Quest for a New Commonwealth* (Lewiston, NY, 1992), and Dean Brackley, *Divine Revolution: Salvation and Liberation in Catholic Thought* (New York, 1996). See also the essays in James W. Skillen, ed., *Political Order and the Plural Structure of Society* (Atlanta, 1991). For his integral humanism, see Sidney Hook, *Reason, Social Myths, and Democracy* (New York, 1940).

On Benedetto Croce, consult the full study by David D. Roberts, *Benedetto Croce and the Uses of Historicism* (Berkeley, 1987). On his antifascism, there is David Ward, *Antifascisms: Cultural Politics in Italy, 1943–1946* (Madison, NJ, 1996). Croce's liberalism is discussed in an essay in Massimo Salvadori, ed., *European Liberalism* (New York, 1972).

CHAPTER 16:
THE WEST: MARXISM VERSUS CAPITALISM

A work that might serve as a good general introduction to the themes treated in this chapter is New Left Review's *Western Marxism: A Critical Reader* (London, 1977), a collection of essays on contemporary Western Marxist thinkers.

Much has been written on all aspects of Sartre's thought. A good biography is Ronald Hayman, *Writing Against: A Biography* (London, 1986), also published under the title *Sartre: A Life* (New York, 1987). On the Marxism of Sartre and the Existentialists, see the following titles: Wilfred Desan, *The Marxism of Jean-Paul Sartre* (Gloucester, MA, 1971); Pietro Chiodi, *Sartre and Marxism* (Hassocks, 1965); James Lawler, *The Existentialist Marxism of Jean-Paul Sartre* (Amsterdam, 1976); Raymond Aron, *Marxism and the Existentialists* (New York, 1965) and, by the same author, *History and the Dialectic of Violence* (Oxford, 1975); and Mark Poster, *Existential Marxism in Postwar France* (Princeton, 1975), a survey from Sartre to Althusser.

Merleau-Ponty has also been the subject of study by English-speaking scholars. See John O'Neill, *Perception, Expression, and History* (Evanston, IL, 1970), a brief consideration of his thought. Samuel B. Mallin, *Merleau-Ponty's Philosophy* (New Haven, 1979), is a longer treatment. Albert Rabil Jr., *Merleau-Ponty: Existentialist of the Social World* (New York, 1967), is a well-documented study.

Louis Althusser has received good introductory treatment by Steven B. Smith, *Reading Althusser* (Ithaca, 1984). Ted Benton, *The Rise and Fall of Structural Marxism: Althusser and His Influence* (New York, 1984), interprets Western Marxism. On aspects of Althusser's influence and Marxism, see Robert Paul Resch, *Althusser and the Renewal of Marxist Social Theory* (Berkeley, 1992); E. Ann Kaplan, ed., *The Althusserian Legacy* (London, 1993); Margaret A. Majumdar, *Althusser and the End of Leninism?* (London, 1995); John O'Neill, *For Marx Against Althusser* (Washington, DC, 1982); Alex Callinicos, *Althusser's Marxism* (London, 1976); *Postmodern Materialism and the Future of Marxist Theory* (Hanover, NH, 1996), a collection of essays; and Stuart MacIntyre, *Althusser and Marxist Theory* (Cambridge, 1975), a very brief treatment. For connections with a particular Western Marxist tradition, see Maria Antonietta Macciocchi, *Letters from Inside the Italian Communist Party to Louis Althusser* (London, 1973).

Michel Foucault has also received extensive treatment in English. Good introductions to his life and thought include Lois McNay, *Foucault: A Critical Introduction* (Cambridge, 1994); J. G. Merquier, *Foucault* (London, 1985); Barry Cooper, *Michel Foucault* (New York, 1981); and David R. Shumway, *Michel Foucault* (Boston, 1989). Edith Kurzweill's survey, *The Age of Structuralism* (New York, 1980), has a good chapter on Foucault. More detailed analyses of particular aspects of the philosopher include the scholarly Charles C. Lemert and Garth Gillan, *Michel Foucault: Social Theory as Transgression* (New York, 1982); and *Michel Foucault: Critical Assessments*, 3 vols. (London, 1994). For Foucault and political theory, see *Foucault and Political Reason: Liberalism, Neo-liberalism, and Rationalities of Government* (London, 1996); Steven Best, *The Politics of Historical Vision* (New York, 1995), which also includes a discussion of Habermas; Thomas L. Dumm, *Michel Foucault and the Politics of Freedom* (Thousand Oaks, CA, 1996); and Honi

Gern Haber, *Beyond Postmodern Politics* (New York, 1994). Mark Poster, *Foucault, Marxism, and History* (Cambridge, 1984), includes a discussion of Sartre. The Frankfurt school is discussed by Zoltán Tar with a focus on Adorno and Horkheimer in *The Frankfurt School* (New York, 1977). More general considerations are Rolf Wiggershaus, *The Frankfurt School* (Cambridge, MA, 1995), and Ronald Jeremiah Schindler, *The Frankfurt School Critique of Capitalist Culture* (Avebury, 1996).

Good introductions to Adorno's philosophy are Willem van Reijen, *Adorno* (Philadelphia, 1992), and Gillian Rose, *The Melancholy Science* (London, 1978). Frederic Jameson's *Late Marxism* (London, 1990) studies Adorno, and Martin Jay, *Adorno* (Cambridge, MA, 1984), explains his thought. Joan Alway's *Critical Theory and Political Possibilities* (Westport, CT, 1995) includes an examination of the thought of Adorno, Horkheimer, and Habermas.

Horkheimer is studied by Peter M.P. Stirk, *Max Horkheimer: A New Interpretation* (Hamal Hempstead, UK, 1992), and Helmut Dubiel, *Theory and Politics* (Cambridge, MA, 1985); consult also *On Max Horkheimer: New Perspectives* (Cambridge, MA, 1993). See also David Held, *Introduction to Critical Theory: Horkheimer to Habermas* (London, 1990); Patrick W. Burman's *The Path of Reason* (Notre Dame, IN, 1974) includes a critical discussion of Horkheimer and Habermas. For Habermas, see in addition Steven K. White, ed., *The Cambridge Companion to Habermas* (Cambridge, 1995), an introduction to his thought through a series of essays. Richard J. Bernstein has also edited a collection of essays, *Habermas and Modernity* (Cambridge, MA, 1985). A good definition of Habermas's thought is also Thomas McCarthy, *The Critical Theory of Jürgen Habermas* (Cambridge, MA, 1979). Other useful works on Habermas are Simone Chambers, *Reasonable Democracy* (Ithaca, 1996); Detlef Horster, *Habermas: An Introduction* (Philadelphia, 1992); Goeff Eley, *Nations, Publics, and Political Cultures: Placing Habermas in the Nineteenth Century* (Ann Arbor, 1990); Robert C. Holub, *Jürgen Habermas: Critic in the Public Sphere* (London, 1991); and Jane Braaten, *Habermas's Critical Theory of Society* (Albany, 1991).

Almost every aspect of Antonio Gramsci's thought has been examined. A massive bibliography of works on Gramsci in all languages has been collected by John M. Cammett, *Bibliografia Gramsciana* (Rome, 1989); see also, by the same author, *Antonio Gramsci and the Origins of Italian Communism* (Stanford, 1967). A standard biography is Giuseppe Fiori, *Antonio Gramsci: Life of a Revolutionary* (New York, 1973). Anne Showstack Sassoon, *Gramsci's Politics* (London, 1980), is a brief introduction to Gramsci's ideas, as is the more recent Roger Simon, *Gramsci's Political Thought: An Introduction* (London, 1991). Aditi Misra has also published a book on his politics, *The Political Philosophy of Antonio Gramsci* (New Delhi, 1991). One of the key elements in Gramsci's thought has been investigated by Benedetto Fontana, *Hegemony and Power* (Minneapolis, 1993). Teodros Kiros has examined the same theme in *Toward the Construction of a Theory of Political Action: Antonio Gramsci: Consciousness, Participation, and Hegemony* (London, 1985), as has John Hoffman, *The Gramscian Challenge: Coercion and Consent in Marxist Political Theory* (Oxford, 1986). Darrow Schecter analyzes another major issue in *Gramsci and the Theory of Industrial Democracy* (Avebury, 1991). Richard Bellamy and Darrow Schecter, *Gramsci and the Italian State* (Manchester, 1993), put Gramsci in his political context.

Gramsci's influence is considered in the following works: Sue Golding, *Gramsci's Democratic Theory: Contributions to a Post-liberal Democracy* (Toronto, 1992); *The Legacy of Antonio Gramsci* (Binghamton, NY, 1987); Renate Holub, *Antonio Gramsci: Beyond Marxism and Postmodernism*; and David Harris, *From Class Struggle to the Politics of Pleasure: The Effects of Gramscianism on Cultural Studies* (London, 1992).

CHAPTER 17: EASTERN EUROPE
VERSUS THE SOVIET SYSTEM

There is an extensive literature on Poland and the opposition to Communism during the period of Soviet domination. On the issue of Soviet control itself, see Stanislaw Mikolajczyk, *The Pattern of Soviet Domination* (London, 1948). Czeslaw Milosz, *The Captive Mind* (New York, 1953), is a classic work, written by a Pole, on the world of Polish, Hungarian, Czech, and Romanian intellectuals under Communism. The concise James F. Morrison, *The Polish People's Republic* (Baltimore, 1968), details the construction of a socialist state in Poland. M. K. Dziewanowski, *The Communist Party of Poland* (Cambridge, MA, 1976), is a comprehensive history of the Polish Communist Party in all its aspects. Maciej Pomian-Srzednicki, *Religious Change in Contemporary Poland* (London, 1982), deals with the religious issue. Janine Wedel, *The Private Poland* (Oxford, 1986), tells how Poles really lived.

Nicholas Bethell, *Gomulka: His Poland and His Communism* (London, 1969), deals with all aspects of Poland under an important leader, and S. L. Schneiderman, *The Warsaw Heresy* (New York, 1959), examines the disorders that took place during Gomulka's tenure.

The literature detailing the opposition to Polish Communism and the rise of the Solidarity movement that finally overthrew it is plentiful. Jane Leftwich Curry and Luba Fajfer, eds., *Poland's Permanent Revolution* (Washington, DC, 1996), consists of a series of essays examining Poland's continuing instability since 1956. Keith John Lepak, *Prelude to Solidarity: Poland and the Politics of the Gierek Regime* (New York, 1988), details Polish conditions between 1971 and 1980, emphasizing political and social opposition. C. M. Hann, *A Village Without Solidarity: Polish Peasants in Years of Crisis* (New Haven, 1985), is about the failure of Polish Communism on the land, and its effects.

More overt forms of opposition may be gleaned from Adam Michnik, *Letters from Prison and Other Essays* (Berkeley, 1985), which describes the growth of resistance to the USSR among intellectuals. Works that illustrate the widespread nature of the opposition are Peter Raina, *Political Opposition in Poland* (London, 1978), and Michael Bernhard and Henryk Szajfer, *From the Polish Underground* (University Park, PA, 1995). The beginnings of the final crisis and the growth of Solidarity can be followed in George Sanford, *Polish Communism in Crisis* (London, 1983); Kevin Ruane, *The Polish Challenge* (London, 1982); Nicholas G. Andrews, *Poland, 1980–1981: Solidarity Versus the Party* (Washington, DC, 1985); Jadwiga Staniszkis, *Poland's Self-Limiting Revolution* (Princeton, 1984); and Lawrence Weschler, *Solidarity: Poland in the Season of Its Passion* (New York, 1981).

Finally, the reader can understand the pull of the Italian Communist Party in Poland and Eastern Europe through Enrico Berlinguer, *After Poland: Toward a New Internationalism* (Nottingham, 1982). General conditions in Hungary regarding the ethnic question may be understood by reading the essays collected by Steven Borsody, ed., *The Hungarians: A Divided Nation* (New Haven, 1988). Bennett Kovrig, *Communism in Hungary* (Stanford, 1979), is a comprehensive overview of Hungarian Communism. Ferenc Nagy, *The Struggle Behind the Iron Curtain* (New York, 1948), is the story of how Hungary came under Soviet domination, by a former prime minister. Thomas Aczel and Tibor Meray, *The Revolt of the Mind* (New York, 1959), examines the resistance to Soviet control by Hungarian intellectuals.

There are many books on the Hungarian Revolution of 1956. Ferenc A. Vali, *Rift and Revolt in Hungary* (Cambridge, MA, 1961), is particularly good because it has long sections on the Hungarian resistance to Soviet Communism before 1956, in addition to a discussion of the revolution itself and its aftermath; he sees the revolution as a case of "Nationalism versus Communism." On Imre Nagy and his fate, there are Nikos Molnar, *The Truth About the Nagy Affair* (New York, 1959), documents from, and comments on, the Nagy trial; and *The Secret Trial of Imre Nagy* (Westport, CT, 1994). Ferenc Feher and Agnes Heller, *Hungary 1956 Revisited* (London, 1983), is interesting because it looks at the meaning of the revolution after twenty-five years.

On György Lukács there is the long and detailed work by Arpad Kadarkay, *Georg Lukács: Life, Thought, and Politics* (Cambridge, MA, 1991). Lee Congdon, *The Young Lukács* (Chapel Hill, 1983), concentrates on his youth. Michael Lowy, *From Romanticism to Bolshevism* (London, 1979), looks at the evolution of his thought, and May Gluck, *Georg Lukács and His Generation, 1900–1918* (Cambridge, MA, 1985), places him in the context of his times. On an important aspect of his thought, there is I. Mészáros, *Lukács' Concept of Dialectic* (London, 1972). See also the collection of essays edited by Agnes Heller, *Lukács Revalued* (London, 1983).

On *Praxis* see Gerson S. Sher, *Praxis: Marxist Criticism and Dissent in Socialist Yugoslavia* (Bloomington, IN, 1977), which is a thorough treatment of the review. There are not many works in English on Milovan Djilas. Consult Stephen Clissold, *The Progress of a Revolutionary* (Hounslow, 1983), an account of his development. He is also considered in *The Soviet Empire: The Challenge of National and Democratic Movements* (Lexington, MA, 1990). Two books that will help the reader to understand the context in which Djilas worked are M. George Zaninovich, *The Development of Socialist Yugoslavia* (Baltimore, 1968), which explains the construction of socialism in the country; and Fred Warner Neal, *Titoism in Action* (Berkeley, 1958), about the practical operation of Titoist Yugoslavia. The reader will have no trouble finding other works on Tito and his times.

Vladimir V. Kusin, *The Intellectual Origins of the Prague Spring* (Cambridge, 1971), is a good, short, account of how reformist ideas grew up in Communist Czechoslovakia. Karen Dawisha, *The Kremlin and the Prague Spring* (Berkeley, 1984), describes how the Prague Spring and the USSR interacted and how the 1968 invasion occurred. H. Gordon Skilling's *Czechoslovakia's Interrupted Revolution* (Princeton, 1976) is a comprehensive account of the theories and developments leading up to and following the Prague Spring.

As might be expected, there is a growing literature on Gorbachev, his reforms, and the Soviet Union's demise. Moshe Levin, *The Gorbachev Phenomenon* (Berkeley, 1988), discusses the social and historical forces that produced Gorbachev. Zhores A. Medvedev, *Gorbachev* (New York, 1986), emphasizes his life and action. Martin McCauley, *The Soviet Union Under Gorbachev* (New York, 1987), is a series of essays on the impact of Gorbachev's policies on different areas of Soviet life. William and Jane Tubman, *Moscow Spring* (New York, 1989), describe the effects of Gorbachev's policies, as do Roy Medvedev and Giulietto Chiesa in *Time of Change: An Insider's View of Russia's Transformation* (New York, 1989). Catherine Merridale and Chris Ward, eds., *Perestroika: The Historical Perspective* (London, 1991), is a collection of essays which lend depth to an understanding of "restructuring." Tatyana Zaslavskaya, *The Second Socialist Revolution* (Bloomington, 1990), is an account of how perestroika might have worked. David Lane, *Soviet Society Under Perestroika* (Boston, 1990), is a good account of perestroika's impact on all aspects of Soviet society. Consult also Mark Galeotti, *Gorbachev and His Revolution* (New York, 1996). Joan Barth Urban, ed., *Moscow and the Global Left in the Gorbachev Era* (Ithaca, 1992), is a collection of essays dealing with perestroika's impact on the world left, including in Europe.

There have also been some good works on the USSR's fall. David Remnick, *Lenin's Tomb* (New York, 1993), is a detailed account of the last days. Important accounts have also been provided by Andrei S. Grachev, *Final Days: The Inside Story of the Collapse of the Soviet Union* (Boulder, 1995); Fred Coleman, *The Decline and Fall of the Soviet Empire* (New York, 1996); and Michael Beschloss, *At the Highest Levels: The Inside Story of the End of the Cold War* (Boston, 1996).

CHAPTER 18: MODELS IN WESTERN EUROPEAN POLITICAL THOUGHT

Unfortunately, the secondary literature in English manifests gaps on some of the authors considered in this chapter—especially the French—and interested readers will have to resort in those cases to articles in specialized journals.

Roland Kley provides a concise analysis of Hayek's ideas in *Hayek's Social and Political Thought* (Oxford, 1994). Andrew Gamble, *Hayek: The Iron Cage of Liberty* (Boulder, 1996), is a recent work with a good bibliography. Hayek's political ideas and liberalism are explored by Calvin M. Hoy, *A Philosophy of Individual Freedom* (Westport, CT, 1984), and John N. Gray, *F. A. Hayek and the Rebirth of Classical Liberalism* (Menlo Park, CA, 1982). See also *The Economics of F. A. Hayek* (Aldershot, UK, 1994). Milton Friedman's ideas are explored in Abraham Hirsch, *Milton Friedman: Economics in Theory and Practice* (New York, 1990).

Raymond Aron's thought has been considered by Daniel J. Mahoney, *The Liberal Political Science of Raymond Aron* (Lanham, MD, 1992), a short introduction. Robert Colquhoun has published a massive biography of Aron with an emphasis on his thought and action, *Raymond Aron*, 2 vols. (Beverly Hills, CA, 1986).

John Gray's *Isaiah Berlin* (Princeton, 1996) is a good introduction to Berlin's thought, analyzing his theme that political and moral life abound in conflicting radical options. Claude J. Galipeau, *Isaiah Berlin's Liberalism* (Oxford, 1994), emphasizes Berlin's focus on pluralism and historical and cultural realism. Alan Ryan, ed., *The Idea of Freedom: Essays in Honour of Isaiah Berlin* (Oxford, 1994), is a collection of essays on different aspects of Berlin's thought, from Liberalism to freedom; the book has a good bibliography of Berlin's publications. Pierre Manent et al., *European Liberty* (The Hague, 1983), includes a good essay on Berlin.

There are several useful introductions to Karl Popper: Roberta Corvi, *Introduction to the Thought of Karl Popper* (New York, 1996), and Jeremy Shearmur, *The Political Thought of Karl Popper* (New York, 1996), are the most recent. Bryan Magee, *Karl Popper* (New York, 1973), is an older, relatively brief introduction. Robert John Ackermann, *The Philosophy of Karl Popper* (Amherst, 1976), is a detailed analysis of his thought. T. E. Burke, *The Philosophy of Popper* (Manchester, 1983), is an investigation of Popper's ideas on several important issues such as historicism and freedom. There is also a book on his methodology, by Ingvar Johansson, *A Critique of Karl Popper's Methodology* (Stockholm, 1975). Bureligh Taylor Wilkins quarrels with Popper's view that a science of society and history is impossible in *Has History Any Meaning?* (Ithaca, 1978); and Maurice Cornforth, *The Open Philosophy and the Open Society* (New York, 1968), is a Marxist refutation of Popper's philosophy.

There are currently only a few secondary works on Dahrendorf. See Dankwart A. Rustow's "Dahrendorf, Reflections on the Revolution in Europe," *Political Science Quarterly* 106:3 (Fall 1991): 564, and the brief "discussion paper" by M. R. Atkinson, *A Critical Interpretation of the Sociology of Ralf Dahrendorf* (Birmingham, 1969).

INDEX